VALUING SERVICES IN TRADE

VALUING SERVICES IN TRADE

A TOOLKIT FOR COMPETITIVENESS DIAGNOSTICS

Sebastián Sáez, Daria Taglioni, Erik van der Marel,

Claire H. Hollweg, Veronika Zavacka

 **WORLD BANK GROUP**

ISBN (paper): 978-1-4648-0155-6
ISBN (electronic): 978-1-4648-0156-3
DOI: 10.1596/978-1-4648-0155-6

Cover design: Debra Naylor, Naylor Design, Inc.

Library of Congress Cataloging-in-Publication Data
Sáez, Sebastián.
Valuing services in trade: a toolkit for competitiveness diagnostics / Sebastián Sáez, Daria Taglioni, Erik van der Marel, Claire H. Hollweg, and Veronika Zavacka.
pages cm
ISBN 978-1-4648-0155-6 — ISBN 978-1-4648-0156-3
1. Service industries. 2. International trade. 3. Competition. I. World Bank. II. Title.
HD9980.5.S24 2014
382'.45—dc23

2014008433

CONTENTS

Tables

FOREWORD

Services trade today represents more than a fifth of global trade measured in volumes and 50 percent if measured in value addition. For some countries, including developing countries, its share in total exports is even bigger. Services are traded along with inputs into other economic activities, with both playing a key role in a country's competitiveness and participation in global value chains. Assessing exactly how competitive these sectors are and how their performance can be improved is therefore critical in designing and implementing trade policies that can increase services' contribution to economic development and growth. *Valuing Services in Trade: A Toolkit for Competitiveness Diagnostics* is a welcome contribution to the empirical analysis of countries' services performance.

Even before our era of "servicification," the importance of services trade for the global economy and country welfare has been widely accepted since the early 1980s. The inclusion of services in the multilateral trading system, which created the World Trade Organization (WTO) in 1995, was a significant step forward. Opening services trade now had a platform. This became clear following the conclusion of the WTO financial services and telecommunication negotiations in 1997. These were important milestones. The role of services in the global trade agenda has been increasing ever since.

Today, services trade has become one of the most important and complex subjects in regional trade negotiations, especially in South-South agreements. Liberalization of services trade, however, has proven very difficult. A lack of data and a limited number of analytical tools for conducting meaningful, rigorous research are major constraints. This problem is particularly severe in some developing and least-developed countries where statistics and knowledge are limited.

As Director General of the WTO, one of my key concerns was to help countries overcome these constraints. Through mutual efforts and close collaboration with World Bank and other trade experts, countries are coming to understand the benefits and challenges of a complex international trade agenda and the importance of a rules-based multilateral trading system. Our support here has been highly valuable for developing country members, but more can still be done.

This book is a significant step forward in filling the existing knowledge and analytical gaps in two important dimensions of the trade in services debate: the role of services as a source of export diversification and its role as a source of competitiveness for the whole economy. It provides a clear, coherent, and innovative framework that policy makers, academics, experts, and anyone interested in trade policy matters will be able to use to analyze the services performance of developing countries. The book begins by providing broad indicators of the services sector, which situate the country in the global context. These indicators can be used to compare a country's performance against its peers', helping to identify potential issues that may explain any differences in performance. It then digs down into the microeconomic indicators, to provide an increasingly precise characterization of the ability and potentialities of a country to be competitive in the export of the services sector and in its ability to use the domestic services industry to enhance the competitiveness of other export sectors.

The book also illustrates the positive contribution of firm-level analysis. The increasing use of firm-level data in service-related analytical work is giving a clearer picture of the characteristics of firms—the real protagonists engaged in services trade. This is helping, in particular, to better understand the size of firms, the skills of employees, the markets where firms export, and the constraints these firms face. Digging down to this level of analysis allows us to compare services firms with firms engaged in goods trade, again helping to identify relevant policy issues and those that could boost services' contributions to trade.

Firm-level analysis is just one example of the refreshing use of new data found in this book. The fragmentation of production in different locations, within countries and abroad, is changing trade patterns. Global value chains, which connect these increasingly fragmented tasks, are creating complex data challenges. The authors recognize these challenges and have provided this book as a toolkit to meet them. The book draws on a new database built specifically to help countries assess the role of services in trade and other economic activities by using value-added data. This database covers a wide range of countries, including least-developed countries. It is in itself a valuable contribution to the empirical work on services trade.

Policies applied by countries and trading partners are particularly important in explaining why performance differs. The toolkit provided in this book highlights the main policies affecting trade and their influences on performance. The authors distinguish three broad categories: regulatory policies, which primarily restrict trade; policies aimed at addressing domestic market failures; and domestic enabling factors, including supply-side factors, such as skills availability, and services-related infrastructure, such as telecommunications and physical infrastructure.

The authors successfully achieve a difficult balance. The user will find a thorough discussion of trade theory, a critical review of the relevant empirical literature, a clear explanation of the indicators used and their relevance, and highly informative case studies where the toolkit has been used. This book is another important contribution from the World Bank to the empirical work on services trade. It will be of particular help to policy makers, trade experts, academics, and all of us interested in trade, growth, and development.

Pascal Lamy
Former Director General
World Trade Organization

PREFACE

Increasingly, as we forge ahead in the 21st century, services will define the ability of countries and their firms to compete on international markets. This toolkit is an effort of the World Bank Group's new Trade and Competitiveness Global Practice to address the needs of countries facing this rising trend, and to help our clients make informed policy choices to better their chances of benefiting from the increasing prominence of services in international trade.

There are two aspects to services' rise. First, thanks to improvements in information and communications technology, services have become more and more tradable; service providers, such as computer programmers or call-center operators, no longer need to be close to their customers. They can operate from a location that provides skilled labor at low costs.

But there's a second component. Not only are more services crossing borders, domestically produced services are also emerging as vital inputs to the production of traded goods and services. Neither a factory nor a call center can operate without reliable electricity and water, for example. And as more and more production enters the just-in-time value chain model, crossing multiple countries in the transition from raw material to finished good, reliable services can mean the difference between a firm's profit and loss. The level of services can also make the case for a firm's investment in one country over another.

This phenomenon, which touches middle-income as well as low-income countries, has important implications for development and for the World Bank Group's twin goals of eradicating poverty and improving the incomes of the bottom 40 percent of populations everywhere. Already, many developing countries export a diverse range of services. They might provide transport services to their neighbors and back-office business services to developing countries, for example. The falling costs of information technology and increasing access to the internet suggest that this trend will only grow, offering the possibility that more and more jobs in the developing world will be in the services sector.

Just as they want to see their exported services thrive, policy makers in many developing countries would like to do more to ensure that all of their industries—producing both goods and services—can be competitive on the world market. Growing and hiring domestic industries, as well as foreign investment, are key components of many countries' strategies for economic growth, job creation, and, ultimately, poverty reduction.

This toolkit is designed to help countries assess their past performance in services as well as areas in which they have comparative advantage. It allows policy makers to improve their understanding of the size, scope, and potential of services production and exports in their countries. It also allows them to identify obstacles to the competitiveness of their services sectors. It is a key pillar of our efforts in the World Bank's Trade and Competitiveness Global Practice to serve our clients and help them have cutting-edge tools in an ever-changing global economy.

Anabel Gonzalez
Senior Director
Trade and Competitiveness Global Practice
The World Bank

ACKNOWLEDGMENTS

Valuing Services in Trade was prepared by the World Bank's International Trade Unit in Poverty Reduction and Economic Management Network. Sebastián Sáez and Daria Taglioni were team coleaders. Erik van der Marel, Claire H. Hollweg, and Veronika Zavacka (consultants) provided invaluable inputs to the report.

The authors would like to thank Michael Engman and Ana Margarida Fernandes, who peer-reviewed the concept note and provided useful comments and suggestions that greatly improved the original idea. The authors are especially grateful to Enrique Aldaz-Carrol, Michael Ferrantino, and Bernard Hoekman, who peer-reviewed the first draft and provided valuable suggestions. Sven Blank, Dale Honeck, Suhail Kassim, and Ivan Rossignol also provided comments on the first draft.

The team would also like to thank Joseph Francois, Miriam Manchin, Olga Pindyuk, and Patrick Tomberger. They compiled the two new cross-country datasets widely used for the applications of the toolkit based on their research on services trade and trade in value added. The team also thanks the staff and consultants of the International Trade Unit who contributed and supported the work at different stages of the project, in particular, Tom Farole, Charles Kunaka, Martin Molinuevo, José-Daniel Reyes, and Jose Guilherme Reis for their discussions and suggestions on how best to tackle the project.

During the development and piloting of parts of the toolkit in different countries and regions across the World Bank, we benefited from the support, comments, and suggestions of Ahmed Ahsan, Julian Latimer Clarke, Sebastian Eckardt, David Gould, Sibel Kulaksiz, Dorsati Madani, Hannah Messerli, Richard Record, Frederico Gil Sander, Rashmi Shankar, John Speakman, Ekaterine Vashakmadze, and Ekaterina Vostroknutova. The team acknowledges the collaboration of experts and consultants who helped to shape the analytical framework and messages of the toolkit, in particular, Guillermo Arenas, Matej Bajgar, Christina Busch, Jose Fernandez, Arti Grover, Beata Javorcick, Carolina Lennon, Saurabh Mishra, Anasuya Raj, Ben Shepherd, and Deborah Winkler.

Shienny S. Lie provided excellent administrative assistance and helped to format the volume. Amir Alexander Fouad provided support during the toolkit's preparation and coordinates the International Trade Unit's publication program.

We also thank Stephen McGroarty, Andrés Meneses, Paola Scalabrin, and Janice Tuten of the World Bank's Publishing and Knowledge Division for their valuable advice and guidance during the publication. The toolkit benefited from the professional editorial work of Barbara Karni.

This project was supported in part by the governments of Finland, Norway, Sweden, and the United Kingdom through the Multidonor Trust Fund for Trade and Development.

Finally, the project and the book would not have been possible without the continuous support and guidance of the staff of the International Trade Unit and its management team, in particular Mona Haddad (Sector Manager) and Bernard Hoekman (former Director), and Jeff Lewis (Director).

ABOUT THE AUTHORS

Sebastián Sáez is a senior trade economist in the International Trade Unit at the World Bank, where he has been responsible for the trade in services agenda since 2009. From 1990 to 1994, he was involved in the General Agreement on Tariffs and Trade's Uruguay Round negotiations as adviser to the Chilean Minister of Finance. He subsequently served as deputy permanent representative in the Chilean Mission to the World Trade Organization (WTO) and as head of the Free Trade Agreement of the Americas Department in the Chilean Ministry of Foreign Affairs. Beginning in 2001, he served as head of the Chilean Department of Foreign Trade, Ministry of Economy, where he participated in trade negotiations with the European Union, Korea, and the United States. Prior to joining the World Bank, he worked in the International Trade and Integration Division at the United Nations Economic Commission for Latin America and the Caribbean (UN–ECLAC).

Claire H. Hollweg is a consultant at the International Trade Unit at the World Bank. She holds a PhD and MA in economics from the University of Adelaide. Prior to studying economics, she worked as a journalist in newspaper and radio, and holds a BS in journalism from the University of Colorado at Boulder. She also has work experience with the Government of South Australia and the Pacific Economic Cooperation Council (PECC) in Singapore. Her research interests include development economics with a recent focus on trade and labor, trade in services, and household responses to shocks.

Daria Taglioni is a senior economist in the International Trade Unit at the World Bank. She has more than 10 years of experience in economic policy analysis on issues of international competitiveness, globalization, and the links between financial markets and trade. Prior to joining the World Bank, she worked at the European Central Bank and at the Organisation for Economic Co-operation and Development (OECD). She holds a PhD in international economics from the Graduate Institute for International Studies in Geneva.

Erik van der Marel is a senior economist at the European Centre for International Political Economy (ECIPE). His main areas of expertise are in services trade, the political economy of services trade policy, the link between total factor productivity (TFP) and regulation, and trade policy in developing countries. Prior to his appointment at ECIPE, he held posts as a lecturer at the London School of Economics and as a research fellow at the Groupe d'Économie Mondiale (GEM) institute in Paris at Sciences-Po, and was a consultant at the Asia-Pacific Economic Cooperation (APEC) forum, the European Commission, the OECD, and the World Bank. He holds a PhD in international economics from Sciences-Po in Paris.

Veronika Zavacka is a board operations officer at the International Monetary Fund (IMF). The focus of her research is on the behavior of international trade under exceptional circumstances, such as financial crises and uncertainty shocks. Prior to coming to the IMF she worked for several other international institutions, including the World Bank, the European Bank for Reconstruction and Development, European Central Bank, and United Nations Development Programme (UNDP). She holds a doctorate in international economics from the Graduate Institute for International Studies in Geneva.

ABBREVIATIONS

ASEAN	Association of Southeast Asian Nations
BPO	business process outsourcing
BRIC	Brazil, Russia, India, China
EBOPS	Extended Balance of Payments Services
EXPY	(revealed) income content of export basket
FATS	Foreign Affiliates Trade Statistics
FDI	foreign direct investment
GATS	General Agreement on Trade in Services
GDP	gross domestic product
GTAP	Global Trade Analysis Project
GVC	global value chain
ICT	information and communication technology
IMF	International Monetary Fund
IT	information technology
ITES	information technology–enabled services
KAM	Knowledge Assessment Methodology
NACE	*Nomenclature statistique des activités économiques dans la Communauté européenne* (Statistical Classification of Economic Activities in the European Community)
NAICS	North American Industry Classification System
OECD	Organisation for Economic Co-operation and Development
PPP	purchasing power parity
PRODY	(revealed) income content of product basket
RCA	revealed comparative advantage
RHCI	Revealed Human Capital Index
RICTI	Revealed Information and Communications Technology–Related Capital Index
STCD	Services Trade Competitiveness Diagnostic
STRI	Services Trade Restrictiveness Index
TCI	Trade Complementarities Index
TFP	total factor productivity
TII	Trade Intensity Index
TiVA	Trade in Value Added
UNCTAD	United Nations Conference on Trade and Development
WDI	World Development Indicators

Note: All dollar amounts are U.S. dollars ($) unless otherwise indicated.

BALANCE OF PAYMENT (BOP) CODES USED IN THIS BOOK

The balance of payments coding system, available at http://www.imf.org/external/np/sta/bopcode/, has been developed by the International Monetary Fund in cooperation with the Statistical Office of the European Union (Eurostat), the Organisation for Economic Co-operation and Development (OECD), and the European Central Bank (ECB). The coding system is designed to facilitate the exchange of data on balance of payments, international investment position, international trade in services, and foreign currency liquidity among these organizations, their member states, and other interested organizations or entities.

Total services		200
1.	Transportation	205
1.1	Sea transport	206
1.2	Air transport	210
1.3	Other transport	214
1.4	Space transport	218
1.5	Rail transport	219
1.6	Road transport	223
1.7	Inland waterway transport	227
1.8	Pipeline transport and electricity transmission	231
1.9	Other supporting and auxiliary transport services	232
2.	Travel	236
2.1	Business travel	237
2.2	Personal travel	240
3.	Communications services	245
3.1	Postal and courier services	246
3.2	Telecommunications services	247
4.	Construction services	249
4.1	Construction abroad	250
4.2	Construction in the compiling economy	251
5.	Insurance services	253
5.1	Life insurance and pension funding	254
5.2	Freight insurance	255

5.3	Other direct insurance	256
5.4	Reinsurance	257
5.5	Auxiliary services	258
6.	Financial services	260
7.	Computer and information services	262
7.1	Computer services	263
7.2	Information services	264
8.	Royalties and license fees	266
8.1	Franchises and similar rights	891
8.2	Other royalties and license fees	892
9.	Other business services	268
9.1	Merchanting and other trade-related services	269
9.2	Operational leasing services	272
9.3	Miscellaneous business, professional, and technical services	273
10.	Personal, cultural, and recreational services	287
10.1	Audiovisual and related services	288
10.2	Other personal, cultural, and recreational services	289
11.	Government services, not included elsewhere	291
11.1	Embassies and consulates	292
11.2	Military units and agencies	293
11.3	Other government services	294

GLOSSARY

asymmetric information. Situation in which one party to a transaction has better information than another, allowing it to exploit the other party's incomplete knowledge.

backward linkage. A "pull" impact of an increase in final demand in a sector on input suppliers to that sector in terms of value added; reveals demand response of a sector from all other (upstream) sectors' supply of inputs.

business process outsourcing (BPO). Contractual agreement of a service to completely manage, deliver, and operate one or more (typically IT–intensive) business processes or functions.

computable general equilibrium model. Model that captures interactions among markets, production, and consumption and which allows estimation of welfare and resource allocation effects resulting from changes in trade policy.

direct method. Assessment of the impact of service regulation on economic performance such as prices and costs on the basis of real information on restrictive policies.

domestic enabling factors. Policies related to the domestic economic and institutional situation within a country, such as institutions, governance, the business environment, labor skills, management and entrepreneurial skills, and trade-related infrastructure.

dyadic gravity equation. Specification for a gravity equation in which the economic mass variable is picked up by importer and exporter fixed effects. This specification controls for all country-specific factors that affect bilateral trade flows and corrects for unobservable omitted variables that could be present in the error term of a specification without fixed effects, potentially biasing the point estimates.

EU KLEMS. Project, funded by the European Commission between 2003 and 2008, that created a database of measures of economic growth, productivity, employment, capital formation, and technological change at the industry level for all member states of the European Union and several other OECD countries from 1970 onward.

Export of Value Added Database. Database of gross and net production and export figures constructed by the World Bank. Data come from the Global Trade Analysis Project (GTAP).

export sophistication/EXPY. Measure of the income content of a country's export basket. Captures whether a country's export basket consists primarily of services typically exported by high-income or low-income economies.

extensive margin. Indicator that assesses whether exports are growing because a country is exporting new goods and services or reaching new markets rather than exporting more of the same goods and services to the same markets.

Foreign Affiliates Trade Statistics (FATS). Indicators of Mode 3 trade in services. Measures the extent to which multinationals sell their service through an affiliate established in a foreign country.

forward linkage. Measure of the contribution of a sector as an input in terms of value added in other sectors; reveals supply response of a sector to all other (downstream) sectors' demand for more inputs.

free-rider problem. Situation in which some individuals or firms either consume more than their fair share or pay less than their fair share of the cost of a common resource. Free-riding can lead to the underproduction of a public good or excessive use of a common property resource.

Gini coefficient. Measure of income distribution or industrial concentration.

global value chain. The full range of activities executed through different stages of production, which are located in various geographical locations, that bring a product or service from conception to delivery to final consumers and disposal after use.

gravity equation. Equation that relates countries' bilateral trade flows to structural determinants such as GDP, geographic distance, and other factors that affect trade costs.

gravity model. Model for predicting the level of interaction between two countries.

Herfindahl-Hirschman Index. Standard concentration index. Measures the size of exports of each sector in relation to each other within a geographical unit.

horizontal measures. Measures that affect services providers across the board. These include measures such as conditions on making foreign investments, regulations on accessing foreign currency, and laws on the entry and stay of individual travelers that affect (services) providers across the board.

indirect method. Assessment of the level of openness, restrictiveness, or contestability of a market based on comparison against a benchmark. Often such assessment is executed by lack of any direct method.

intensive margin. Indicator that assesses whether exports are growing because a country is exporting more of the same goods and services to the same market rather than exporting new goods and services or reaching new markets.

inward FATS. Indicator of operations of foreign-owned firms in the host economy under Mode 3 trade in services.

joint venture. Company whose equity is owned by both a foreign and a domestic firm; form of business organization often required before a foreign firm is allowed to operate in a country.

jointness in production. Requirement for proximity of the consumer and the producer.

Knowledge Assessment Methodology (KAM). Interactive benchmarking tool created by the Knowledge for Development Program of the World Bank to help countries identify the challenges and opportunities they face in making the transition to the knowledge economy.

knowledge economy. Economy in which knowledge is the main engine of economic growth.

knowledge process outsourcing (KPO). Contractual agreement to completely manage, deliver, and operate one or more (typically IT–intensive) business processes or functions that are knowledge intensive, such as business consulting, business analytics, market intelligence, and legal services.

ladder of comparative advantage. Stages of development in which countries move from an economy of production and trade largely based on agriculture, to one based on industry, and finally services following relative prices and adoption of new technologies.

leapfrogging. Skipping of one or more of the sequential stages in a process.

moral hazard. Tendency of a person to be more willing to take a risk if he or she knows that the potential costs of doing so will be borne, in whole or in part, by others.

national treatment. Nondiscriminatory treatment of nationals, foreigners, investors, goods, and services.

natural monopoly. Situation in which the long-run average cost of production decreases with output, implying that costs are lowest when a single firm produces a good or service, making participation by more than one firm unviable. Natural monopolies exist where investment costs are very high, creating huge economies of scale and high barriers to entry. Examples include public utilities.

network externalities. Situation in which access to essential facilities is a critical ingredient and the overall benefit for the economy depends on how many other individuals or firms also have access to the facilities or knowledge provided. Sectors characterized by network externalities include telecommunications, transport and logistics services, and financial services.

outward FATS. Indicator of operations of affiliates of domestic firms established abroad under Mode 3 trade in services.

positive externality. Benefit created for one party by an activity performed by another. Examples include the effect of one person's education on others.

PRODY. Measure of the income content of a product or service; income level associated with a product or service.

prudential regulations. Regulations aimed at achieving a legitimate policy objective such as consumer protection without being protectionist. In the case of the financial services sector, they ensure financial soundness of licensed financial institutions to prevent financial system instability and losses of deposits by unsophisticated investors. Examples include capital adequacy requirements, liquidity requirements, and loan-loss provisioning mandates.

public good. Good or service that is both nonexcludable (individuals cannot be effectively excluded from use) and nonrival (use by one individual does not reduce the availability of the good to others). Examples include national defense and lighthouses.

public-private partnership. Private sector business venture that provides a service traditionally provided by the government and is funded and operated through a partnership of government and one or more private sector companies.

Revealed Comparative Advantage (RCA) Index. Measure that compares the share of a sector's exports of a country in the country's total exports with the share of exports of all countries in that sector in the world's total exports for all sectors.

revealed factor intensity. Measure of intensities of factors, such as human and physical capital, in a sector.

Revealed Human Capital Index (RHCI). Adjusted version of the RCA Index multiplied by a country's human capital stock.

Revealed Information and Communications Technology–Related Capital Index (RICTI). Adjusted version of the RCA Index multiplied by a country's ICT-related capital stock.

Revealed Physical Capital Index (RPCI). Adjusted version of the RCA Index multiplied by a country's physical capital stock.

Theil Entropy Index. Standard diversification measure. Measures the size of exports of each sector in relation to each other within a geographical unit.

Tradability Index. Measure of the probability of trade taking place in a particular sector between partner countries.

Trade Complementarities Index (TCI). Index indicating extent to which a country's export profile is similar to a partner country's import profile.

Trade in Services Database. Data set of bilateral services flows aggregated by the World Bank. Data come from the Organisation for Economic Co-operation and Development (OECD), Eurostat, the United Nations, and the International Monetary Fund (IMF).

trade-in-tasks paradigm. Paradigm in which trade patterns consist of flows of goods, services, investment, and know-how necessary to produce goods and services fragmented in multiple tasks located in different countries.

Trade Intensity Index (TII). Index indicating the extent to which a country is present in the export market of a trading partner relative to other trade partner countries.

World Development Indicators (WDI). World Bank's primary collection of development indicators, compiled from officially recognized international sources. Indicators, which include national, regional, and global estimates, are the most current and accurate global development data available.

INTRODUCTION

Globalization continues to create opportunities, in particular for competitive developing countries. But it also presents new challenges. Because the global economy is changing rapidly, countries need to continuously reposition themselves on the global trade and production map.

The Role of Services in Trade and Competitiveness: Key Issues and Debates

In an ever-more globalizing and competitive world, it is important for countries to understand how they fare relative to competitors and to their own past export performance.

Trade indicators have been used extensively as a measure of competitiveness. Balassa (1965) used them to measure revealed comparative advantage. Hatsopoulos, Krugman, and Summers (1988) and Markusen (1992) tied trade balances to rising real income. Sharpe (1985, 1986), Krugman and Hatsopoulos (1987), Fagerberg (1988), and Mandeng (1991) used them to estimate market shares or increases in market share.

Competition can also be measured by relative prices. In competitive economies, equilibrium factor prices are lower than those of international competitors. The real exchange rate and the real effective exchange rate are measures of competitiveness based on relative prices. Durand and Giorno (1987), Helleiner (1989), and Lipshitz and McDonald (1991) use them to measure competitiveness.

Other studies (Buckley, Pass, and Prescott 1988; Porter 1990; WEF 2004) use multidimensional definitions of competitiveness. Although these measures are unsuitable for deriving robust quantitative measures, they have the advantage of capturing several aspects of competitiveness.

Services are an important component of competitiveness in two respects. First, a country with a comparative advantage in tradable services can export them, thereby diversifying the economy and expanding the country's exports. Second, services can be a strategic driver of competitiveness for the whole economy.

What's Special about Trade in Services?

Trade of goods and trade of services differ in several important ways (Francois and Hoekman 2010; Copeland and Mattoo 2008). Goods trade involves shipping goods from one country to another, whereas cross-border trade in services (known as Mode 1) is only one of the modes by which services are traded. Trade in services also occurs when the consumer crosses the border (Mode 2). Trade also occurs when a producer establishes a commercial presence in the consumer's country (Mode 3) or the producer temporarily moves across borders to provide the service (Mode 4). In services trade, then, the international movement of factors of production—capital, in the form of foreign direct investment (FDI), and labor, in the form of temporary labor mobility—are critical.

How important are the different modes of supply? In 2005, the most important mode of supply was commercial presence (Mode 3), suggesting that firms serve foreign markets primarily through in-house offshored services activities (table I.1). In addition to the need for face-to-face interaction between the producer and the consumer of many services, the fact that services often have a very high level of intellectual property content (and rights) may explain this preference.

Modes of supply may be either substitutes or complements. When modes are perfect substitutes, liberalization of one of them should be sufficient to fully reap the gains of liberalization. When modes are imperfect substitutes, their competitiveness normally requires more than one set of reforms and a framework that takes into account the mix of cross-border and locally supplied services.

The mix of reforms needed is likely to change over time and to be location specific. The evolving patterns of technology underpinning services trade and the new possibilities they open require recognition of the fact that policies need to adapt. A new technology that allows the cross-border provision of a wide range of professional services, for example, makes nationality or local

1

Table I.1. Share of Total Trade in Services, by Mode of Supply, 2005

Mode	Description	Share of total trade in services (percent)
1	Cross-border trade	25–30
2	Consumption abroad	10–15
3	Commercial presence	55–60
4	Presence of natural persons	Less than 5

Source: Magdeleine and Maurer 2008.

presence requirements increasingly irrelevant and ineffective (Francois and Hoekman 2010).

For many services (and goods), the relationship between investment and trade is complex. For some services, there is strong complementarity: investment facilitates trade (Helpman 2011). The empirical literature on services indicates a robust complementary relationship between trade and FDI that has increased over time. The sign and magnitude of the relationship differs across categories. The categories for which a significant complementary relationship have been found—banking; insurance; business, professional, technical, and legal services (Lennon 2009)—account for the bulk of services exports. These services are also the most dynamic in terms of export growth.

Services provision also requires complementary inputs (financial services, for instance, require professional and telecommunication services). In order to export, it is thus not sufficient to have an advantage in a particular service if other required inputs are not in place. Examples of this interdependency abound: logistics services depend on the interaction among transportation, freight-forwarding services, warehousing, and cargo handling (Kunaka, Antoci, and Sáez 2013). The success of tourism depends on the provision of other services and physical infrastructure, such as airports and roads.

Many services require the proximity of the consumer and the producer—what is known as **jointness in production.** Customers often provide information to producers regarding their needs that is critical for effective delivery of the service (Hoekman and Kostecki 2009).

Jointness has important implications for policy design. For example, regulatory regimes are important determinants of the feasibility of trade in services. Cross-border trade restrictions may diminish FDI incentives, and restrictions on the operations of foreign firms may limit cross-border trade in services. Cross-border service exports are thus linked to inward FDI flows. FDI policies are key for promoting exports of services (Francois and Hoekman 2010).

Service industries are usually characterized by market failures, such as imperfect and **asymmetric information**, lack of competition, and natural barriers to entry, particularly in sectors with significant **network externalities.** Problems of imperfect and asymmetric information arise if buyers and service providers face difficulties assessing the standing of providers or consumers. Regulation and infrastructure, including competition laws and independent regulatory bodies, are necessary in sectors in which market failures are prevalent. Regulating in a way that does not unnecessarily restrict trade is therefore complex.

Services as a Source of Export Diversification

Many developing countries export a diversified range of services, both within their own regions and to high-income countries. Although services are intrinsically less tradable than most goods (because they typically require the face-to-face presence of buyer and seller), the falling costs of travel, communications, and information technology and increasing access to the Internet are making it easier to produce a service in one location and consume it in another, thus creating new opportunities for trade in services.

As a result, exports of services have increased for all country income groups and regions (figure I.1). Developing countries' share of world services exports increased from 18 percent in 1990 to 30 percent in 2012.[1] India's exports of software and business process services accounted for about 33 percent of its total services exports. In Latin America, Brazil, Costa Rica, and Uruguay export professional and information technology–related services; Mexico exports communication and distribution services; and Chile exports distribution and transportation services. Exports of professional services to Europe by Kenya, South Africa, and Tunisia are growing. The Philippines, Singapore, and Thailand are exporting medical services, and Malaysia is increasing its exports of education, Islamic banking, and telecommunication services.

The increasing tradability of services is one the most important changes in trade patterns of the last quarter of the 20th century. The tradability of services is driven by changes in technology and regulatory reforms. Improvements in information and communication technologies (ICT) have reduced—and for a range of services eliminated—the need for proximity between consumer and producer. They have done so by increasing storability and allowing greater use of outsourcing and offshoring in the context of global and regional production chains. Breakthrough reforms that increased the tradability of services include the elimination of monopoly providers and restrictions that affected foreign investors. These changes have allowed the private sector and foreign investors to provide services traditionally provided by the state (Francois and Hoekman 2010).

Figure I.1. Services Trade as Share of GDP, by Region

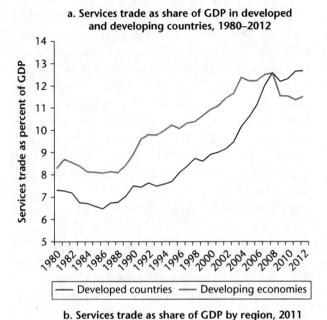

a. Services trade as share of GDP in developed and developing countries, 1980–2012

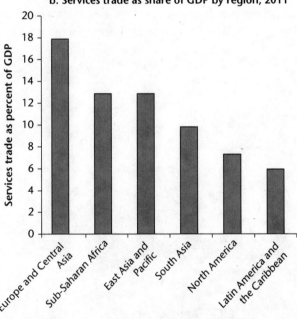

b. Services trade as share of GDP by region, 2011

Source: United Nations Conference on Trade and Development (UNCTAD) and World Development Indicators.

As the number of champions of services exports from middle- and lower-income country groups has grown, policy makers increasingly recognize the unexploited potential of services trade. Developing countries were initially reluctant to embrace the services trade agenda. During negotiation of the Uruguay Round of the General Agreement on Tariffs and Trade (GATT), the conventional wisdom was that developing countries lacked a comparative advantage in services trade and the capacity to deal with the complex nature of trade liberalization, deregulation, and the required policy reforms. Since the mid-1990s, this perception has slowly changed. Policy makers now ask for guidance on identifying areas of potential comparative advantage over peer countries in the services sector.

Services as a Source of Competitiveness to the Whole Economy

Services play a strategic role in countries' competitiveness agenda not only because they are a source of export diversification but also because they are used in the production of many downstream competitive products. The competitiveness of most goods exports depends not only on access to raw material inputs but also on critical services inputs, including efficient, competitively priced utilities, financial services, and other commercial services. Because of the importance of services to the economy as a whole, more and more governments want to improve their understanding of the size, scope, and potential of services production and exports and to identify obstacles that need to be removed to unlock the competitiveness of their services sectors.

Increasing the competitiveness of the services sector is important, particularly given internationally fragmented models of production. Trade in the 20th century was mainly about selling goods to customers in another country. In the 21st century, trade is increasingly about flows of the goods, services, ideas, investment, training, know-how, and intellectual property needed to produce goods and services in multiple locations (Baldwin 2011, 2012; Jones 2000; Grossman and Rossi-Hansberg 2008; Feenstra 2010; Helpman 2011).

Global value chains internationalize the nexus of flows, giving rise to the trade-investment-service-intellectual property nexus. Global value chains can be thought of as factories that cross international borders. Traditional factories clustered most stages of production into a single building or industrial district. Coordinating complex production processes involves continuous, two-way flows between goods, people, ideas, investment, training, know-how, and other inputs. Factories traditionally minimized the cost of such flows by keeping all stages of production as close to one another as possible.

The ICT revolution of the 1990s reduced the cost of coordinating complexity over long distances, allowing production stages that previously had to be within walking distance to be dispersed internationally. Some stages of production were offshored to lower-wage countries, giving rise to global value chains, transforming the nature of international commerce.

Global value chains did not end the need for the intra-stage flows of goods, people, ideas, investment, and know-how; they internationalized them. Flows that used to take place only within factories in high-income countries are now a key part of international commerce.

Services trade coordinates the dispersed production. Thanks to the ICT revolution, production stages can be coordinated at a distance, allowing production stages to be dispersed geographically and to benefit from price, cost, and wage differentials.

Easy access to efficient services and infrastructure in the host country—inexpensive and reliable power, reliable telecommunications and transport, finance and trade support—is critical to domestic and particularly foreign investors. Among firms surveyed, 52 percent cited access to finance and 39 percent cited transport infrastructure and services as the most serious supply-side constraint among global value chain suppliers in developing countries (OECD–WTO 2013). For all types of services,

the organization of the domestic segment of the value chain is as important as the international one.

The "servicification" of manufacturing is apparent from figure I.2, which shows that about 40 types of services are involved when a manufacturing firm internationalizes its production. This example indicates that even in the manufacturing sector, a country cannot be competitive and join global value chains if it does not have efficient domestic services or is closed to the imports of such services. Managing the complexity of the chain and preserving the production standards throughout requires coordination of efficient services and the movement of key personnel across borders.

Recent data suggest that services represent more than 30 percent of the value added of trade in manufactures (figure I.3).

The central role of services becomes more apparent when one looks at trade through the lens of the new **trade-in-tasks paradigm** proposed by Grossman and Rossi-Hansberg (2008). As figure I.4 shows, firms' location decisions are task specific. Country strategies should move away from paradigms in which development means evolving in terms of sectors, focusing instead on the tasks they

Figure I.2. Services Involved in the Internationalization of Production

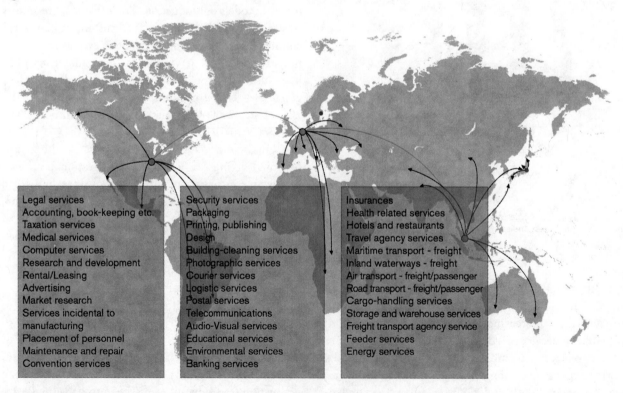

Legal services
Accounting, book-keeping etc.
Taxation services
Medical services
Computer services
Research and development
Rental/Leasing
Advertising
Market research
Services incidental to manufacturing
Placement of personnel
Maintenance and repair
Convention services

Security services
Packaging
Printing, publishing
Design
Building-cleaning services
Photographic services
Courier services
Logistic services
Postal services
Telecommunications
Audio-Visual services
Educational services
Environmental services
Banking services

Insurances
Health related services
Hotels and restaurants
Travel agency services
Maritime transport - freight
Inland waterways - freight
Air transport - freight/passenger
Road transport - freight/passenger
Cargo-handling services
Storage and warehouse services
Freight transport agency service
Feeder services
Energy services

Source: Swedish National Board of Trade (Kommerskollegium) 2010.
Note: Figure displays production by Sandvik Tooling, a Swedish producer of construction equipment and tools.

Figure I.3. Value Added of Services as Share of Value Added of Manufacturing, by Sector, 2009

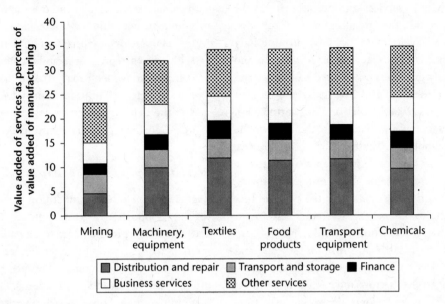

Source: OECD-WTO 2013.
Note: Distribution and repair does not include distribution of final goods.

Figure I.4. From Sector-Based to Task-Based Development Strategies

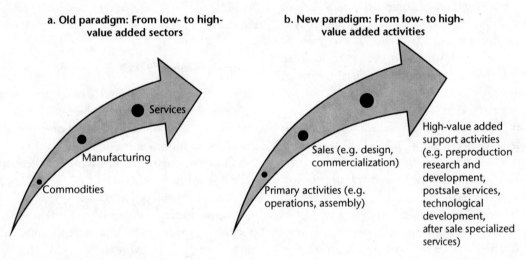

Source: Adapted from Cattaneo and Miroudot 2013.

can perform within sectors, which may serve as inputs to multiple sectors.

The new paradigm brings to the forefront the fact that the range of activities necessary to 21st century manufacturing is very broad and includes many services. The classical literature on value chains (Porter 1985) distinguishes between primary, support, and sales activities. Primary activities range from manufacturing of inputs, outputs, and assembly operations to inbound and outbound logistics, marketing, sales, and a range of other service activities. Support activities include the production of other inputs (machinery and equipment as well as many services activities, including research

and development); technological development; and activities aimed at organizing the firm's infrastructure, human resources management, and procurement.

The Role of Regulation

Where the domestic services sector is weak, access to imports of services (through all modes of production) must be liberalized in order to increase access to efficient, world-class services. Liberalization allows an economy to increase both the services intensity and the value addition of the goods and services it produces and exports.

The empirical literature finds a positive relationship between productivity in services and productivity in the overall economy. Within the Organisation for Economic Co-operation and Development (OECD), productivity growth in services has been a key driver of growth, and general productivity growth can be traced to market and business services (Hoekman and Kostecki 2009; Inklaar, Timmer, and Ark 2007, 2008; Triplett and Bosworth 2004). Services imports serve as a transmission channel for the transfer of new technologies. These imports both improve the performance of services exports in skill-intensive industries and increase the value added of manufacturing exports (Francois and Woerz 2008; for the positive link between trade liberalization of services sectors and manufacturing productivity, see Arnold, Mattoo, and Narciso 2008; Arnold and others 2010; and Arnold, Javorcik, and Mattoo 2011). Services trade plays a key role in increasing the productivity of services sectors and has a strong impact on overall productivity and economic growth over time (van der Marel 2012).

For these reasons, services matters to a country's competitiveness, and investment barriers to services matter to trade. Lack of clarity and predictability in domestic laws or deficiencies in domestic services may reduce productivity and the attractiveness of a country to foreign investors.

Following Goswami, Mattoo, and Sáez (2012), one can distinguish three broad types of policies affecting services competitiveness:

- Regulatory policy affecting trade, investment, and labor mobility in services includes all policies affecting cross-border trade and the domestic provision of services.[2] These policies do not explicitly target trade in services but nevertheless affect it.
- Trade barriers that target trade, investment, and labor mobility in services include policies designed to promote exports and investment. They include the creation of special economic zones and privileged access to land, infrastructure, and imported inputs; fiscal incentives for exporters and investors, in the form of subsidies or tax

exemptions; and other forms of trade-promotion activities, such as trade fairs and information dissemination.
- **Domestic enabling factors** include a country's endowments of factors, especially of human capital, including skills and entrepreneurial ability; natural resources and cultural endowments that attract tourists; infrastructure, especially telecommunications networks, which facilitate the delivery of services; and institutional quality, especially the regulatory environment for services.

Regulatory Policy and Trade Barriers

Regulation, including competition laws and independent regulatory bodies, is necessary in sectors in which market failures are prevalent. Such regulation is often implemented to deal with limited competition, asymmetric information, and differences between private and social utility (externalities and **public goods**). Putting in place regulations that do not unnecessarily restrict trade is difficult.

A wide set of limitations affect imports and exports of services explicitly. These measures can be discriminatory or nondiscriminatory in intent and direct or indirect. They are likely to pertain to market access, **national treatment**, domestic regulations, and other regulations (table I.2).

Domestic Enabling Factors

Good regulatory policies stand to gain from other measures a government can implement. These policies are related to the domestic economic and institutional situation inside the country (fundamentals) rather than the explicit policies in place. **Horizontal measures** complement specific trade and domestic policies.

Domestic enabling factors are broad in scope. They include institutions, governance, business environment, labor skills, management and entrepreneurial skills, and trade-related infrastructure (table I.3).

A shared language, cultural history, or colonial history is likely to increase services exports, because such factors make it easier to establish business ties.

Table I.2. Types and Examples of Trade Barriers

Type of barrier	Example	Nature of effect
Market access	Measures, usually quantitative, that make it difficult for foreign firms to enter the domestic market	Direct
National treatment	Legal (de jure) restrictions against foreign firms	Direct
	Discrimination through nondiscriminatory barriers (de facto)	Indirect
Domestic regulation	Regulations that do not explicitly target foreign firms or restrict trade but may constitute de facto trade barriers if they are more burdensome than necessary to achieve a legitimate policy objective. These measures include both nondiscriminatory entry regulations and regulations affecting ongoing operations.	Indirect

Table I.3. Domestic Enabling Factors

Policy area	Objective
Labor skills	Increase capacity to produce sophisticated services exports; climb up ladder of comparative advantage in services (or from goods to services), especially in professional, computer and computer-related, and business services.
Management and entrepreneurial skills	Enhance adoption and use of modern technologies that are essential for producing a service or good.
Trade-related infrastructure	Reduce costs related to delivery of services (transportation, telecommunications, export, transactions, and search costs).
Institutions	Establish governance arrangements to foster relationships between private parties rather than between private parties and the government (Acemoglu and Johnson 2005).
Governance	Increase ability of governments to formulate and implement sound policies and regulations that allow and promote private sector development.
Business environment	Attract foreign direct investment and multinational corporations in order to expand exports and increase domestic competitiveness.

These characteristics cannot be changed. By contrast, institutions, governance, the business environment, labor skills, management and entrepreneurial skills, and trade-related infrastructure can be enhanced, albeit only in the medium to long term.

Institutions reduce transaction costs, disproportionately benefitting sectors that engage in a complex web of transactions with the rest of the economy (Amin and Mattoo 2006). Certain institutions play a particularly significant role in the development of services sectors, for three reasons:

- Asymmetric information is greater in services markets than in goods markets, because it is harder for consumers to evaluate the quality of services before they purchase them. Regulatory institutions therefore matter more.
- Services sectors that require specialized distribution networks (such as roads and rails for land transport, cables and satellites for communications, and pipes for energy distribution) are likely to be **natural monopolies** or oligopolies. Regulations are needed to ensure that monopolistic suppliers do not exploit consumers or undermine market access (Mattoo, Stern, and Zannini 2007).
- For customized services, both consumers and suppliers must make relationship-specific investments, raising the cost of switching from one supplier or consumer to another. Contract-enforcing institutions therefore assume greater importance in services than in goods. A firm's willingness to outsource medical transcription or confidential financial information, for example, is much greater if it has confidence in the privacy and data protection laws of the host country and therefore of the firm responsible for processing the information (Amin and Mattoo 2006).

Molinuevo and Sáez (2014) provide a methodology for assessing both the regulatory environment and the governance of service regulations. A Regulatory Assessment of Services Trade and Investment (RASTI) can help policy makers assess regulations consistently, streamline the regulatory framework, and set up a process for introducing new regulations. A RASTI provides the information required to finalize the competitive diagnostic and provide relevant policy recommendations regarding policies affecting services trade.

Assessing the business environment for FDI and the ability to attract and protect foreign investors is a critical part of the diagnostic. Empirical research finds a positive correlation between services openness and growth (Mattoo and Rathindran 2006; Francois and Hoekman 2010). Because one of the most relevant modes of supply for services trade is commercial presence (which includes investment decisions of foreign and domestic providers), the analysis should focus on the following:

- openness and degree of foreign participation
- government policy toward foreign capital (risk of expropriation, investment protection)
- degree to which private property rights are guaranteed and protected
- procedures required to set up a new business and freedom of existing businesses to compete
- legal environment (contract enforcement, piracy rates, intellectual property protection and laws governing ICT) and perceptions of corruption.

Because many services activities are skill intensive, assessing the skill level of the country's workforce, the availability of specific skills, and overall skill intensity, including managerial skills, of services sectors is critical. Many sectors (business services, banking, telecommunications) are significantly more skill intensive than most goods sectors. Cross-country evidence suggests that endowments of human capital are an important determinant of output and growth (figure I.5). Sustaining growth in South Asia may require addressing the serious systemic weaknesses in higher education. In the Philippines, the success of **business process outsourcing (BPO)** exports may soon be hampered by the dearth of skilled workers. Moving from BPO to **knowledge process outsourcing (KPO)** activities requires higher levels of skills to attract investors.

Managerial skills also play a key role in the adoption of modern technologies, which are critical for producing high-quality services for export. Experience working in a multinational firm has been found to develop such skills. Development of the Indian software industry is attributed largely to entrepreneurs of Indian origin who had world-class training in management skills or experience working abroad in multinational firms (Gregory, Nollen, and Tenev 2009).

Trade-related infrastructure is also important (figure I.5). Transport and tourism are intensive in physical infrastructure and sensitive to institutions such as customs and border management. These characteristics make these subsectors more similar to goods exports than to other services exports. In contrast, commercial services that are usually traded across borders rely on telecommunication infrastructure and are sensitive to contract enforcement. The diagnostic should identify the state of the infrastructure sectors required to develop specific services; assess their efficiency; and review the role of proactive policies, such as the creation of information technology (IT) parks, in addressing infrastructure needs.

Some governments promote specific services sectors by providing trade-related infrastructure. To address key infrastructure and regulatory constraints, such as weak supply of electricity, telecommunications/Internet broadband, and real estate services as well as burdensome regulations that affect the local business environment, some developing country governments have created special regimes, such as IT parks. Export-oriented firms in such facilities enjoy dedicated infrastructure and streamlined administration.

Telecommunications growth is the most powerful symbol of vitality of the services sector. It is also critical to the development of other services. ICT has reduced the cost of delivering many cross-border services to virtually zero.

Organization of the Toolkit

A diagnostics analysis of services trade assesses the enabling factors and obstacles to services competitiveness. Conducting the assessment requires a number of preparatory steps, including defining the objectives of the assessment, evaluating the main actors, assessing how it relates to a country's overall pro-competitiveness strategies, and defining the scope of the assessment.

This toolkit provides general guidance, based on the methodology developed by Reis and Farole (2012) for goods. It provides guidance on finding answers to at least six broad questions:

- How can one assess the trade performance of a country's services sector?
- How can one assess the role of services as inputs in the traded sectors of an economy?
- What factors determine services trade performance?

Figure I.5. Cross-Country Regression of Services Exports versus Gross Tertiary Enrollment and Internet Penetration

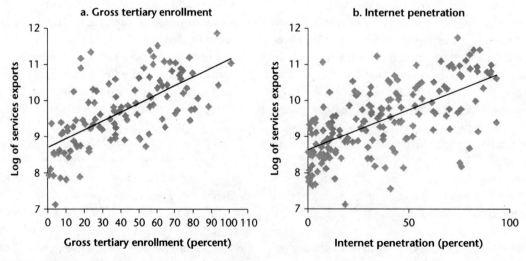

Source: World Development Indicators and Goswami, Mattoo, and Sáez 2012.

- What is the relative importance of these determinants for different services?
- How do policies affect the efficiency of these determinants and of services exports?
- What are the main policy constraints to the growth and development of trade in services?

It does so by providing a methodology and instruments for (a) assessing countries' performance and potential in services, both as exports and as inputs into other traded activities, and (b) identifying key constraints that affect services trade. Its objective is to help policy makers improve services trade and facilitate countries' integration into global markets by increasing their competitiveness. To achieve this objective, the toolkit provides a framework for analyzing and assessing the performance of the services industry and identifying specific enabling factors or obstacles that affect the efficiency of services. It complements the analytical framework of trade in goods provided by the Trade Competitiveness Diagnostic Toolkit (Reis and Farole 2012), allowing policy makers in developing countries to better integrate services into their overall trade strategies.

The toolkit consists of four modules. Module 1 proposes measures of outcomes in trade in services. Module 2 assesses the existence and importance of a domestic services sector. Module 3 assesses countries' potential for expanding trade in services. Module 4 examines broad policy areas and options for addressing the constraints identified in Modules 1, 2, and 3. It distinguishes between sectoral policies that can be implemented in the short to medium term (mostly technical regulations and barriers) and horizontal measures and strategies related to the domestic economy and institutions, which can be implemented only over a longer time horizon.

Conducting a Services Trade Competitiveness Diagnostic (STCD) requires six sequential steps:

- desk-based assessment of trade outcomes
- initial desk-based research on and formulation of hypotheses on failures and policy areas to address in detail
- planning of and preparation for fieldwork
- in-country field research
- follow-up investigation of issues that emerge during field analysis
- preparation of final synthesis STCD report.

The STCD is designed to be completed within four months, including between two to six weeks of fieldwork. It should be conducted by a core team of three or four people. At least one team member should be a trade economist with an understanding of trade policy and competitiveness issues and technical skills in analyzing services trade data. The team leader should have in-depth country knowledge and experience and, ideally, some trade experience. It should not be necessary to involve technical experts for each component of the diagnostic. However, if certain topics are considered critical at the outset, it may be useful to bring in specialized technical expertise to lead those components.

Input from a wide variety of stakeholders in the country, including government officials and the private sector, is critical to the success of an STCD. Consultation should take place through individual and focus group interviews. In some cases, it may also be useful for key stakeholders from government, business, and labor to participate in the assessment.

Notes

1. See http://unctadstat.unctad.org/TableViewer/tableView.aspx.

2. Trade policies in services are all government measures that limit the international transaction of services by foreign providers. The General Agreement on Trade in Services (GATS) of the World Trade Organization (WTO) applies to measures affecting trade in services. The focus of negotiations is on market access limitations and discrimination between domestic and foreign services and services providers (national treatment). The GATS defines market access limitations as measures that affect the number of services suppliers, transactions, operations, number of people that may be employed in a particular sector, the types of legal entity through which a supplier may provide a service, and the participation of foreign capital. Measures that limit national treatment are domestic regulations that imply de jure or de facto discrimination of foreign services and providers.

References

Acemoglu, Daron, and Simon Johnson. 2005. "Unbundling Institutions." *Journal of Political Economy* 113 (5): 949–95.

Amin, Mohammad, and Aaditya Mattoo. 2006. "Do Institutions Matter More for Services?" Policy Research Working Paper 4032, World Bank, Washington, DC.

Arnold, Jens, Beata Javorcik, Molly Lipscomb, and Aaditya Mattoo. 2010. "Services Reform and Manufacturing Performance: Evidence from India," CEPR Discussion Paper 8011, Centre for Economic Policy Research, London.

Arnold, Jens, Beata Javorcik, and Aaditya Mattoo. 2011. "Does Services Liberalization Benefit Manufacturing Firms? Evidence from the Czech Republic." *Journal of International Economics* 85 (1): 136–46.

Arnold, Jens M., Aaditya Mattoo, and Gaia Narciso. 2008. "Services Inputs and Firm Productivity in Sub-Saharan Africa: Evidence from Firm-Level Data." *Journal of African Economies* 17 (4): 578–99.

Balassa, B. 1965. "Trade Liberalisation and Revealed Comparative Advantage." *The Manchester School* 33 (2): 99–123.

Baldwin, R. 2011. "Trade and Industrialisation after Globalisation's 2nd Unbundling: How Building and Joining a Supply Chain Are Different and Why It Matters." NBER Working Paper 17716, National Bureau of Economic Research, Cambridge, MA. http://www.nber.org/papers/w17716.

———. 2012. "Global Supply Chains: Why They Emerged, Why They Matter, and Where They Are Going." CEPR Discussion Paper 9103, Centre for Economic Policy Research, London.

Buckley, Peter J., Christopher L. Pass, and Kate Prescott. 1988. "Measures of International Competitiveness: A Critical Survey." *Journal of Marketing Management* 4 (2): 175–200.

Cattaneo, O. and S. Miroudot. 2013. "From Global Value Chains to Global Development Chains: An Analysis of Recent Changes in Trade Patterns and Development Paradigms." In *21st Century Trade Policy: Back to the Past?* edited by E. Zedillo and B. Hoekman. New Haven, CT: Yale University Press.

Copeland, Brian, and Aaditya Mattoo. 2008. "The Basic Economics of Services Trade." In *A Handbook of International Trade in Services*, edited by Aaditya Mattoo, Robert M. Stern, and Gianni Zanini. Oxford: Oxford University Press.

Durand, M., and C. Giorno. 1987. "Indicators of International Competitiveness: Conceptual Aspects and Evaluation." *OECD Economic Studies* 9: 147–82.

Fagerberg, J. 1988. "International Competitiveness." *Economic Journal* 391: 355–74.

Feenstra, Robert C. 2010. *Offshoring in the Global Economy: Microeconomic Structure and Macroeconomic Implications.* Cambridge: MIT Press.

Francois, Joseph, and Bernard Hoekman. 2010. "Services Trade and Policy." *Journal of Economic Literature* 48 (3): 642–92.

Francois, Joseph, and Julia Woerz. 2008. "Producer Services, Manufacturing Linkages, and Trade." *Journal of Industry, Competition and Trade* 8 (3): 199–229.

Goswami, Arti Grover, Aaditya Mattoo, and Sebastián Sáez. 2012. "Service Exports: Are the Drivers Different for Developing Countries?" In *Exporting Services: A Developing Country Perspective*, edited by Arti Grover Goswami, Aaditya Mattoo, and Sebastián Sáez, 25–81. Washington, DC: World Bank.

Gregory, Neil, Stanley Nollen, and Stoyan Tenev. 2009. *New Industries from New Places: The Emergence of the Hardware and Software Industries in China and India.* Redwood City, CA: Stanford University Press and Washington, DC: World Bank.

Grossman, Gene M., and Esteban Rossi-Hansberg. 2008. "Task Trade between Similar Countries." NBER Working Paper 14554, National Bureau of Economic Research, Cambridge, MA.

Hatsopoulos, George N., Paul R. Krugman, and Lawrence H. Summers. 1988. "US Competitiveness: Beyond the Trade Deficit." *Science* 241: 200–307.

Helleiner, G. K. 1989. "Transnational Corporations and Direct Foreign Investment." In *Handbook of Development Economics,* edited by Hollis Chenery and T. N. Srinivasan, 1441–80. Amsterdam: Elsevier.

Helpman, Elhanan. 2011. *Understanding Global Trade.* Cambridge, MA: Belknap Press of Harvard University Press.

Hoekman, Bernard, and Michel Kostecki. 2009. *The Political Economy of the World Trading System,* 3rd. edited by Oxford: Oxford University Press.

Inklaar, Robert, Marcel Timmer, and Bart van Ark. 2007. "Mind the Gap! International Comparisons of Productivity in Services and Goods Production." *German Economic Review* 8 (5): 281–307.

———. 2008. "Market Services Productivity across Europe and the US." *Economic Policy* 23: 141–94.

Jones, Ronald W. 2000. *Globalization and the Theory of Input Trade.* Cambridge, MA: MIT Press.

Krugman, Paul, and George N. Hatsopoulos. 1987. "The Problem of US Competitiveness in Manufacturing." *New England Economic Review* (January/February).

Kunaka, Charles, Monica Alina Antoci, and Sebastián Sáez. 2013. "Trade Dimensions of Logistics Services: A Proposal for Trade Agreements." *Journal of World Trade* 47(4): 925–50.

Lennon, Caroline. 2009. "Trade in Services and Trade in Goods: Differences and Complementarities." WIIW Working Paper 53, Vienna Institute of International Economics Studies (WIIW), Vienna.

Lipschitz L., and D. McDonald. 1991. "Real Exchange Rates and Competitiveness: A Clarification of Concepts and Some Measurement for Europe." IMF Working Papers, Washington, DC.

Magdeleine, Joscelyn, and Andreas Maurer. 2008. "Measuring GATS Mode 4 Trade Flows." WTO Staff Working Paper ERSD-2008-05, World Trade Organization, Geneva.

Mandeng, O. 1991. "International Competitiveness and Specialization." *CEPAL Review* 45: 39–52.

Markusen, J. 1992. "Productivity, Competitiveness, Trade Performance and Real Income: The Nexus among Four Concepts." Minister of Supply and Services, Ottawa, Canada.

Mattoo, Aaditya, and Randeep Rathindran. 2006. "Measuring Services Trade Liberalization and Its Impact on Economic Growth: An Illustration." *Journal of Economic Integration* 21: 64–98, Center for Economic Integration, Sejong University, Seoul.

Mattoo, Aaditya, Robert M. Stern, and Gianni Zanini, eds. 2007. *A Handbook of International Trade in Services.* Oxford: Oxford University Press.

Molinuevo, Martin, and Sebastián Sáez. 2014. *Regulatory Assessment Toolkit: A Practical Methodology for Assessing Regulation on Trade and Investment in Services.* Washington, DC: World Bank.

OECD (Organisation for Economic Co-operation and Development) and WTO (World Trade Organization). 2013. "OECD-WTO Database on Trade in Value Added First Estimates." January 16, Organisation for Economic Co-operation and Development, Paris.

Porter, Michael. 1985. *Competitive Advantage: Creating and Sustaining Superior Performance.* New York: Free Press.

———.1990. *The Competitive Advantage of Nations.* New York: Free Press.

Reis, José Guilherme, and Thomas Farole. 2012. *Trade Competitiveness Diagnostic Toolkit.* Washington, DC: World Bank.

Sharpe, A. 1985. "Can Canada Compete? Part 1." *Canadian Business Review* 12 (4).

———. 1986. "Can Canada Compete? Part 2." *Canadian Business Review* 13 (1).

Swedish National Board of Trade (Kommerskollegium). 2010. *At Your Service: The Importance of Services for Manufacturing Companies and Possible Trade Policy Implications.* Stockholm. http://www.kommers.se/Documents/dokumentarkiv/publikationer/2010/skriftserien/report-2010-2-at-your-service.pdf.

Triplett, Jack E., and Barry P. Bosworth. 2004. *Productivity in the US Services Sector: New Sources of Economic Growth.* Washington, DC: Brookings Institution Press.

van der Marel, E. 2012. "Trade in Services and TFP: The Role of Regulation." *The World Economy* 35 (11): 1387–429.

WEF (World Economic Forum). 2004 "The Global Competitiveness Index." *Global Competitiveness Report.*

ASSESSING SERVICES TRADE AND COMPETITIVENESS OUTCOMES

Services are important because they are a source of export diversification and a source of competitiveness for the economy as a whole. This module describes instruments that quantify where countries stand in the former respect.

The methodology for assessing services trade outcomes focuses on the size and scope of trade in services. It provides a quantitative and qualitative assessment of historical performance in trade in services.

Both dimensions present important challenges. Measuring services trade faces more constraints than measuring trade in goods, because detailed industry, product, geographical, and time series data are limited. Standard statistics for trade in services are wholly unsatisfactory for describing the competitiveness of the services sector. For emerging markets and developing countries, even standard statistics for trade in services are scant.

The World Bank's **Trade in Services Database** provides better data than were previously available (box 1.1). Because of the difficulty of recording international transactions of services, however, even this data set does not provide the degree of disaggregation that can be found in goods trade data.

Analysis of services trade outcomes is largely a desk-based exercise that involves assessing a series of indicators and analytical tools. The construction of indicators must be complemented by focused, in-depth analysis of specific research questions and by targeted field analysis, to ensure the correct interpretation of the results and to reveal more subtle trends and developments that may not be evident from the data. Firm-level statistics are also a powerful complementary tool. They include census-type information, balance sheet data, and records of export and import transactions. The availability of this information differs from country to country.

The indicators analyzed in this module focus on services export performance. The export performance measures include export growth compared with goods and peer countries, services exports relative to services value added, measures of revealed comparative advantage (RCA), measures of the evolution of exports and world demand that reveal whether specialization observed in a country is moving into the most dynamic sectors, and firm-level measures of exports and imports of services.

The indicators in this module are built mainly on the basis of balance of payments data, which broadly reflect cross-border transactions through Modes 1 and 2. Other data sources for other modes of supply are discussed through Modules 2 and 3. Modules 2, 3, and 4 use additional indicators and other data sources to enrich the analysis.

Size of Trade in Services

The toolkit starts with an analysis of services trade outcomes. It provides a quantitative and qualitative assessment of the historical performance of trade in services. The focus is on determining and comparing the size and scope of trade in services.

Exports of Services

Measuring the Value of Services Exports
Several indicators are critical to assessing the value of services exports. They include the services and goods trade balance, the value of trade in services, and the value of exports and imports of services, all as shares of GDP. Data on these indicators should be collected for specific years for all countries. Useful sources of information include the following:

- World Development Indicators (services trade balance, GDP)
- IMF (balance of payments statistics)
- UNCTADstat (trade balance in services and trade balance in goods).

Box 1.1. Modes of Services Trade and Data on Trade in Services

Services have unique characteristics, such as intangibility and nonstorability, that greatly affect their tradability. They typically also require differentiation and **jointness in production**—that is, the participation of customers in the production process.

In order to capture these aspects and allow for trade in services that also require joint production, the General Agreement on Trade in Services (GATS) of the World Trade Organization (WTO) defines four modes of supply of services:

- **Mode 1**: Cross-border trade (services supplied from the territory of one country into the territory of another)
- **Mode 2**: Consumption abroad (services supplied in the territory of one country to the consumers of another)
- **Mode 3**: Commercial presence (services supplied in the territory of one country by any type of business or professional establishment in another [foreign direct investment])
- **Mode 4**: Presence of natural persons (services supplied by nationals of a country in the territory of another).

(For more on these modes, see Module 3.) Only data on cross-border services trade in Modes 1 and 2 are reported in balance of payments statistics. Foreign direct investment (FDI) is not covered. About 60 percent of the global FDI stock is in the service sector, with finance and trade the most important sectors. Services are also traded through cross-border movement of persons (Mode 4). On the consumer side, Mode 2 covers, for example, Germans going to Poland for dental work, as well as tourism. On the producer side (Mode 4), it includes the temporary cross-border movement of skilled labor, such as accountants and software engineers who work across Europe. It also includes Polish construction workers relocating temporarily to work in the Netherlands or France.

Trade through affiliates (Mode 3) includes exports that pass through affiliates. Indeed, given the nature of services trade and the role of FDI in the sector, the activities of affiliates include a mix of cross-border and local activities.

The quality of trade data in services is far from comparable to the data for goods. Because of the long tradition of tariff revenues, the quality of trade data for goods is high. Because of the intangibility and nonstorability of services, at-the-border-duties cannot be collected. As a result, the data are much less accurate. Particularly with respect to Modes 3 and 4, up-to-date measurement is difficult and incomplete. Ongoing revisions and refinements of the balance of payments classifications are trying to improve the quality of the data.

To create a data set covering bilateral services flows (Trade in Services Database), the World Bank aggregated data collected by the Organisation for Economic Co-operation and Development (OECD), Eurostat, the United Nations, and the International Monetary Fund (IMF) (Appendix B describes the data set). IMF data cover only trade with the world as a partner. The OECD, Eurostat, and United Nations provide data on bilateral services trade flows by partners and balance of payments codes. The most comprehensive coverage is by the United Nations, which provides data on 190 reporters. Eurostat and the OECD provide data for a limited number of countries: Eurostat covers 27 members of the European Union plus Croatia, Iceland, Japan, Norway, Turkey, Switzerland, and the United State; the OECD covers 28 countries (all OECD members except Chile, Iceland, Israel, Slovenia, and Switzerland). WTO data on services trade were not included because they provide limited coverage of sectors and partners; the data are reported for only three sectors and for the world as a partner.

Historically, most services sectors were considered nontradable. This concept changed dramatically over the last two decades, as trade increased in both traditional services sectors (such as transport and postal services) and modern services (such as business services, telecommunications, and information and communications technology [ICT]).[1] However, compared with goods, services trade remains modest for all income groups, as shown in figure 1.1.

Trade in and exports of services are increasing rapidly for all income groups, as shown in figure 1.2. The share of developing countries in world exports of services increased from 18 percent in 1990 to 30 percent in 2012.[2]

Figure 1.2 shows the normalized values of exports of each income group in order to highlight growth differences across income groups during the first decade of the 21st century. Growth was highest for the lower-middle-income group, but all groups grew steadily throughout the period. However, in absolute terms, the high-income group remained dominant. The growth of

services exports was linked to the falling costs of trading, as a result of declines in the costs of transportation and travel; reductions in trade barriers; and improvements in technology. Technological change has been particularly important for services: increased use of ICT, including the Internet, significantly reduced some of the costs associated with trade in services (Freund and Weinhold 2002).

Services are intrinsically less tradable than most goods, because many of them require that buyer and seller meet. But technological advances are enhancing the ability to produce services in one location and consume them in another. ICT and other Internet-related technologies, such as cloud computing, create new opportunities for trade in services and expand the scope of services trade.

Figure 1.3 shows how the increased tradability of services has affected the contributions of different income groups to total world exports in services. It reveals that

Figure 1.1. Shares of Exports of Goods and Services, by Country Income Level, 2011

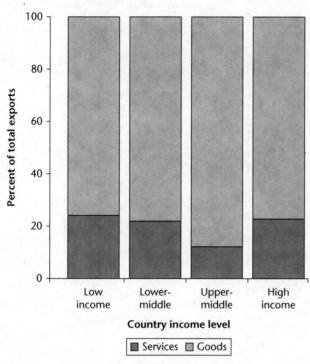

Source: World Development Indicators.
Note: Income classification is as of July 1, 2012.

Figure 1.2. Index of Services Exports, by Country Income Level, 2000–10

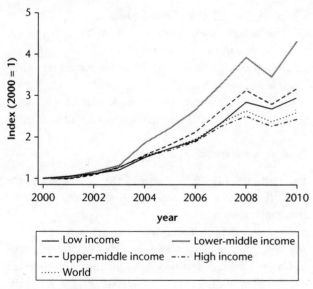

Source: World Development Indicators.
Note: Income classification is as of July 1, 2012.

Figure 1.3. Contribution to World Services Exports, by Income Level, 1990–2010

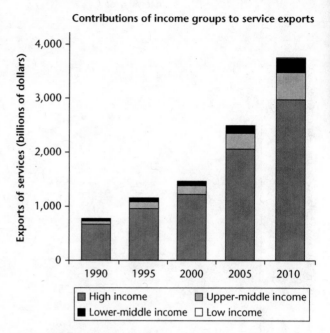

Source: World Development Indicators.
Note: Income classification is as of July 1, 2012.

despite their rising participation, low- and lower-middle-income countries still make only a very modest contribution to total trade. Their minor participation in services trade explains why average world growth in services exports is almost identical to growth in high-income countries. The modest contributions by low- and middle-income countries compared with their rapid economic growth figures can also be explained by the fact that these country groups start from a lower base, reflecting significant potential for the future development of services trade.

The trade balance indicates whether a country is a net importer or net exporter of services. Panel a of figure 1.4 shows that this indicator, taken as a percentage of gross domestic product (GDP), ranges widely across country income groups, with only the high-income group being net exporters.

Panel b of figure 1.4 reports the services trade balance for five middle-income countries: three from Latin America (Chile, Costa Rica, and Paraguay) and two comparators from Asia (India and Malaysia). The indicators vary even more widely than by income groups. Costa Rica and Paraguay record a consistent and growing surplus over the period 2001–10, Malaysia's trade balance increased steadily, and Chile's trade balance was consistently negative.

MODULE 1

MODULE 1

Figure 1.4. Services Trade Balance as Percent of GDP, by Income Group and in Selected Countries, 2001–10

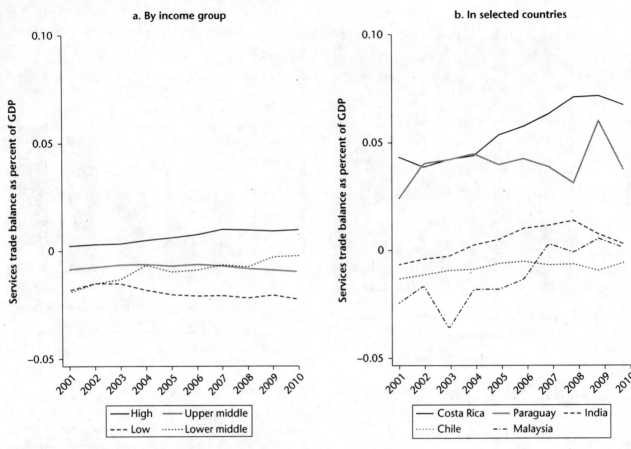

Source: World Development Indicators.
Note: Income classification is as of July 1, 2012. GDP = gross domestic product.

Trade Balance for Services and Goods

It is useful to compare the trade balance for goods and services. Figure 1.5 shows that high-income countries have a positive trade balance in services but a negative trade balance in goods. This picture is exactly the opposite for upper-middle income countries, where the goods balance is positive and the services balance negative. Figure 1.5 also shows that although the services trade balance of the lower-middle-income group is negative, it increased over the last 10 years. This group's share of services exports relative to total goods was comparable to that of low-income countries.

Figure 1.6 shows the trade balance of three countries in Central Asia between 2000 and 2010. With respect to trade in goods, oil exporter Kazakhstan (and other large economies) ran a trade surplus. Tajikistan (and other small economies) ran a deficit most of the time. For services, the only country with a positive net balance was Uzbekistan, which is not shown in the figure, because not all data were available. The services trade balance deficit ranged between

4–9 percent of GDP in Kazakhstan and 2–12 percent of GDP in Tajikistan. Except in 2010, since 2002, the Kyrgyz Republic has shown a relatively balanced services trade account. Overall, however, the size of the deficits tend to be much lower for services than for total trade in the Kyrgyz Republic and Tajikistan, suggesting that at least for these countries, services are a marginal component of total trade.

Trade in Services and Development

The trade balance yields limited information about the absolute importance of services trade for the economy. Other indicators must be examined.

Figure 1.7 depicts one such indicator: total trade in services (the sum of exports and imports) divided by population (per capita) and measured against the economic development of the country (measured as GDP per capita in purchasing power parities [PPPs]). Trade in services per capita is used to obtain a normalized measure of the importance of services in each country, rather than analyzing by country size.

Figure 1.5. Trade Balance for Goods and Services, by Income Group, 2000–10

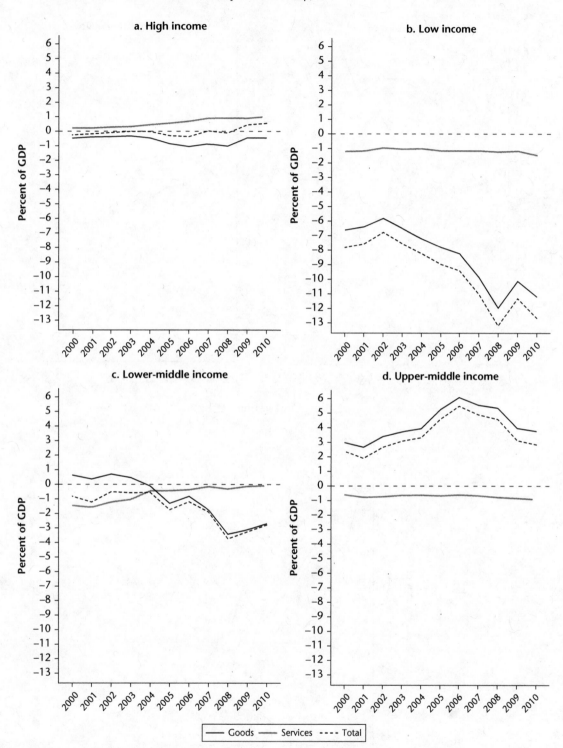

Sources: Trade data are from UNCTADstat. GDP data are from World Development Indicators (accessed in June 2012).
Note: Trade and GDP data are in current U.S. dollars.

Figure 1.6. Trade Balance in Kazakhstan, the Kyrgyz Republic, and Tajikistan, as Percent of GDP, 2000–10

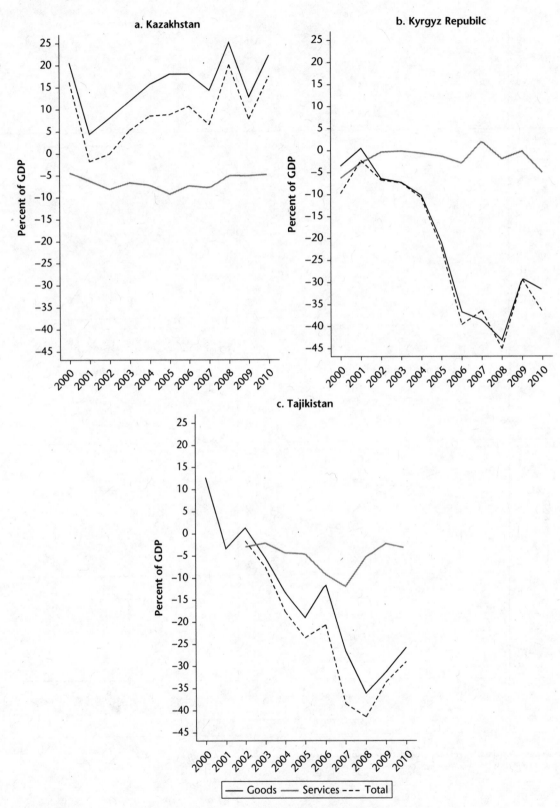

Sources: Trade data are from UNCTADstat. GDP data are from World Development Indicators (accessed in June 2012).
Note: Trade and GDP data are in current U.S. dollars.

Figure 1.7. Per Capita Trade in Services and Per Capita GDP, 2002–04 and 2008–10

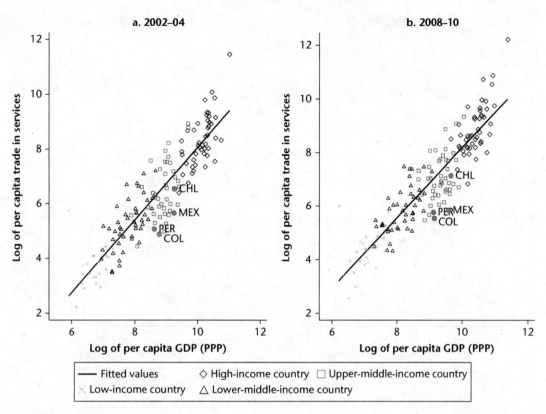

Source: World Development Indicators.
Note: Income classification is as of July 1, 2012. CHL = Chile, COL = Colombia, MEX = Mexico, PER = Peru, PPP = purchasing power parity.

The figure shows that the importance of trade in services increases with the level of development. Many countries—such as Chile, Colombia, Mexico, and Peru, and also highly developed ones—actually export less than one might expect based on the level of development. Figure 1.7 shows that between 2002–04 and 2008–10, trade openness seemed to increase for Colombia and Peru. Most other countries, including some high-income ones, however, seem to be stuck in their initial situation.

Other structural factors may also help explain these results. Figure 1.8 plots the residuals of the regression shown in table 1.1, which regresses the log of trade in services per capita against log of population and log of per capita income in PPP. Both population and GDP are significant variables in table 1.1, but there is substantial variance in the performance of countries not explained by these variables, as shown by the large residuals from this regression plotted on the horizontal axis of figure 1.8. There is also a strong correlation between the log of trade in services per capita and the residuals, suggesting that the more important services are for the economy, the higher the residuals (or, the more important other structural factors are in explaining this performance).

Figure 1.9 shows more specifically the relationship between exports and development. Note, however, that both imports and exports are important in trade patterns. Openness of countries is also explained by larger import shares, which implies greater export potential. This is true particularly when considering the capabilities of developing countries to join a **global value chain** (GVC), because a country cannot become a major exporter within GCVs without first becoming a major importer: exports within GVCs require imports (box 1.2).

As stated, both imports and exports are of vital importance; both indicate the extent to which a country participates in the globalization process. Yet, because the main purpose of this diagnosis is to assess external competitiveness, the focus is on exports.

Share of Services versus Share of Services Exports in GDP

The share of services exports in GDP indicates whether the importance of the services sector in the domestic economy translates into competitiveness externally. If it does not, the diagnostic should reveal whether the reason is the

Figure 1.8. Per Capita Trade in Services and Ordinary Least Squares Residuals, 2002–04 and 2008–10

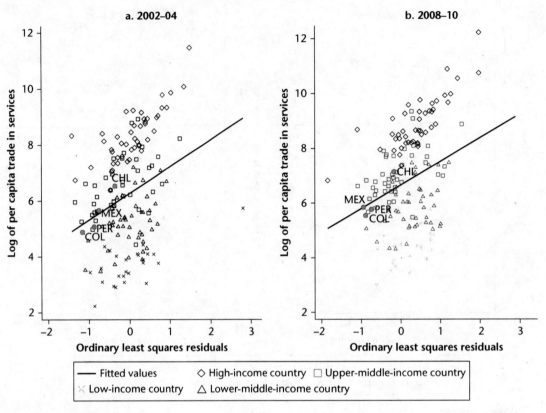

Source: World Development Indicators.
Note: Income classification is as of July 1, 2012. CHL = Chile, COL = Colombia, MEX = Mexico, PER = Peru.

Table 1.1. Results of Regression of Trade in Services against Development and Population

Item	ln(services trade pc)
ln(population)	–0.243***
	(0.0175)
ln(gdp_pc_ppp)	1.280***
	(0.0274)
Observations	321
R-squared	0.891
Root mean square deviation	0.610

Note: Standard errors are in parentheses. *** $p < 0.01$.

nontradability of services produced in the economy or other causes, such as regulatory obstacles.

Figure 1.10 shows a positive relationship between the value added of services in the domestic economy and the share of services exports in GDP. A negative relationship is evident for industry and agriculture. The figure also shows that in many important economies, the size of the services export sector is smaller than would have been predicted based on the size of services in the domestic economy. (Module 3 further explores the export potential of services.)

Figure 1.10 suggests that countries are becoming more competitive on the world market in goods and hence are exporting more goods but that such exports add only marginally to their GDP. While exports of goods increase, the share of industry in GDP declines. Similarly, although the share of exports of agriculture products in GDP increases, the share of agriculture value added decreases. The value added of goods rose significantly in Mauritius; Hong Kong SAR, China; and Lebanon, but the increase did not reflect increased exports of goods. In contrast, larger shares of services exports in GDP appear to be associated with larger shares of value added in GDP. This indicator does not, however, provide information on who is actually involved in trade in services. Box 1.3 discusses the characteristics of exporters using firm-level data.

Comparing a Country's Trade in Services with Peers and the World

An important starting point in diagnosing the competitiveness of individual countries is the scale of services exports. Figure 1.11 compares Turkey's commercial services exports to BRICS countries (Brazil, Russia, India,

Figure 1.9. Per Capita Exports in Services and Per Capita GDP, 2002–04 and 2008–10

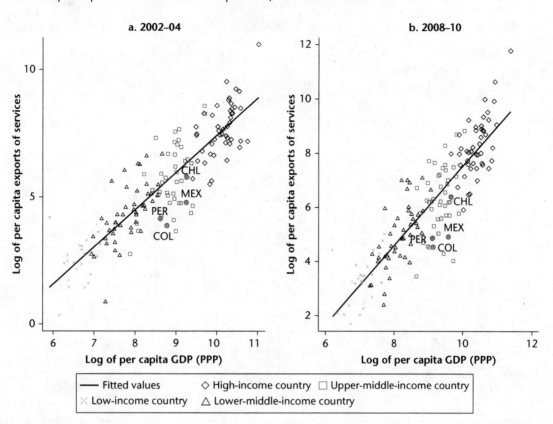

Source: World Development Indicators.
Note: Income classification is as of July 1, 2012. CHL = Chile, COL = Colombia, MEX = Mexico, PER = Peru, PPP = purchasing power parity.

Box 1.2. How Can Developing Countries Join and Climb the Ladder of Global Value Chains?

In recent years, global value chains (GVCs) have profoundly affected international trade and development. Developing countries now need to figure out how they can join different segments of this process rather than enhance the development of entire industries.

Joining a GVC can be facilitated by policies such as low tariffs on intermediate goods, an efficient transport and logistics network, a good business and regulatory environment, and the ability to meet product standards. Good policies on these factors can help boost competitiveness, increase connectivity with international markets, and improve the business and investment climate. A World Bank toolkit (*Making Global Value Chains Work for Development* [Taglioni and Winkler 2014]) focuses on GVCs.

Services play a crucial role in GVCs: they represent about 30 percent of the value added in goods trade (OECD and WTO 2013). Efficient domestic services and the availability of imported services are therefore vital. The reduction in supply chain barriers such as transport, logistics, and communication infrastructure and related services have a greater impact on growth of GDP and trade than the elimination of tariffs (WEF 2013).

Upgrading within GVCs is also important. Upgrading processes, products, or skills can increase the services content of production by moving away from traditional production (assembly stage) into pre- and postfabrication stages that are more services intensive and contribute more value added in the production cycle (see Cattaneo and others 2013; Milberg and Winkler 2013).

China, and South Africa) plus Poland and Romania. Turkey's exports in services reached $34 billion in 2010, 28 percent of the value of goods exports and 22 percent of the value of all goods and services exports. The scale of Turkey's commercial services export sector compares well with BRICS's and regional peers'. The share of commercial services in the total goods and services export basket is larger in Turkey than in all of its comparators except India. However, this measure of services exports divided by exports in goods may give a distorted picture for India, whose industrial sector is underdeveloped because of historical policy goals.

One way to correct this picture is to use a different measure, such as market size, to normalize services exports.

Figure 1.10. Size of Sector and Exports of Sector as Share of GDP in Selected Economies, 2008–10

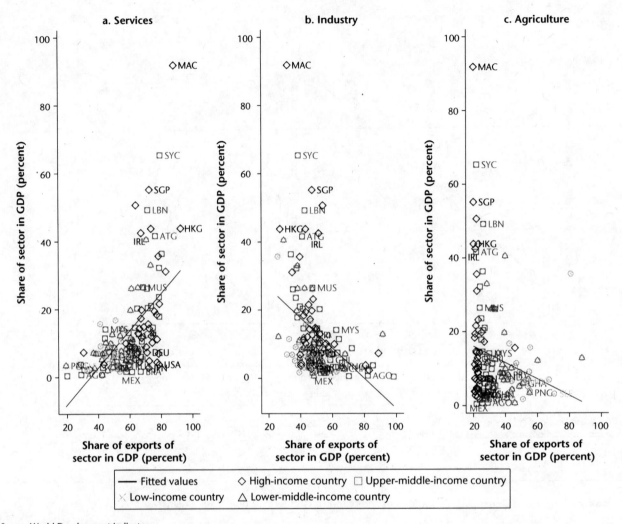

Source: World Development Indicators.
Note: The vertical axis is expressed in value added terms. The horizontal axis is expressed in gross values. Income classification is as of July 1, 2012. For the International Organization for Standardization (ISO) abbreviations, see appendix B.

Based on this metric, India performs worse than Poland and even Romania. As exports per capita show how much a country exports relative to its own market size (as measured by population), it gives a good indication of the presence in foreign markets, according to Wignaraja and Taylor (2003). Poland performs very well in foreign markets given the size of its domestic market.

The extent of presence in foreign markets is only one dimension of external competitiveness. Diversification is another. Ideally, exports should come from a well-diversified set of sectors rather than a few sectors, such as minerals or textiles. A well-diversified economy can generally expect a more sustainable growth path (see, for instance, Sachs and Warner 1999).

Figure 1.12 plots the per capita services export earnings (the vertical axis) against the combined share of manufacturing and services value added in GDP (the horizontal axis). The horizontal axis is a rough proxy of economic diversification. Earning more services exports (per capita) from an economic base that is more diversified is expected to generate a more sustainable growth pattern; diversifying away from natural resources or agriculture is usually a sign of development (McKinsey 2010).

Not all countries have diversified their economies. Countries such as Ethiopia or Cambodia, in the top left corner, have above-average services export income, but their economies are relatively undiversified. In contrast, China, India, and Malaysia, also in the upper left quadrant, have more diversified economies. Figure 1.12 also shows that a substantial number of upper-middle- and lower-middle-income countries, such as Brunei and Mauritius (bottom right corner), still have much scope for increasing

Box 1.3. What Kind of Firms Export Services?

Analysis of firm- and plant-level data from many countries shows that exporters, including exporters of services, are more productive than nonexporters (Bernard and Jensen 1999; Melitz 2003). Services exporters tend to be larger (as measured by the number of employees) than nonexporters (figure B1.3.1). This finding for exporters of goods is consistent with empirical studies by Iacovone, Mattoo, and Zahler (2013) and Brienlich and Criscuolo (2011) that analyze the characteristics of services exporters in Chile and the United Kingdom, respectively.

Figure B1.3.1. Number of Employees of Exporting and Nonexporting Firms, 2009

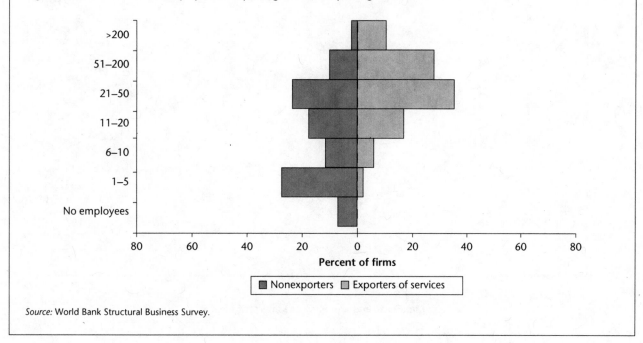

Source: World Bank Structural Business Survey.

Figure 1.11. Commercial Services Exports by Turkey and Selected Comparator Countries, 2010

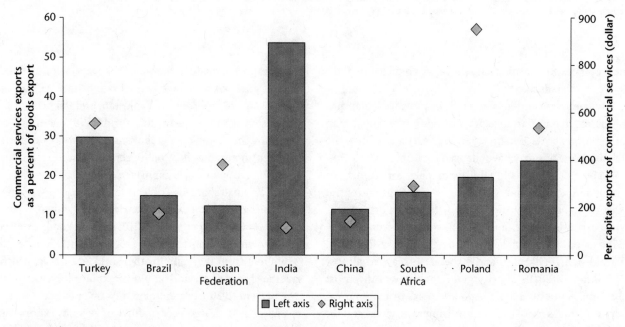

Source: World Development Indicators.

Figure 1.12. Services Exports and Diversification in Selected Economies, 2008–10

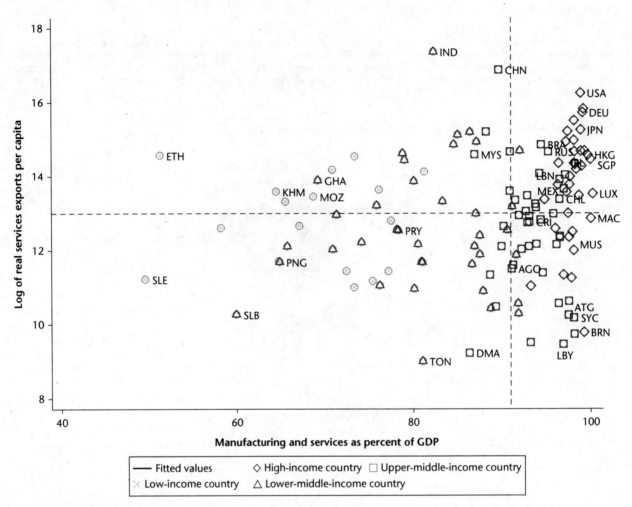

per capita export earnings in services as predicted by their levels of diversification.

Dynamics are also important. Scale provides a snapshot of the relative importance of countries in the global map of services exports; dynamic trends give a sense of how the relative positions may have changed over time.

Table 1.2 shows annual growth rates for exports of goods and services and export growth rankings in Central Asia over the last decade. In all of them, exports of services expanded more rapidly than world services exports. Exports of commercial services by the Kyrgyz Republic, Kazakhstan, Tajikistan, and Uzbekistan reached almost $6 billion in 2010. The Kyrgyz Republic was the most dynamic economy in the region: exports of commercial services (total services minus government services) grew at an annual rate of 24.7 percent between 2000 and 2010, the

fastest rate of increase in the world. Exports of commercial services grew at an average annual rate of 14.6 percent in Kazakhstan, 10.7 percent in Tajikistan, and 9.8 percent in Uzbekistan. The average for the world was 9.3 percent.

Although the region's global share of services exports has been increasing, it remains very low, accounting for just 0.16 percent of world exports of commercial services in 2010. The small share also reflects the fact that the region's services share in total exports has declined, from 10.0 percent in 2000 to 7.6 percent in 2010, because goods exports have grown even more rapidly (16.2 percent). This trend is different from the trend for the world as a whole, which saw the shares of services in global exports increase from 19.7 percent to 20.7 percent over the same period.

Figure 1.13 shows the dynamics of services exports by India, Turkey, and comparator countries in the region

Table 1.2. Growth of Exports of Goods and Services in Central Asia, by Country, 2000–10

	Exports of goods			Exports of commercial services	
Country	Rank among 207 countries	Average annual growth rate	Country	Rank among 165 countries	Average annual growth rate
Kazakhstan	12	18.7	Kyrgyz Republic	1	24.7
Uzbekistan	48	14.1	Kazakhstan	30	14.6
Kyrgyz Republic	69	12.4	Tajikistan	69	10.7
Turkmenistan	103	9.5	Turkmenistan	—	—
			Uzbekistan	83	9.8
World	n.a.	8.6	World	n.a.	9.3
Tajikistan	164	4.3			
Central Asia	n.a.	16.2	Central Asia	n.a.	13.9

Source: UNCTADstat Database online, accessed in June 2012.
Note: Annual growth rates were calculated as logarithmic compounded returns. Commercial services are total services minus government services.
n.a. = Not applicable. — = Not available.

Figure 1.13. Annual Growth of Exports of Services by India, Turkey, and Regional and Income-Group Comparators, 1994–2010

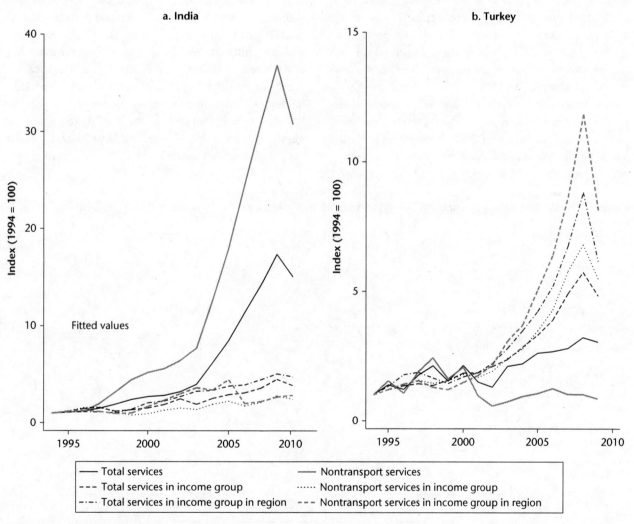

Source: Trade in Services Database.
Note: Regions are South Asia for India and Europe and Central Asia for Turkey. Income groups are lower-middle for India and upper-middle for Turkey.
Regional classifications are from World Development Indicators.

between 1994 and 2010. During the period, the value of India's services exports increased by a factor of more than 17; excluding transport services, the value of services exports increased by a factor of 37. India performed far better than other lower-middle-income countries.

In Turkey, the average annualized rate of growth was just 6.8 percent over the decade—below the global average, below the average for all peer countries (both other countries at the same income level and other countries in the region), and below Turkey's own performance in goods exports. Between 1994 and 2007, the value of total services exports, excluding transport, increased by just 2.6 percent a year. Over the same period, upper-middle-income countries from the rest of Europe and Central Asia recorded a growth in exports of services excluding transport of 339 percent. Turkey's overall services exports increased by 195 percent—far lower than for upper-middle-income countries in the region.

A useful way to look at the evolution of services exports over time is to relate it to world demand, measured as total imports of services by all countries. The solid line in figure 1.14 shows total world demand (imports). The separate country lines represent the extent to which each country can meet this demand (exports). The figure shows that world demand for services is growing too quickly for most countries to meet. Only in India did exports of services rise more rapidly than world imports. For the world as a whole, demand fell after 2007. However, as India still falls above the world line, it is still better able than its comparators to meet world demand.

Is a country exporting services for which global demand is growing? To which part of the world is a country exporting—to countries that are growing rapidly or to countries that are already relatively rich and in which growth is limited?

Figure 1.15 investigates these questions for India. As expected, India's export share is very high for other commercial services, business services, and computer and information services (panel a). Global demand for computer and information services is high. Global demand is also high in the rail transport; road transport; advertising and market research; and agricultural, mining, and on-site processing services sectors; India's share of exports is lower in these sectors. Ideally, the two indicators would be positively correlated, so that the rest of the world can "pull" India's service exports.

Panel b in figure 1.15 shows the link between India's export share in services and the bilateral increase in demand by partner countries in India's services overall. This relationship is negative: India's services exports go mainly to destinations in which demand growth was weak in 2000–08, such as the Germany, the United Kingdom, and the United States. Higher growth in services trade is observable in, for instance, Bulgaria, Latvia, and Romania, countries in which India's stake as a services exporter is modest. Although India's trading partners for services are not the countries that enjoyed the highest rates of services import growth, they still represent large markets, so that the negative impact as the result of the decline in growth will likely be limited.

Figure 1.14. World Demand for Imported Services and Exports of Services by India, Malaysia, and Mexico, 2002–09

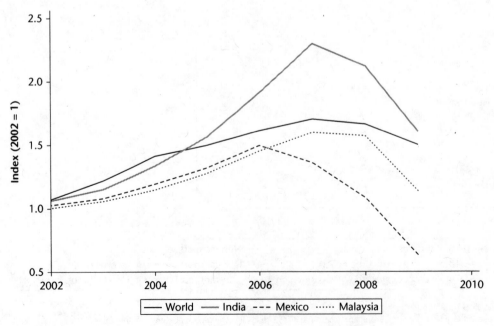

Source: Trade in Services Database.

Figure 1.15. Services Exports by India, by Sector and Destination, 2000–08

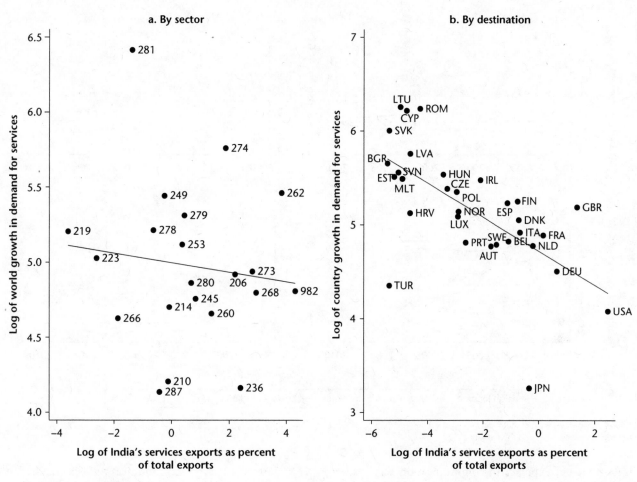

Source: Trade in Services Database.
Note: For the IMF balance of payments categories, see page xxi; for the country codes of the International Organization for Standardization (ISO), see appendix B.

Structure of Services Exports by Sector

Assessing the Sectoral Composition of Services Exports

Several indicators are critical to assessing the structure of services exports. They include the services and goods trade balance, the value of trade in services, and the value of exports and imports of services, which can be calculated as shares of GDP. Data on these indicators should be collected for specific years for all countries. Useful sources of information include the following:

- World Development Indicators (services trade by sector and GDP)
- IMF (balance of payments statistics)
- UNCTADstat (trade balance in services)
- World Bank's Trade in Services Database (see appendix B).

After assessing aggregate services exports, the next stage is to look at their sectoral composition. Which services are exported? Are all exports concentrated in one or a few

sectors? Is the country exporting low value-added services, or is it competitive in sectors requiring high-level skills and strong domestic infrastructure?

Several data sets can provide answers to these questions. One is the World Bank's **World Development Indicators (WDI)**. It provides information, based on balance of payments statistics from the IMF, on the travel, transport, financial and insurance, communication, and computer services sectors. The WDI groups all services other than government, travel, and transport services in the "other commercial services" category.

As figure 1.16 shows, all income groups are net importers of transport services. Only high-income countries are net importers of travel services. Only high-income economies are net exporters of financial services. The positive balance in trade in communications services has been driven largely by low- and lower-middle-income countries in recent years.

Figure 1.17 shows the structure of services exports by selected lower-middle-income countries. India is an

Figure 1.16. Balance of Trade in Services, by Country Income Level and Sector, 2000–10

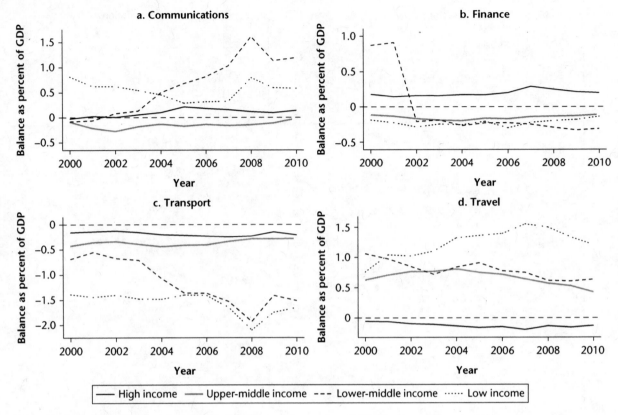

Source: World Development Indicators.
Note: Income classification is as of July 1, 2012.

important net exporter of communication services, an importer of most transport services, and neither a net exporter nor a net important of travel services. Ukraine increased it exports of communication services but saw a decline in exports of transport services. (This pattern is also evident in other emerging countries within this income group, such as the Philippines and, to a lesser extent, Indonesia.) Other lower-middle-income economies, such as Bolivia, Nicaragua, and Senegal, show few differences across sectors. Some low-income countries have been able to increase services exports through travel/tourism services rather than finance or transportation.

Table 1.3 shows the export growth rate of communications, finance, transport, and travel services between 2000 and 2010 for selected countries in Central and South Asia and the Caucasus as well as the averages for the income groups to which these countries belong. What immediately stands out is the impressive expansion of services exports in the Kyrgyz Republic, propelled by travel services, which increased by a factor of almost 18 between 2000 and 2010. In Mongolia, exports of financial services increased by a factor of 53. In Tajikistan, exports of communication services rose by a factor of more than 12. Growth rates in the Caucasus

region were high for communications in Azerbaijan (940 percent), finance in Georgia (490 percent), and travel in Armenia (980 percent) and Azerbaijan (940 percent).

Figure 1.18 puts these figures into perspective by showing the composition of services exports for each of the selected countries in Central Asia. It shows that Tajikistan drastically changed its export specialization, from transport to communications, which accounted for more than 70 percent of services exports by 2010. Kazakhstan and Mongolia reduced their dependence on travel services and increased their exports of transport services. Each of the Central Asian economies specializes in a different services sector. Kazakhstan specializes in exports of transport services, the Kyrgyz Republic in travel services, and Tajikistan in communications services.

As countries become richer, the role of services in the economy increases, in terms of both value added and exports. However, not all services sectors grow in importance as a country develops, as shown in figure 1.19. The share of transport and travel services in total exports is only marginally associated with the level of development. For both sectors, the fitted value line is almost horizontal, meaning that the share of transport and travel services in a country's total

Figure 1.17. Balance of Trade in Services in Selected Lower-Middle-Income Countries, by Sector, 2001–11

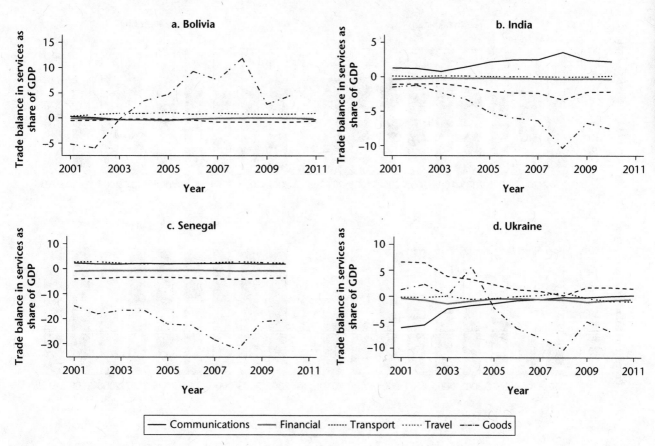

a. Bolivia

b. India

c. Senegal

d. Ukraine

———— Communications ———— Financial ·········· Transport ········· Travel —··— Goods

Source: World Development Indicators.
Note: Income classification is as of July 1, 2012.

Table 1.3. Growth Rate of Services Exports by Selected Countries in Central Asia, South Asia, and the Caucasus Region, by Sector, 2000–10
(rate)

Region/country	Communications	Finance	Transport	Travel
Central and South Asia				
Kazakhstan	2.9	6.0	3.9	1.8
Kyrgyz Republic	7.8	3.8	8.0	17.6
Mongolia	4.0	53.4	4.8	5.8
Pakistan	9.8	5.3	0.7	2.8
Tajikistan	12.1	6.9	0.1	1.8
Average	8.1	5.5	3.2	6.0
Caucasus				
Armenia	4.7	3.6	1.5	9.8
Azerbaijan	9.4	1.6	4.4	9.4
Georgia	2.4	4.9	3.5	3.7
Turkey	–0.6	2.0	2.2	1.7
Average	4.0	3.0	2.9	6.2
Income group				
Low	1.7	4.7	2.5	2.0
Lower-middle	3.0	2.7	2.2	1.8

Source: UNCTADstat.
Note: Income classification is as of July 1, 2012.

MODULE 1

Figure 1.18. Sectoral Shares of Services Exports by Selected Countries in Central Asia, 2002–10

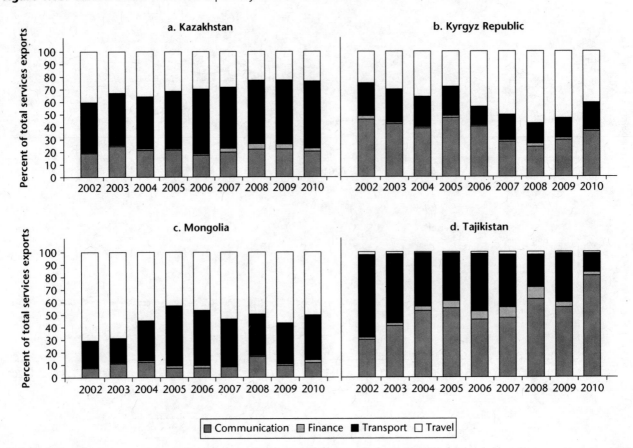

Source: UNCTADstat.
Note: Income classification is as of July 1, 2012.

services export basket is not correlated with the level of development. Both communications and construction services seem to decline in importance as countries become richer.

In contrast, insurance, finance, computer, distribution (which includes leasing), and business services all show a positive correlation between the level of development and the share of total exports. (In the insurance, finance, and computer sectors, some outliers—such as Luxembourg for finance and India for computer services—were taken out because their high values would have given a distorted picture. Others outliers, such as the United Kingdom in financial services, were included. In outlier countries, the skewed specialization pattern often reflects very specific policies or historical reasons.) Had all outliers been omitted, the positive correlation would have been even stronger. Some outliers are visible in each sector, possibly indicating successful policy choices.

Figure 1.20 depicts the relationship between upper- and lower-middle-income countries' trade balance and their level of development. Only some sectors reveal a clear association between the two variables. Upper-middle-income countries are likely to have a balanced or negative trade

balance in transport, construction, insurance, financial, and business services. One reason why these countries may be less likely to run trade surpluses in these services is that high-income countries probably are net exporters of them. Higher per capita GDP for upper-middle-income countries is associated with larger positive trade balances in travel, computer, and distribution services.

Middle-income countries at all levels of income have been successful at exporting particular services. For example, Bolivia, Mongolia, and Ukraine are situated low on the ladder of development but have large trade surpluses for business services. This high ratio could be biased by the fact that least-developed countries often lack complete data coverage, so that not all data flows are recorded. Services are difficult to tax at the border. If least-developed countries were included, the correlation between the ratio of exports to imports and per capita GDP would probably have been positive.

The importance of sectoral exports can also be presented by showing the breakdown of services for each country and looking at how the composition changes

Figure 1.19. Sectoral Shares of Services Exports and GDP Per Capita in Selected Countries, 2009

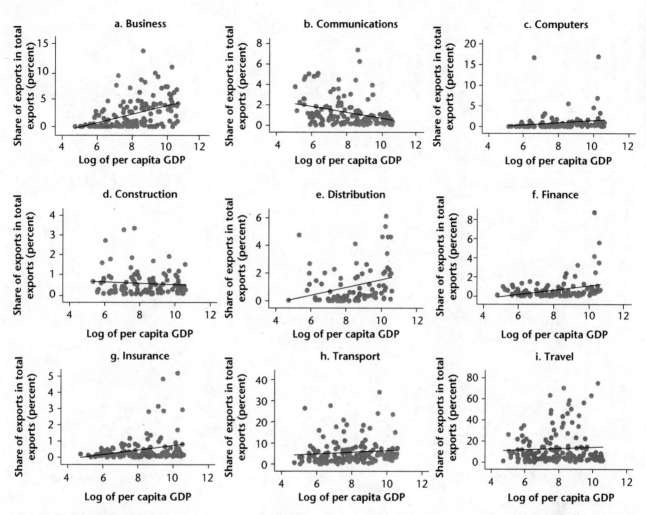

Source: Trade in Services Database.

over time. The sectoral breakdown for a country can then be compared with that of its peers. Figure 1.21 shows the changes in the composition of services exports for India and Turkey between 2001 and 2009.

The bulk of India's exports is concentrated in a single sector—computer and information services—which accounted for about 53 percent of its total services exports in 2009. This share is much larger than in any of India's comparators. For lower-middle-income countries as a whole, for example, computer and information services accounted for just 2.5 percent of total service exports. For the world as a whole, computer and information services accounted for 4.7 percent of total services trade.

The second-largest services export sector in India is "other business services." Traditional services sectors, such as transport and travel, play only a small role in India compared with other lower-middle-income countries or the world as a whole.

Turkey's services exports are also concentrated in a single sector: travel services. The share of this sector peaked in 2004, at 66 percent of total services exports; in 2009, its share was 63 percent. The share of tourism is much larger than in comparators: worldwide, travel services accounted for only 23 percent of total services exports in 2009.

"Other business services" accounted for a relatively small share of Turkey's services exports. In the prerecession year of 2007, its share of total services exports was 7 percent, much lower than the 22 percent for upper-middle-income countries in the Europe and Central Asia region.

More detailed analyses provide a more nuanced picture. Turkey, for example, has some small but very dynamic sectors. Exports of insurance, computer and information services, and post and telecommunication services experienced double-digit annual growth between 1994 and 2007. Table 1.4 separates growth in the precrisis and crisis periods, given the trade collapse of 2008–09, which affected

MODULE 1

Figure 1.20. Trade Balance and Level of Development in Selected Upper- and Lower-Middle-Income Countries, 2009

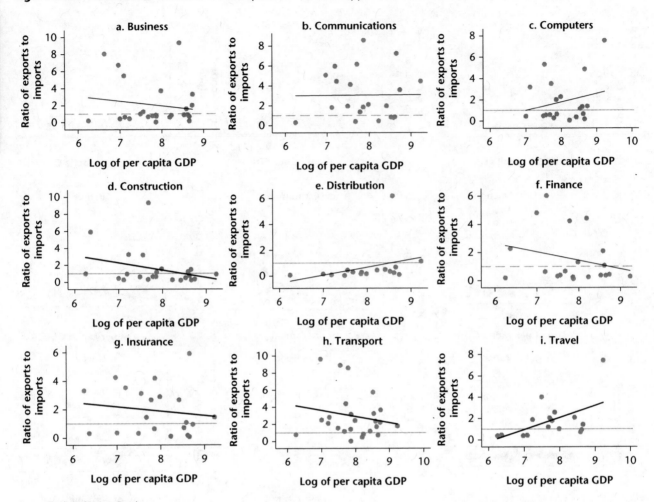

Source: Trade in Services Database.
Note: Dotted line indicates that ratio of exports to imports is 1. Solid line shows fitted values. Trade values of less than $1 million and ratios above 10 were excluded.

primarily goods and only marginally services (Borchert and Mattoo 2009). It is possible, however, that some services categories were affected more than others, given the differences in the linkages between services and downstream goods sectors. For this reason, the growth computations are separated. Notable in the 2008–09 period is the exceptional growth not only of certain sectors but also of royalties and license fees, which represent an increasingly sought after segment of services exports.

Figure 1.22 explores this dynamic aspect of services. It compares an upper-middle-income country (Malaysia) with a high-income country (the United Kingdom). Malaysia's main services exports are travel and transport services. Before 2009, Malaysia saw a steady expansion of its business services sector. During the great trade collapse of 2009, this sector shrank by more than 73 percent. In contrast, both travel and transport services performed relatively well.

The United Kingdom specializes in business and financial services. Business services proved resilient to

the collapse, increasing more than 12 percent in 2010. Financial services also held strong, shrinking only marginally, from 24 percent of total services export in 2009 to about 21 percent in 2010. Travel and transport also fared relatively well in the United Kingdom during the great trade collapse.

Export Concentration

The Herfindahl-Hirschman and Theil Entropy Indexes
Several indicators are critical to assessing export concentration. They include measures of concentration (such as the Herfindahl-Hirschman Index) and dispersion (such as the Theil Entropy Index). Data on these indicators should be collected for specific years for all countries. Useful sources of information include the following:

- World Development Indicators (GDP)
- IMF (balance of payments statistics)
- World Bank's Trade in Services Database (see appendix B).

Figure 1.21. Composition of Services Exports by India and Turkey, 2001–09

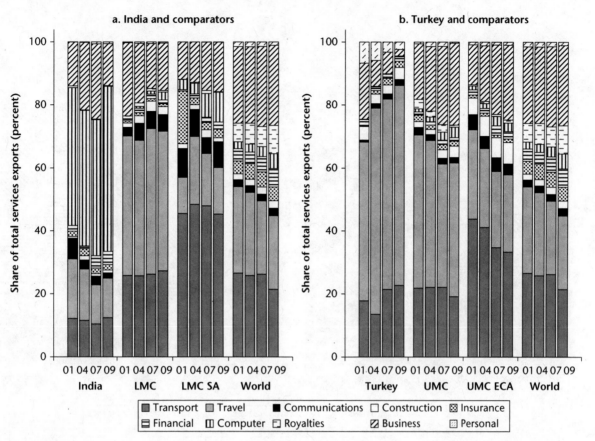

Source: Trade in Services Database.
Note: 01 = 2001; 04 = 2004; 07 = 2007; 09 = 2009. LMC SA = lower-middle-income country in South Asia; UMC ECA = upper-middle-income country in Europe and Central Asia.

Table 1.4. Average Annual Growth of Services Exports, 1994–2007 and 2008–09
(percent)

Sector	Turkey		Upper-middle income		Upper-middle income Europe and Central Asia		World	
	1994–2007	2008–09	1994–2007	2008–09	1994–2007	2008–09	1994–2007	2008–09
Transport	13.7	7.6	11.8	–6.7	13.0	–2.1	9.0	–7.3
Travel	11.7	7.2	10.5	2.3	13.7	2.2	7.4	–1.5
Post and telecommunications	12.0	11.9	6.5	–2.0	17.5	1.2	13.3	2.3
Construction	–3.1	22.2	17.3	9.9	9.8	5.3	10.4	7.3
Insurance	38.1	1.4	6.2	–3.3	29.3	8.8	10.7	–6.0
Financial	9.3	8.4	22.0	–9.9	18.9	–10.1	16.4	–11.3
Computer and information	15.3	39.4	44.1	11.2	42.1	12.0	27.4	5.7
Royalties and license fees	1.6	25.6	36.9	–41.7	26.5	27.5	12.0	5.8
Other business services	–0.3	–42.3	13.2	0.2	12.9	–1.3	12.1	–4.1
Total	8.3	4.3	11.9	0.5	12.9	0.8	10.1	–2.7

Source: Trade in Services Database.

MODULE 1

Figure 1.22. Value of Services Exports in Malaysia and the United Kingdom, by Sector, 2000–10

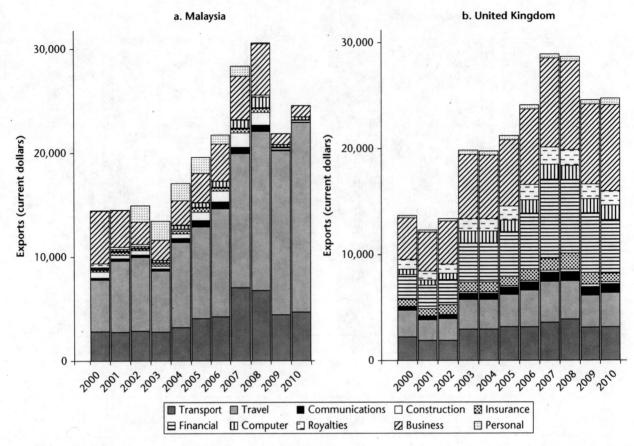

Source: Trade in Services Database.

Diversification is important because it prevents economies from being too dependent on one sector. Despite the importance of diversifying, however, countries tend to specialize. Software and business process services represent about a third of total exports by India. Brazil, Costa Rica, and Uruguay specialize in professional and information technology–related exports, Mexico in communication and distribution services, and Chile in distribution and transportation services. In Morocco, Tunisia, Kenya, and South Africa, exports of professional services to Europe are growing. In Asia, the Philippines and Thailand are exporting health services, and Malaysia is increasing its export of education, Islamic banking, and telecommunication services.

One standard measure of concentration is the share of total exports by the most important sector. This index—the **Herfindahl-Hirschman Index**—is calculated as follows:

$$H_i = \sum_{k=1}^{N} S_{ik}^2$$

where S_{ik} refers to the share of industry k in the total exports of country i. The index ranges from $1/N$ to 1, with

N representing the number of sectors in which the economy exports. The higher the value of the index, the more concentrated are the country's exports.

For easier interpretation, it is useful to compute the normalized version of this index. This index ranges from 0 to 1, with higher values indicating higher concentration. It is calculated as follows:

$$H_i^* = (H_i - 1/N)/(1 - 1/N).$$

A second measure of concentration of exports is the **Theil Entropy Index**. This index is calculated as follows:

$$E_i = -\sum_{k=1}^{N} S_{ik} \log(S_{ik})$$

where i stands for country, k for industry, and S for the share in total exports. A larger value of this index (which ranges from 0 to infinity) indicates greater export diversification. A country that exports only one service would have a Theil Entropy Index of zero. If all services have an equal share (n) in the export basket, the index would have a maximum value that is $-\log(n)$. Figure 1.23 shows the Herfindahl-Hirschman Index and the Theil Entropy Index for nine countries from different income groups. It shows some changes between 2002 and 2010. For instance, Cambodia's services sector became relatively less concentrated (more diversified) and Jordan's export sector became much less diversified (more concentrated).

In the lowest-income countries, the number of services exports and their values tends to be very low; adding just one sector can therefore change the index dramatically. In such cases, it is useful to look at simple shares, the number of sectors involved, and the absolute levels of exports. Firm-level data can help determine concentration ratios at a more micro-level. Box 1.4 provides an illustration, using data on Romania.

Are services exports in developing countries concentrated in one or two sectors? Is Malaysia, where one sector dominates (see figure 1.22), typical of developing countries? Or is Malaysia a special case because travel is the dominant sector? Do all developed countries have an export range that looks like that of the United Kingdom (see figure 1.22)?

To answer these questions, figure 1.24 plots the Theil Entropy Index against the log of GDP per capita PPP, a proxy for development. No clear pattern is evident, although export portfolios tend to be more diversified among higher-income countries. Higher-income countries also export more, as shown by the size of the circles in figure 1.24. Low-income countries seem to have a lower Theil Entropy Index overall, but the index varies widely. The relationship between development and more diversified exports becomes weaker when developing countries are taken into account.

Revealed Comparative Advantage

Assessing Revealed Comparative Advantage
Several indicators are critical to assessing revealed comparative advantage. They include the value, shares, and growth rates of exports by sector. Data on these indicators should be collected for specific years for all countries. Useful sources of information include the following:

- World Bank's Trade in Services Database (see appendix B)
- IMF (balance of payments statistics).

Figure 1.23. Concentration and Diversification Indexes for Selected Countries, 2002 and 2010

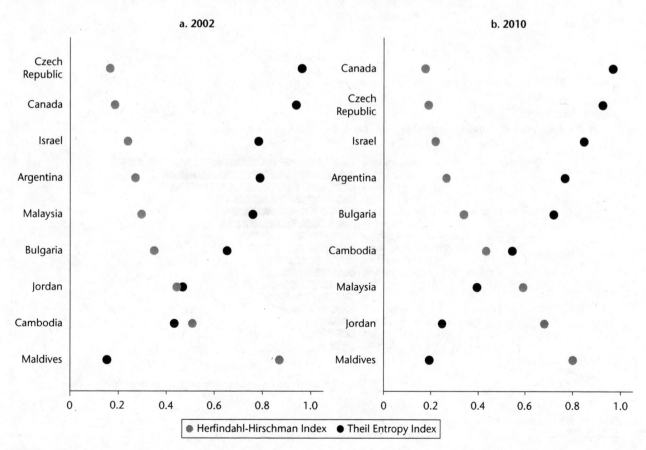

Source: Trade in Services Database.

Box 1.4. Using Firm-Level Data to Estimate Concentration Ratios: Evidence from Romania

Concentration ratios can be calculated from firm-level data. Figure B1.4.1 shows a normalized **Herfindahl-Hirschman Index** for Romania.

Romania's exports are concentrated in several sectors, including recreation, computer and modern communication, and computer repair. Other important sectors include education, food, and administrative and support services.

Another way to show concentration is to show the share of production of the top five firms in each sector (figure B1.4.2). By this measure, some services, such as computer and modern communications, are extremely concentrated. The top five firms in Romania represent almost 50 percent of output production in computer and modern communication.

Figure B1.4.1. Herfindahl-Hirschman Index for Romania, by Sector, 2008

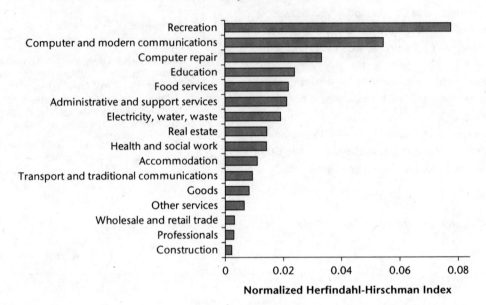

Source: World Bank Structural Business Survey.

Figure B1.4.2. Share of Output Produced by Top Five Firms in Romania, by Sector, 2008

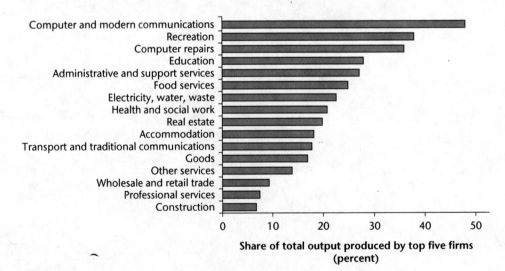

Source: World Bank Structural Business Survey.

Figure 1.24. Relationship between Theil Entropy Index and Level of Development, 2010

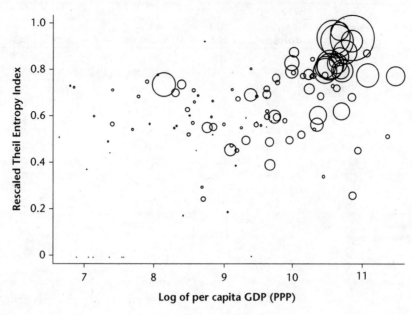

Source: Trade in Services Database.
Note: The size of the circles reflects the dollar value of exports. PPP = purchasing power parity.

Sectoral data enable users to identify sectors in which a country has a competitive edge, or revealed comparative advantage (RCA). The **RCA Index** compares the share of a sector's exports in a country's total exports with the average share of exports of all countries in the sector in total world exports. The higher the ratio, which can range from zero to infinity, the more competitive the country is in the sector.

The RCA Index is calculated follows:

$$RCA_{ik} = \frac{\frac{x_{ik}}{X_i}}{\frac{x_{wk}}{X_w}}$$

where x_{ik} are country *i*'s exports of sector *k*, X_i are total exports of country *i*, x_{wk} are world exports of sector *k*, and X_w are total world exports. An RCA Index above 1 indicates that a country's share of services exports in a sector is larger than the global share of exports in that sector. A high value of this indicator should not be confused with net exports of a sector. A country could have an RCA Index below 1 but still be a net exporter of a service. The RCA Index helps identify sectors in which it is less costly for a country to specialize based on "opportunity costs" (the cost associated with the next-best alternative).

Table 1.5 gives the RCA Indexes for various services sectors, the real values of those exports, and the share of those exports in total services exports in Argentina.

It shows that between 2002 and 2010, Argentina increased its RCA Index in travel, computer and information, business, and personal services and reduced its RCA in communications. The share of transport services in Argentina's exports declined.

As evident from table 1.5, comparative advantage is a dynamic process. For business services, Argentina had an RCA Index below 1 in 2002 but above 1 in 2010. While the country increased its potential in this sector, it also maintained an RCA Index above 1 in travel, communications, computer, and personal, cultural, and recreational services sectors. However, there is huge variation by services sector over time, as figure 1.25 shows for Costa Rica.

Costa Rica had a strong export presence in travel services in 2000. The RCA Index increased slightly before decreasing in 2009. Business services and computer services became stronger over time, pointing to Costa Rica's strong export potential in these sectors. Other services, such as finance, still lag behind.

The determinants that make or shape comparative advantage are economywide variables on which firms in specific services sectors can capitalize (see Module 3). Policy variables such as regulation can also affect comparative advantage. Other policies, such as undervalued exchange rates or subsidies, have less of an effect on comparative advantage (subsidies aim to increase export volumes rather than exploit productivity differences) (Siggel 2006).

Table 1.5. Value, Export Share, and Revealed Comparative Advantage Index of Services Exports by Argentina, 2002 and 2010

	2002			2010			
	Value (U.S. dollars)	Share (percent)	RCA	Value (U.S. dollars)	Share (percent)	RCA	Average annual growth (2002–10)
Transport	1,538.0	21.3	0.9	4,042.9	15.4	0.7	12.8
Travel	3,070.2	42.5	1.5	9,883.8	37.7	1.8	15.7
Communications	300.0	4.2	1.8	670.9	2.6	1.0	10.6
Construction	46.7	0.7	0.3	126.6	0.5	0.2	13.3
Insurance	86.9	1.2	0.3	150.6	0.6	0.2	7.1
Financial	25.6	0.4	0.1	30.6	0.1	0.0	2.2
Computer	254.5	3.5	1.1	2,496.9	9.5	1.7	33.0
Royalties and licenses	276.9	3.8	0.6	270.0	1.0	0.1	0.3
Business	1,430.0	19.8	0.8	7,819.9	29.8	1.1	23.7
Personal, cultural, and recreational	190.7	2.6	1.8	711.6	2.7	2.7	17.9

Source: Trade in Services Database.
Note: RCA = revealed comparative advantage.

Figure 1.25. Revealed Comparative Advantage Index for Costa Rica, 2000, 2005, and 2009

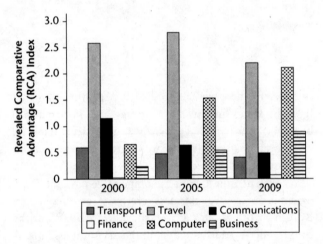

Source: Trade in Services Database.

Export Sophistication

Assessing Export Sophistication

Several indicators are used to assess export sophistication. Data on these indicators should be collected for specific years for all countries. Useful sources of information include the following:

- World Bank's Trade in Services Database (see appendix B)
- World Development Indicators (GDP)
- IMF (balance of payment statistics).

The sophistication of exports, or **EXPY** (the revealed income content of the export basket), is calculated for a country's export basket by ranking each service exported by the income levels of the countries that export the service.

Controlling for overall economic size, products exported by higher-income countries are ranked higher than products exported by lower-income countries. These product-specific calculations are then aggregated to construct the countrywide indexes of **export sophistication**.

Specifically, let countries be indexed by i and products by k. Let p be an export category (goods, manufacturing, services). Total exports of category p by country i equal $X_i^p = \sum_k x_{ik}^p$. Let Y_i denote the per capita GDP of country i. Then the income level associated with product k in category p equals the weighted average of per capita GDP, where the weights represent the RCA of each country exporting that product. **PRODY** (the revealed income content of the product) thus represents the income level associated with that product. PRODY is a weighted average of the per capita GDP of countries exporting that good. Weights in PRODY are based on the RCA. PRODY values of all products that a country exports are then weighted by each product's share in the country's total export basket and summed to derive a country's level of GDP per capita as inferred from the sophistication of its export basket (EXPY).

$$PRODY_k^p = \sum_i \frac{(x_{ik}^p/x_i^p)}{\sum_i (x_{ik}^p/x_i^p)} * Y_i.$$

The numerator of the weight, x_{ik}^p/x_i^p, is the value share of the product in the country's category p export basket. The denominator of the weight, $\sum_i(x_{ik}^p/x_i^p)$, aggregates the value shares across all countries exporting that product in that category. The PRODYs are used to compute the income level associated with each product k in category p (all goods, manufactured goods, or services). Specifically, $EXPY_i^p$ is the average income level associated with all products in a category exported by a country. It is computed as the weighted average of all relevant PRODYs, where the weights represent the share of the relevant product in the country's export basket of category k:

$$EXPY_i^p = \sum_k \left(\frac{x_{ik}^p}{x_i^p} \right) * PRODY_k^p.$$

An increase in EXPY indicates a country's shift from low-PRODY to high-PRODY products. It means that the share of high-PRODY goods, manufactures, and services in the export basket has increased. Box 1.5 identifies some shortcomings of this measure.

There is a positive relationship between GDP per capita and the sophistication of services exports (figure 1.26).

Box 1.5. Services Sophistication: Handle with Care

Calculating export sophistication (EXPY) is a two-stage process. The first stage is to measure the income level associated with each service (or product) (PRODY). The PRODY of a particular service is the gross domestic product (GDP) per capita of the typical country that exports that service. Typical GDP is calculated by weighting the GDP per capita of all countries exporting the service. The weight given to each country is based on its revealed comparative advantage (RCA). The PRODY for a single service is calculated by weighting the GDP per capita of all countries exporting that service. Therefore, a service that typically makes up a large percentage of a poor country's export basket will be more heavily weighted by poor countries' GDP per capita.

The second stage is to measure the income associated with a country's export basket as a whole (EXPY). The EXPY is calculated by weighting the PRODYs of each service by the share each service contributes to total exports. For example, if tourism makes up 15 percent of a country's exports, its PRODY is given a weight of 0.15. Countries whose export baskets are made up of "rich-country goods" will have higher EXPYs; export baskets made up of "poor-country goods" will have lower EXPYs.

The concepts of PRODY and EXPY are not free of criticism (see Lederman and Maloney 2012). To begin with, classification of services trade is not well developed. In the balance of payments statistics, for example, a professional services category may include activities that are entirely different across countries.

Furthermore, categories can include a wide range of services. An activity such as accounting may refer to a highly commoditized activity (such as preparing simple tax returns) or a highly sophisticated service (such as providing tax advice to a multinational corporation); there is no way to differentiate. If these problems are not taken into account, EXPY may overestimate the importance of sophisticated products from low-income countries.

The sophistication of a particular country's export basket may be increasing over time even though the country does not show an RCA in high-value-added services exports, such as information and communication technology (ICT) or business-related services, as illustrated in the table and figure in this box.

Chile shows an RCA Index greater than 1 only for transportation services as shown in table B1.5.1. Yet figure B1.5.1 shows that Chile's services exports sophistication is above what would be expected given its level of development. In India, the high RCA in ICT exports and to a lesser extent "other business services" accounts for the sophistication of its services exports.

Table B1.5.1. Revealed Comparative Advantage Index of Selected Countries for Goods and Services Exports, 2009–11

	Brazil	Chile	Egypt, Arab Rep.	Hungary	India	Malaysia	Philippines	South Africa	Ukraine
Goods	1.1	1.2	0.7	1.1	0.7	1.1	0.9	1.2	1.0
Transportation	0.5	2.0	3.9	0.9	0.9	0.6	0.5	0.4	2.9
Travel	0.5	0.5	5.2	1.0	0.7	1.7	0.9	2.0	1.2
Other commercial services	0.8	0.3	0.7	0.8	2.1	0.4	1.4	0.3	0.7
Communication	0.3	0.4	3.2	0.7	0.7	5.6	1.0	0.4	1.3
Information and communication technologies	0.1	0.1	0.3	0.9	11.7	0.6	2.6	0.3	0.6
Construction	0.0	—	2.6	0.7	0.3	0.8	0.2	0.1	0.7
Financial	0.6	0.0	0.3	0.1	0.9	0.0	0.1	0.6	0.4
Government (not indicated elsewhere)	1.8	0.4	1.1	0.3	0.3	0.1	—	1.1	2.3
Insurance	0.4	0.8	0.4	0.1	1.0	0.4	0.2	0.6	0.1
Other business	1.4	0.5	0.6	1.0	1.2	0.4	2.2	0.2	0.8
Personal, cultural, and recreation	0.3	0.8	1.4	6.8	0.8	2.4	0.4	0.5	0.9
Royalties and license fees	0.2	0.1	—	0.7	0.0	0.1	0.0	0.0	0.1

Source: IMF various years.
Note: — Not available.

(continued on next page)

Box 1.5. *(continued)*

Figure B1.5.1. Export Sophistication and GDP in Selected Countries, 2009–11

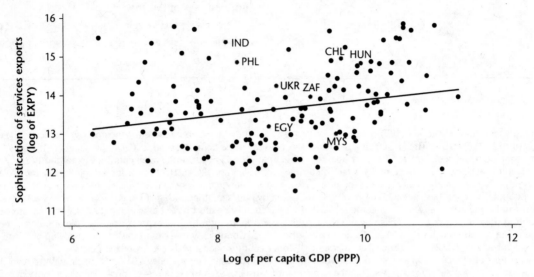

Source: IMF 2009.
Note: CHL = Chile, EGY = Arab Republic of Egypt, EXPY = (revealed) income content of export basket, HUN = Hungary, IND = India, MYS = Malaysia, PHL = Philippines, PPP = purchasing power parity, UKR = Ukraine, ZAF = South Africa.

The composition of services exports moves in the direction of modern activities, such as ICT, professional services, and other higher value added services that are normally exported by high-income countries. Trade models based on comparative advantage are agnostic about whether welfare gains accrue from producing a particular product or service. Using the RCA Index therefore reveals little about which sector most growth would come from.

In general, higher value added goods and services have higher PRODYs. Figure 1.26 shows that many lower-income countries exhibited little change in the type of goods they exported. In contrast, the PRODYs of Latin American countries rose steadily between 2001 and 2007 (this trend ended with the onset of the global financial crisis) (figure 1.27).

The apparent decline in the sophistication of services exports between 2007 and 2009 was not necessarily driven by a change in the composition of services exports of these countries; it may instead reflect the construction of the sophistication measure (see box 1.5). Moreover, figures 1.26 and 1.27 say nothing about the direction of causation between export sophistication and per capita GDP.

Yet, one can note that India, for instance, exports the type of services that would normally appear in the export portfolio of higher-income countries (see figure 1.26). Based on a large pool of countries and exported goods, Hausmann, Hwang, and Rodrik (2007) find that it is likely

that countries above the fitted line will see higher economic growth rates in the future.

Revealed Factor Intensities

Physical, human, and ICT-related capital are relevant for services. Useful sources of information on them include the following:

- World Bank's Trade in Services Database (see appendix B)
- IMF (balance of payments statistics)
- Barro and Lee (2012) data set on educational attainment
- Conference Board data on physical and ICT capital.

The **Revealed Human Capital Index (RHCI)** is an adjusted version of the RCA Index multiplied by a country's factor endowments. It can range from zero to infinity. Human capital is the average years of education. Physical and ICT-related capital is the capital stock per capita for a country corrected using the perpetual inventory method. The index for human capital is calculated as follows where k denotes product, i denotes country, and H denotes average years of education:

$$RHCI_k = \sum_i \frac{\left(\dfrac{x_{ik}}{x_i}\right)}{\sum_i \dfrac{x_{ik}}{x_i}} * H_i.$$

Figure 1.26. Sophistication of Services Exports and Per Capita GDP in Selected Countries, 2001 and 2009

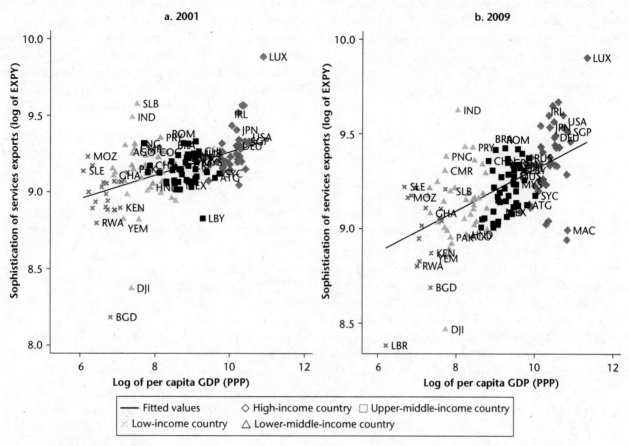

Source: Trade in Services Database.

Note: Income classification is as of July 1, 2012. For the International Organization for Standardization (ISO) abbreviations, see appendix B. PPP = purchasing power parity, PRODY = (revealed) income content of product basket.

Figure 1.27. Sophistication of Services Exports by Six Countries in Latin America, 2001–09

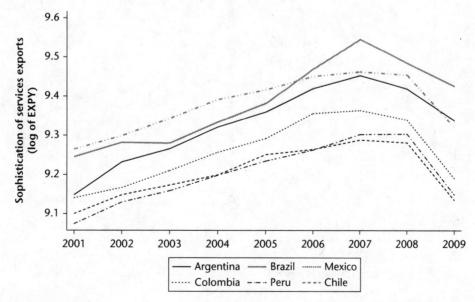

Source: Trade in Services Database.

Note: EXPY = (revealed) income content of export basket.

The indexes for the **revealed physical capital (RPCI)** and the **revealed information and communications technology–related capital (RICTI)** are calculated as follows, where K is the physical capital stock, ICT is the ICT-related capital stock, and L is population:

$$RPCI_k = \sum_i \frac{\left(\frac{x_{ik}}{x_i}\right)}{\sum_i \frac{x_{ik}}{x_i}} * \frac{K_i}{L_i}$$

$$RICTI_k = \sum_i \frac{\left(\frac{x_{ik}}{X_i}\right)}{\sum_i \frac{x_{ik}}{X_i}} * \frac{ICT_i}{L_i}.$$

Another more direct measure of factor intensities for services can be taken from the **EU KLEMS** (O'Mahony and Timmer 2009), which uses a methodology based on growth accounting. This database of growth and productivity covers mostly developed countries. Table 1.6 shows factor intensities, which are calculated for each sector directly rather than computed based on **revealed factor intensities**. The sectors are ranked from high to low, based on factor calculations, using the methodology of Shepherd and van der Marel (2013).

Figure 1.28 uses the revealed factor intensities calculated using the equation for $RHCI_k$. It shows a positive relationship between human capital and the export value of services. In both South Africa and Turkey, services exports are associated with a higher index of human capital. The size of each sector (the circle) indicates the extent to which a sector is intensive in ICT capital, showing a strong correlation with the level of ICT capital and human capital within sectors.

Table 1.6. Factor Intensities of Selected Services Exports

Service	ICT intensity	Service	High-skill labor intensity
Travel	0.30	Travel	0.17
Transportation	0.30	Transportation	0.20
Personal services	0.30	Personal services	0.19
Other business	0.43	Other business	0.24
Insurance	0.28	Insurance	0.21
Information and communications technology	0.25	Information and communications technology	0.20
Finance	0.39	Finance	0.25
Construction	0.27	Construction	0.16
Communication	0.23	Communication	0.25

Source: EU KLEMS (O'Mahony and Timmer 2009).
Note: ICT = information and communication technology.

Figure 1.28. Revealed Factor Intensities for Human and ICT-Related Capital in Selected Services Sectors in South Africa and Turkey, 2009

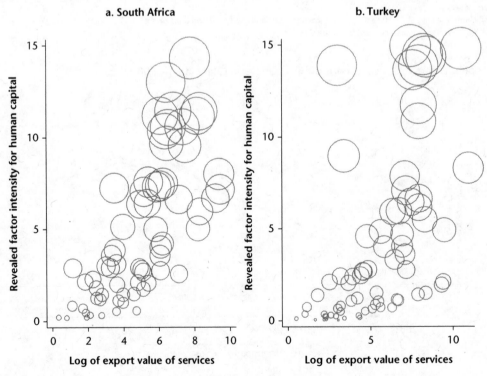

Source: Trade in Services Database.
Note: The size of each circle indicates the revealed information and communication technology (ICT) capital intensity of each sector, which tends to be higher the more intensive human capital services become.

Table 1.7 shows that the indexes for both human capital (RHCI) and ICT-related capital (RICTI) have significant effects on future growth, which is used as a dependent variable. Countries specializing in services that are intensive in factor inputs that are usually abundant in developed countries thus have better growth prospects.

Table 1.7. Regression Results of Future Growth between 1999 and 2008 on Revealed Human Capital Index (RHCI) and Revealed ICT-Related Capital Index (RICTI)

Item	(1)	(2)
log (RHCI)	1.283***	
	−0.266	
log (RICTI)		0.701***
		−0.222
log GDP pc "99	−7.003***	−9.696***
	−0.366	−0.471
Observations	2,790	1,983
R-squared	0.154	0.337

Note: log GDP pc "99 = log of per capita GDP in 1999. Cross-country regression used robust clustered standard errors. *** $p < 0.01$.

Export Markets

The ability to diversify should be judged not only in terms of the sectoral distribution of services exports but also in terms of the markets importing these services. Exporting to a range of markets not only helps mitigate the effects of asymmetric shocks that might hit some but not all importers, it also helps exporters improve the competitiveness of their products.

Success can be evaluated along two dimensions. The first, the **intensive margin**, looks at how volumes of exports to existing partners developed over time. It evaluates the depth of the relationship with each importer. The second, the **extensive margin**, looks at the number of existing relationships and markets and examines their dynamics over time. It assesses whether exports are growing because a particular country is exporting to new markets or new products.

Figure 1.29 depicts one way of analyzing the intensive margin. It shows that between 2002 and 2010, Germany maintained its position as the top importer of Turkey's

Figure 1.29. Intensive Margin of Turkey, 2002 and 2010

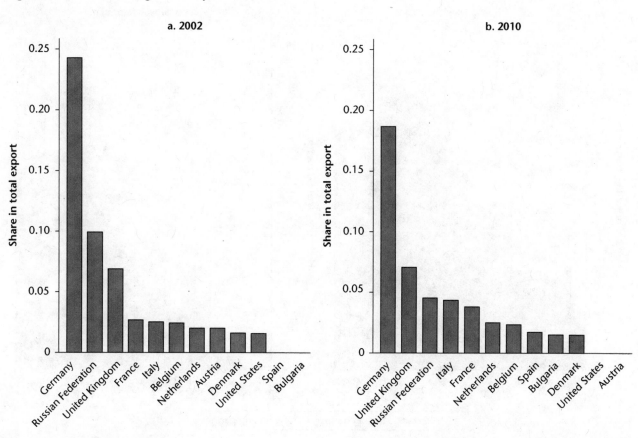

Source: Trade in Services Database.

services, despite some decline in its imports of Turkish goods. The United Kingdom's share of services exports from Turkey did not change much. In 2010, other countries, such as Italy and the Netherlands, were also important export destinations for Turkish services. Bulgaria also increased in importance. These findings suggest that Turkey may have expanded to new markets or that countries with previously low levels of services imports from Turkey became more important export destinations.

The bilateral data included in appendix B provide insights on the dynamics of the extensive margin. They allow researchers to assess the total number of relationships as well the number by sector. For trade in goods, detailed disaggregated data are available for most trading pairs. For services, the quality of bilateral data varies, for the reasons described earlier. The Trade in Services Database offers the best coverage of services trade.

Figure 1.30 looks at the number of trading relationships for Mexico and the Slovak Republic. Mexico added partners rather steadily until the 2008 crisis. The changes in the Slovak Republic were more erratic. Part of the explanation

could be the strong transition dynamics experienced there, possibly in combination with the expected accession to the European Union.

Services exports to unknown markets increased in 2002, however, suggesting that the observed dynamics may reflect data rather than market issues. Data problems are particularly problematic in analyzing the extensive margin for export markets (that is, services sectors rather than trading partners).

These problems notwithstanding, the data can help understand the dynamics and relative position of pairs of trading partners. Researchers should keep an eye on the residual category, however, and probably focus only on the most recent years, for which bilateral coverage is strongest.

Figure 1.31 plots the intensive margin against the extensive margin for Mexico, the Slovak Republic, and Turkey. It shows that over time, Mexico relied much more on its intensive margin than its extensive margin. One explanation for this result could be Mexico's strong ties with the United States through the North American Free Trade

Figure 1.30. Extensive Margins of Mexico and the Slovak Republic, 1994–2010

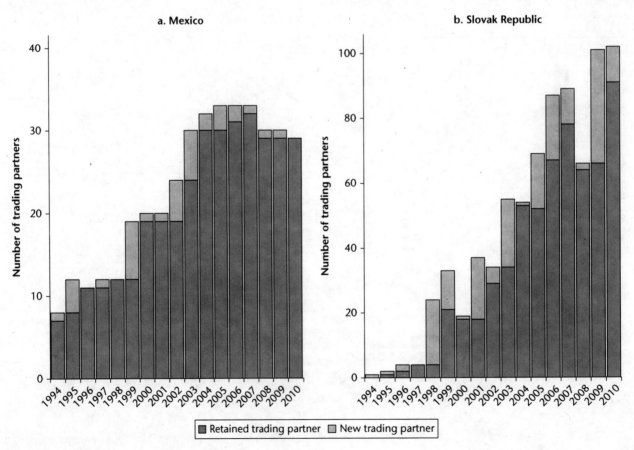

Source: Trade in Services Database.

Figure 1.31. Extensive and Intensive Margins of Mexico, the Slovak Republic, and Turkey, 2010

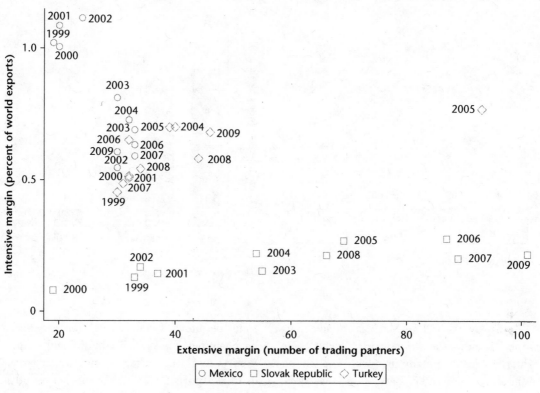

Source: Trade in Services Database.

Agreement (NAFTA), which may reduce its incentive to explore new markets. Over time, the extensive margins in the Slovak Republic and to some extent in Turkey had broader reach than their intensive margins. Generally, years of trade experience translates into more trading partners, although this relationship is bumpy. For most countries, there is a positive relationship between the two margins over time.

Trade Intensity, Trade Complementarities, and Gravity Models

> **Indicators Used to Measure Trade Opportunities**
> Several indicators are critical to assessing trade opportunities. They include the Trade Complementarities Index, the Trade Intensity Index, and the difference between predicted and actual services exports (determined using a theory-grounded gravity model). Data on these indicators should be collected for specific years for all countries. Useful sources of information include the following:
>
> - World Bank's Trade in Services Database (see appendix B)
> - *Centre d'Etudes Prospectives et d'Informations Internationales* (CEPII) (gravity model–related variables)
> - World Development Indicators
> - Stata.

Computing the **Trade Complementarities Index (TCI)** can help identify markets with export potential. It identifies whether a potential importer buys services that an economy exports abroad. The TCI complements the RCA Index. Ideally, a country would export those services in which it has a comparative advantage and import services in which it has a comparative disadvantage, as outlined in Cadot, Carrère, and Strauss-Kahn (2011).

The TCI is calculated by summing the (absolute) difference between a country's share of imports of a service in its total imports and the exporter's share of a service in its total exports:

$$TCI_{ij} = 100\left[1 - \sum_k \frac{\left|m_k^i - x_k^j\right|}{2}\right]$$

where k stands for services sectors, i for countries that import the service, and j for countries that export the service. In this index, which ranges from 0 to 100, a higher score indicates that two countries are a better "fit" as trading partners and that their trade baskets are complementary. A lower score indicates that two countries are similar in their trade structure and therefore lack scope to develop additional bilateral exports.

Figure 1.32. Trade Complementarities Index between Malaysia and Selected Trade Partners, 2004–10

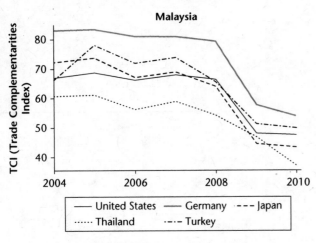

Source: Trade in Services Database.

Figure 1.33. Trade Intensity Index for Turkey and Selected Trade Partners, 2008

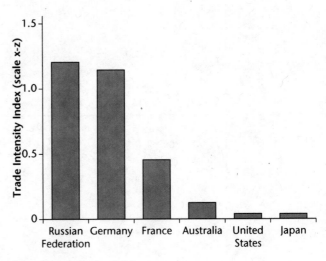

Source: Trade in Services Database.

Figure 1.32 displays the TCI for Malaysia and five of its trading partners. It shows that Malaysia shares higher trade complementarities with Germany than with Thailand, a country in the same region and income group as Malaysia. Thailand seems to have an export structure that is similar to Malaysia's. The TCI can help policy makers evaluate whether trade barriers are preventing a country from reaching the full potential provided by trade opportunities with a trading partner or whether there is a scope to negotiate a bilateral trade agreement to reduce barriers. It can also help in the analysis of potential gains from a bilateral or regional trade agreement.

A second index for measuring trade opportunities is the **Trade Intensity Index (TII)**. It focuses on total trade rather than trade by sector.

The TII is measured as country i's exports to country j relative to its total exports divided by world exports to country j relative to total world exports. It is calculated as follows:

$$TII_{ij} = \frac{\frac{x_{ij}}{X_i}}{\frac{x_{wj}}{X_w}}$$

where x_{ij} are country i's exports to country j; X_i are total exports of country i; x_{wj} are world exports to country j, and X_w are total world exports. The TII thus indicates the extent to which a country is present in the export market of a trading partner.

Figure 1.33 displays the TII for Turkey. It shows high values for Germany, France, and the Russian Federation. It shows low values for Australia, Japan, and the United States, despite the fact that these countries are in a different income group and specialize in different sectors. Turkey's exports to Germany represent a much larger share of its total exports than the share of the rest of the world's exports to Germany.

Japan's TII is much lower, even though Japan's import structure should make it an ideal trading partner for Turkey. Why is Turkey's trade with Japan not greater? Is the fact that Turkey is geographically closer to Germany than it is to Japan relevant?

A **gravity model** (box 1.6) can be used to assess whether a country is actually exporting what it "should" be exporting to its partners. Malaysia exports more to Australia because Australia is geographically closer than most of Malaysia's other partner countries. In contrast, Germany imports a large share of Turkey's exports because Germany has a very large market. These factors can be taken into account by performing a regression analysis using a gravity model.

The gravity model does a good job of predicting Malaysia's trade relationships with partner countries (figure 1.34). Market size and distance are good determinants of Malaysia's strong export relationships with Australia and Japan. Malaysia trades less than would be expected with Poland, Portugal, and Turkey. It trades more than predicted with France.

The reasons for such deviations could lie outside standard gravity explanatory variables, which this time are not incorporated in the regression but could be included. Policy barriers that are not captured by the distance proxy—such as specific tariffs or domestic logistics

Box 1.6. What Is a Gravity Model?

The **gravity equation**—introduced by Nobel laureate Jan Tinbergen, in 1962—is one of the most successful empirical tools in international trade. It posits that bilateral trade is explained largely by (a) distance between any pair of countries (which proxies for transport costs, policy barriers, behind-the-border barriers, and informational asymmetries) and (b) the market size or mass of the exporting and importing countries (proxied by the countries' GDPs). The gravity equation often includes additional control variables, such as common language, border, currency, and legal systems and whether the countries have signed a free trade agreement. Based on these factors, it predicts the value of exports between countries and compares it with the actual value of trade.

Recent advances in the empirical trade literature have refined the gravity model in various ways. First, the volume of trade between partners depends not only on direct (or absolute) trade costs between partners but also on the (indirect) relative trade costs with respect to third countries. These "multilateral resistance terms," developed by Anderson and van Wincoop (2003), should be incorporated into the model.

Second, several new techniques allow analysts to take stock of zero-trade flows. One way of doing so is to include the Heckman sample selection correction method, which takes the probability of being included in the sample as an explanatory variable into account. When performing ordinary least squares regressions, researchers usually drop zero observations by taking their logs. Such a procedure can create sample selection bias, as the probability of having nonzero trade flows could be correlated with GDP or distance. Another way of correcting for zero trade flows is by using the Poisson pseudo-maximum likelihood (PPML) estimator, introduced by Santos Silva and Tenreyro (2006).

Figure 1.34. Gravity Model for Malaysia and Selected Trade Partners, 2008

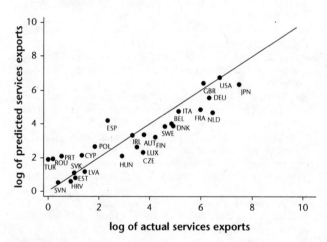

Figure 1.35. Trading Partners and Development, 2008

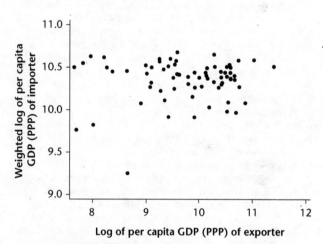

Source: Trade in Services Database.
Note: For the International Organization for Standardization (ISO) abbreviations, see appendix B.

Source: Trade in Services Database.
Note: PPP = purchasing power parity.

performances (Arvis and others 2010)—may explain why countries "over" or "under" trade with Malaysia.

The previous section established that the type of service a country exports matters. Does the destination also matter? Higher-income countries export more sophisticated services than do lower-income countries. It may therefore make sense for developing countries to try to specialize in these services. A similar argument could be made for export markets. Figure 1.35 shows that there is no clear relationship between the levels of development and trading partners—that is, a high-income country

is no more likely to trade with a low-income or high-income country.

A limitation of figure 1.35 is that the Trade in Services Database does not record all trade relationships for services. Part of the reason why the data are spotty is that services are intangible and therefore difficult to tax at the border, particularly in developing countries. For this reason, trade in services, particularly between developing countries, is probably underestimated, possibly explaining why there are more dots on the right side of figure 1.35 than on the left.

MODULE 1

Notes

1. For the purpose of this toolkit, *modern services* are services that can be traded across borders without the buyer and seller being in the same place. Delivery of these services is less dependent on physical infrastructure and more dependent on telecommunications and electric supply. Examples of such services include communication, banking, insurance, business, and remote access services; transcription of medical records; call centers; and education. These services differ markedly from traditional services, which demand face-to-face interaction.

2. Trade figures do not reflect the true importance of services trade. When trade is measured in terms of value added, the share of services may increase by as much as 50 percent by some estimates (Francois, Manchin, and Tomberger 2013).

References

Anderson, J. E., and E. van Wincoop. 2003. "Gravity with Gravitas: A Solution to the Border Puzzle." *American Economic Review* 93 (1): 170–92.

Arvis, Jean-François, Monica Alina Mustra, Lauri Ojala, Ben Shepherd, and Daniel Saslavsky. 2010. *Connecting to Compete 2010: Trade Logistics in the Global Economy. The Logistics Performance Index and Its Indicators.* Washington, DC: World Bank.

Barro, Robert J., and Jong-Wha Lee. 2012. "A New Dataset of Educational Attainment in the World, 1950–2010." NBER Working Paper 15902, National Bureau of Economic Research, Cambridge, MA.

Bernard, A., and J. B. Jensen. 1999. "Exceptional Exporter Performance: Cause, Effect, or Both?" *Journal of International Economics* 47 (1): 1–25.

Borchert, Ingo, and Aaditya Mattoo. 2009. "The Crisis-Resilience of Services Trade." Policy Research Working Paper 4917, World Bank, Washington, DC.

Brienlich, Holger, and Chiara Criscuolo. 2011. "International Trade in Services: A Portrait of Importers and Exporters." *Journal of International Economics* 84: 188–206.

Cadot, Olivier, Céline Carrère, and Vanessa Strauss-Kahn. 2011. "OECD Imports Diversification of Suppliers and Quality Search." Policy Research Working Paper 5627, World Bank, Washington, DC.

Cattaneo, Olivier, Gary Gereffi, Sébastien Miroudot, and Daria Taglioni. 2013. "Joining, Upgrading and Being Competitive in Global Value Chains: A Strategic Framework for Developing Countries." World Bank Policy Research Paper 6406, Washington, DC.

Francois Joseph, Miriam Manchin, and Patrick Tomberger. 2013. "Services Linkages and the Value Added Content of Trade." Policy Research Working Paper 6432, World Bank, Washington, DC.

Freund, Caroline, and Diana Weinhold, 2002. "The Internet and International Trade in Services." *American Economic Review* 92 (2): 236–40.

Hausmann, Ricardo, Jason Hwang, and Dani Rodrik. 2007. "What You Export Matters." *Journal of Economic Growth* 12 (1): 1–25.

Iacovone, Leonardo, Aaditya Mattoo, and Andrés Zahler. 2013. "Trade and Innovation in Services: Evidence from a Developing Economy." Policy Research Working Paper 6520, World Bank, Washington, DC.

IMF (International Monetary Fund). 2009. *Balance of Payments and International Investment Position Manual,* 6th ed. Washington, DC: IMF.

———. Various years. Balance of Payments Statistics. Washington, DC. http://elibrary-data.imf.org/finddatareports.aspx?d=33061&e=170784.

Lederman, D., and W. Maloney. 2012. "Does What You Export Matter? In Search of Empirical Guidance for Industrial Policies." World Bank, Washington, DC.

McKinsey. 2010. *Lions on the Move: The Progress and Potential of African Economies.* McKinsey Global Institute, Washington, DC.

Melitz, Marc. 2003. "The Impact of Trade on Intra-Industry Reallocations and Aggregate Industry Productivity." *Econometrica* 71 (6): 1695–725.

Milberg, William, and Deborah Winkler. 2013. *Outsourcing Economics: Global Value Chains in Capitalist Development.* Cambridge: Cambridge University Press.

OECD (Organisation for Economic Co-operation and Development) and WTO (World Trade Organization). 2013. "OECD-WTO Database on Trade in Value Added First Estimates." January 16, Organisation for Economic Co-operation and Development, Paris.

O'Mahony, Mary, and Marcel P. Timmer. 2009. "Output, Input and Productivity Measure at the Industry Level: The EU KLEMS Database." *Economic Journal* 119 (538): 374–403.

Sachs, Jeffrey D., and Andrew M. Warner. 1999. "The Big Push, Natural Resource Booms and Growth." *Journal of Development Economics* 59 (1): 43–76.

Santos Silva, J. M. C., and S. Tenreyro. 2006. "The Log of Gravity." *Review of Economics and Statistics* 4 (88): 641–58.

Shepherd, Ben, and Erik van der Marel. 2013. "International Tradability of Services." Policy Research Working Paper 6712, World Bank, Washington, DC.

Siggel, Eckhard. 2006 "International Competitiveness and Comparative Advantage: A Survey and a Proposal for Measurement." *Journal of Industry, Competition and Trade* 6 (2): 137–59.

Taglioni, Daria, and Deborah Winkler. 2014. *Making Global Value Chains Work for Development.* Washington, DC: World Bank.

Tinbergen, Jan. 1962. *Shaping the World Economy: Suggestions for an International Economics Policy.* New York: Twentieth Century Fund.

Trade in Services Database. World Bank, Washington, DC.

UNCTADstat Database. http://unctadstat.unctad.org/ReportFolders/reportFolders.aspx.

WEF (World Economic Forum). 2013. *Enabling Trade: Valuing Growth Opportunities.* Geneva: World Economic Forum.

Wignaraja, Ganeshan, and Ashely Taylor. 2003. "Benchmarking Competitiveness: A First Look at the MECI." In *Competitiveness in Developing Countries: A Manual for Policy Analysis,* edited by Ganeshan Wignaraja. London: Routledge.

World Development Indicators (database). World Bank, Washington, DC. http://data.worldbank.org/data-catalog/world-development-indicators.

SERVICES AS A SOURCE OF COMPETITIVENESS IN THE WHOLE ECONOMY

Before a country can export services, it needs to develop a competitive domestic services sector. Cross-country comparisons of basic indicators, such as the share of a country's value added from services activity, provide a first assessment of the existence and importance of a domestic sector.

Services in the Domestic Economy

Assessing the Role of Services in the Domestic Economy

Several indicators are critical to assessing the role of services in the domestic economy. They include the value added of the services, industry, and agriculture sectors as a percent of gross domestic product (GDP) versus the log of GDP per capita; employment by sector; and the openness of services trade. Data on these indicators should be collected for specific years for all countries. World Development Indicators provides the following information:

- value added by sector as a percent of GDP
- GDP and GDP per capita
- employment per sector
- total services trade.

Table 2.1 shows a simple cross-country regression between the share of services value added in GDP in 1985 and the share of services trade in GDP in 2010. It shows that the size of the domestic services sector is a robust precondition for specialization in services exports in later years. However, this relationship weakens when more recent data are used for the independent variable, suggesting that over time, other forces, such as policy, play roles.

Value Added of Services

Figure 2.1 shows scatter plots of per capita value added of services (in logs) against the log of GDP per capita purchashing power parity (PPP) for two periods, 2000–02 and 2008–10. The fitted line reflects the stylized fact that services tend to grow in importance for the economy as the level of a country's development rises.

Figure 2.1 indicates whether the services sector is larger or smaller than predicted based on a country's level of development. It shows that most developed countries are highly dependent on services, even controlling for per capita income. In contrast, per capita value added of services are much smaller in countries such as Peru, which falls below the fitted line.

Value added also reveals substantial differences in the size of the services sector at all levels of development. Although the share of services in GDP generally increases with economic development, it varies across economies at the same level of development. The share of services is about 70 percent in Brazil, for example, but just 40 percent in Malaysia, even though per capita income is similar in the two countries.

Comparison of the two panels of figure 2.1 shows that there has been little change in the relative positions of most countries, although all countries, including low-income countries, have become somewhat richer.

Other structural factors may help explain these results. Figure 2.2 plots the residuals of the regression shown in table 2.2, which regresses the log of per capita value added of services against the log of population and the log of per capita income in PPP. The population variable does not show a significant correlation with value added per capita, but GDP per capita does. These variables do not fully explain the wide variance in the performance of countries; figure 2.2 illustrates the large residuals. Within each income group there is a correlation between the log of per capita services value added and the residuals, suggesting that the more important services are for the economy, the

Table 2.1. Cross-Country Regression of Size of Services Sector against Specialization in Services Export

Item	ln(STR perc GDP 2010)
log (SVA perc GDP "85)	0.837***
	(0.280)
Observations	111
R-squared	0.085

Note: STR perc GDP 2010 = services trade as percent of GDP in 2010. SVA perc GDP "85 = services value added as percent of GDP in 1985. Robust clustered standard errors are in parentheses. *** $p < 0.01$.

larger are the residuals. This result is somewhat weaker in more recent years. Nonetheless, the correlations seem to imply that other structural factors explain the growth of services as countries develop.

This pattern of specialization across stages of development was first observed in the late 1930s. Fisher (1939, 1952) and Clark (1940) observed that countries at the first stage of development tend to specialize in agriculture,

countries at the second stage in manufacturing, and countries at the most advanced stage of development in services. This pattern is captured by the slopes of the curves in figure 2.3, which plots log of per capita value added of each of these sectors against level of development.

In 2012, the share of services value added represented 75 percent of total value added in high-income economies. It accounted for 49 percent of value added in low-income countries and 56 percent in upper-middle-income countries. In many low- and lower-middle-income countries in Africa, the figure is just 20 percent. The countries with the smallest shares of services tend to be countries with a history of conflict, such as Angola, Iraq, and Libya. The only country classified as high income that has a very small share of services in value added is Equatorial Guinea.

Since 1990, the share of services in value added has increased steadily across all income groups (figure 2.4). Even low-income economies, which have not yet attained

Figure 2.1. Per Capita Services Value Added and Per Capita GDP in Selected Countries, 2000–02 and 2008–10

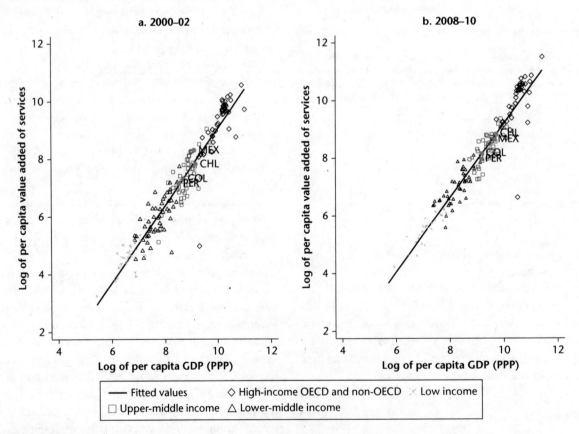

Source: World Development Indicators.
Note: Income classification is as of July 1, 2012. In the WDI database, services correspond to International Standard Industrial Classification (ISIC) divisions 50–99. The sector is derived as a residual (GDP less agriculture and industry) and may not reflect the sum of services output. For some countries, values include product taxes (minus subsidies) and may reflect statistical discrepancies. CHL = Chile, COL = Colombia, MEX = Mexico, OECD = Organisation for Economic Co-operation and Development, PER = Peru, PPP = purchasing power parity.

MODULE 2

Figure 2.2. Services Value Added and Structural Factors in Selected Countries, 2000–02 and 2008–10

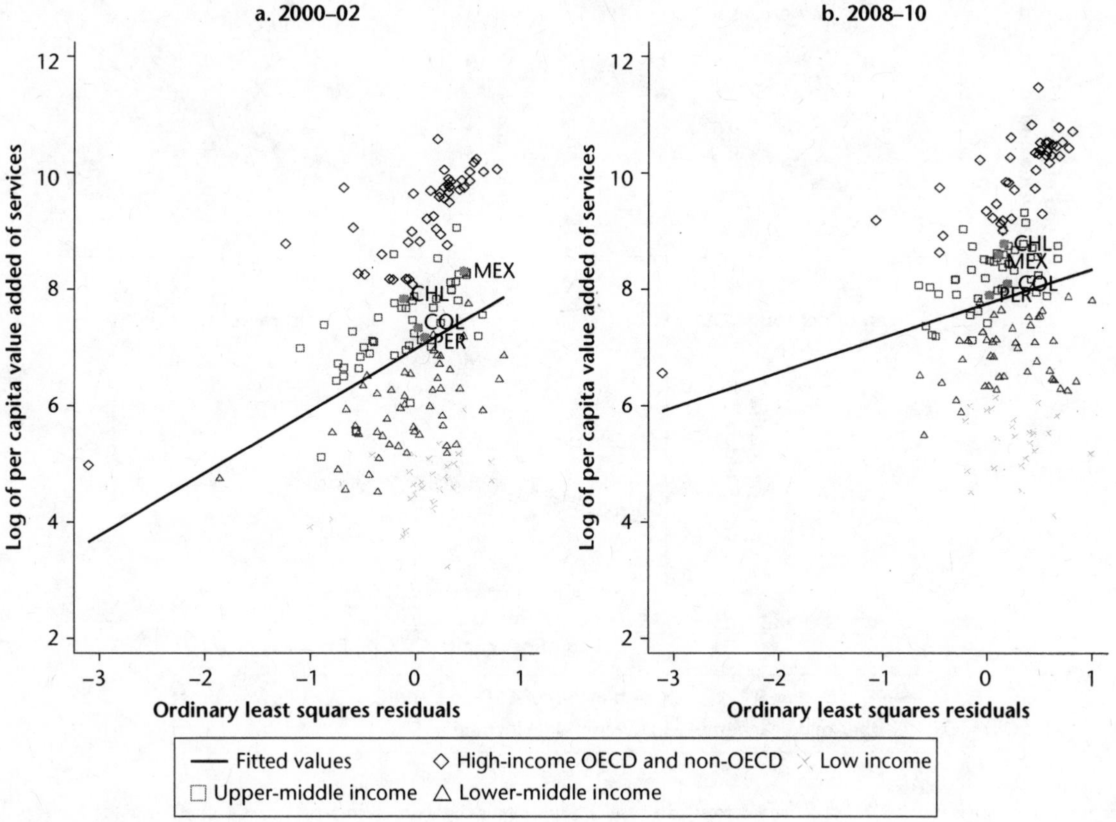

Source: World Development Indicators.
Note: CHL = Chile, COL = Colombia, MEX = Mexico, OECD = Organisation for Economic Co-operation and Development, PER = Peru.

their full production potential in industry, have seen the services sector grow (box 2.1).

These observations suggest that it is difficult to say whether a country's share of services in the economy is small or large without putting other characteristics in context. Income is only a partial explanation of why the services sector thrives in some countries but is relatively underdeveloped in others.

Table 2.2. Cross-Country Regression of Per Capita Services Value Added against Level of Economic Development

Item	ln(services VA pc)
ln(population)	–0.0236*
	(0.0141)
ln(gdp_pc_ppp)	1.330***
	(0.0222)
Observations	329
R-squared	0.919
Root mean square deviation	0.510

Note: Standard errors are in parentheses. * $p < 0.1$, *** $p < 0.01$.

Structural characteristics, such as the level of regulation, the availability of specific skills, and urbanization, also matter. In India the services that were most underdeveloped were also the most regulated and grew fastest after deregulation, according to Eichengreen and Gupta (2011, 2012). Part of the reason the services sector is less developed in China than in India is that India is more urbanized, according to Liping and Evenett (2010).

The tradability of a service also matters. When trading is not burdened by regulatory obstacles, tradable services tend to grow faster than their nontradable counterparts. Amin and Mattoo (2006, 2008) show that services output is greater in Indian states with larger bases of skilled workers and that countries with good institutions have larger and more dynamic services sectors (see Module 4).

Figure 2.5 shows the sectoral composition of value added expressed in GDP in several Central Asian economies in 1990, 2000, and 2010. Over this period, the services share increased in some of these economies. By 2010, it represented the main economic activity in three out of the five economies (Tajikistan, the Kyrgyz Republic, and

Figure 2.3. Per Capita Value Added of Agriculture, Industry, and Services versus Per Capita GDP, 2008–10

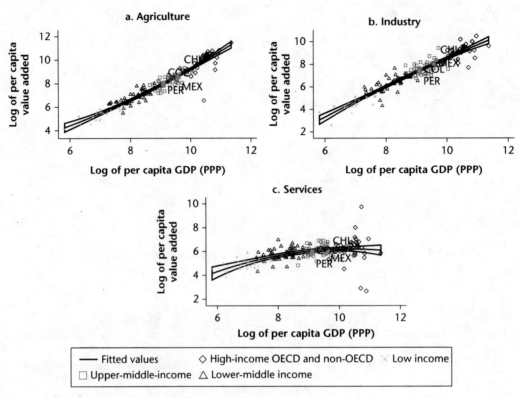

Source: World Development Indicators.
Note: Income classification is as of July 1, 2012. Linear regression is based on a quadratic GDP term. Each panel shows a fitted line of the scatter plot. The lines above and below it are the 95 percent confidence intervals. CHL = Chile, COL = Colombia, MEX = Mexico, OECD = Organisation for Economic Co-operation and Development, PER = Peru, PPP = purchasing power parity.

Uzbekistan). In Azerbaijan and Turkmenistan, industry is the main economic sector, and the share of services in the economy declined over the past two decades. This pattern probably reflects the fact that these economies are largely dependent on the gas and petroleum sector, which prevents them from climbing the **ladder of comparative advantage**. Other factors, such as infrastructure or regulatory problems, could also play roles.

In the lower-middle-income countries of the Kyrgyz Republic and Uzbekistan, the relative importance of agriculture shrank. However, in Uzbekistan the growth of services was accompanied by the simultaneous growth of industry, which was not the case in the Kyrgyz Republic or Tajikistan. The continuously growing services sector in Uzbekistan may be directly related to its industry.

The steady increase in the share of services over the past two decades was not experienced in many countries in the Middle East and North Africa, including the Arab Republic of Egypt, the Islamic Republic of Iran, and the Syrian Arab Republic (figure 2.6). In all countries in the region, the relative importance of agriculture shrank considerably. Except in Lebanon, Tunisia, and Turkey, the decline of

agriculture was accompanied by a decline in the share of services and an increase in the share of industry. In Turkey and Tunisia, the value added from services increased significantly. Their economic structure is similar to that of other upper-middle-income countries.

The services sector is still the main economic activity in almost all countries in the region for which data are available. The exceptions to this trend are Iraq and Libya in 2000, where the industrial sector represented the main economic activity. Lebanon has the most services-intensive economy in the region, with a services share of 71 percent in 2010.

Employment

The services sector is also an important source of employment. Unfortunately, employment data are very limited; the latest observations from **World Development Indicators** for a large number of countries are from 2005. Nevertheless, figure 2.7 shows that services are the dominant employer in developed countries and that their importance has been sizable in middle-income countries. As much as 71 percent of the workforce in high-income countries was employed in

Figure 2.4. Sectoral Share of Value Added, by Income Group, 1990, 2000, and 2010

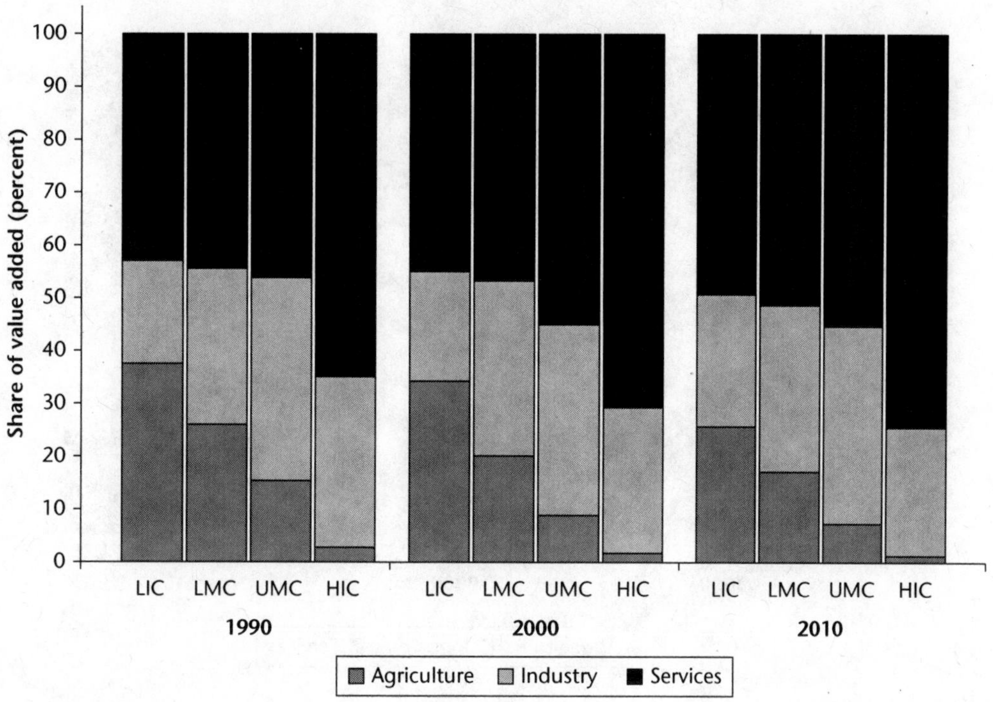

Source: World Development Indicators.
Note: LIC = low-income country; LMC = lower-middle-income country; UMC = upper-middle-income country; HIC = high-income country. Data for 2009 instead of 2010 were used for high-income countries.

Box 2.1. Does India Defy the General Pattern of Ladders of Comparative Advantage?

In general, countries first develop a strong domestic services sector before they begin to export services. Not all countries follow this path, however. India, for example, did not have a large domestic services sector before it became a major provider of international call services. Its cost and skill advantage led straight to a strong external sector. India also has a relatively large pool of people in the agricultural sector who, because of policies, cannot move into industry. In the meantime, India's services sector has expanded.

---

services in 2005 (up from 65 percent in 1994). In 2005, the share of employment generated by services was 31 percent in lower-middle-income and 40 percent in upper-middle-income countries (up from 27 percent in lower-income and 29 percent in upper-middle-income countries in 1994). Data are not available for low-income countries.

Employment by a sector can be assessed by comparing it with employment in other countries at the same level of income. In Senegal, a lower-middle-income country, for example, the services sector employs 43 percent of the labor force. In most other peer countries, agriculture is the main employer (figure 2.8). The services sector accounts for just 16 percent of employment in Mozambique and 19 percent in Tanzania.

Figure 2.8 reveals that the sectoral employment shares of a few countries are in line with their development.

For example, in Senegal, Vietnam, and to a lesser extent Ghana, which are lower-middle-income countries, their sectoral shares of employment are close to the average for their income group. In contrast, in Cambodia, Mozambique, and Tanzania, which are low-income countries, the agricultural sectors account for a large share of employment, especially relative to industry. In Kenya, the services sector is in line with the average low-income country.

Assessing the employment absorption capacity of each sector and comparing them to the value added contribution can also be insightful. Figure 2.3 showed that the richer a country becomes, the more value added in services it produces. Figure 2.9 suggests that employment in services rises with value added.

Figure 2.9 shows that the services sector generates less employment in Turkey than in countries with

Figure 2.5. Value Added of Agriculture, Industry, and Services as Share of GDP in Central Asian Countries, 1990, 2000, and 2010

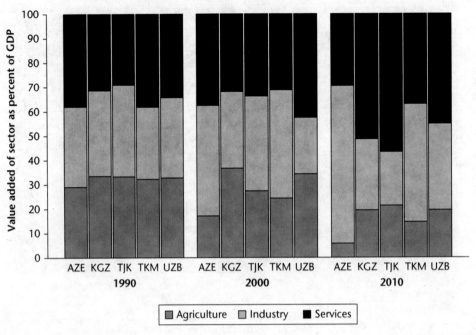

Source: World Development Indicators.
Note: AZE = Azerbaijan, KGZ = Kyrgyz Republic, TJK = Tajikistan, TKM = Turkmenistan, UZB = Uzbekistan. For the Kyrgyz Republic, data for 1992 instead of 1990 were used.

Figure 2.6. Value Added of Agriculture, Industry, and Services as Share of GDP in Selected Countries in the Middle East and North Africa, 1990, 2000, and 2010

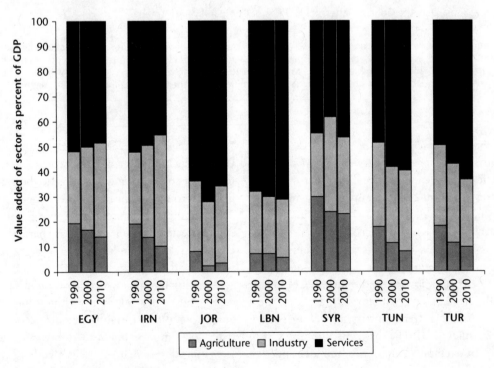

Source: World Development Indicators.
Note: EGY = Arab Republic of Egypt, IRN = Islamic Republic of Iran, JOR = Jordan, LBN = Lebanon, SYR = Syrian Arab Republic, TUN = Tunisia, TUR = Turkey. Data were not available for Iraq in 1990 and 2010 or Libya in 1990.

Figure 2.7. Employment in Agriculture, Industry, and Services, by Income Group, 1994, 2000, and 2005

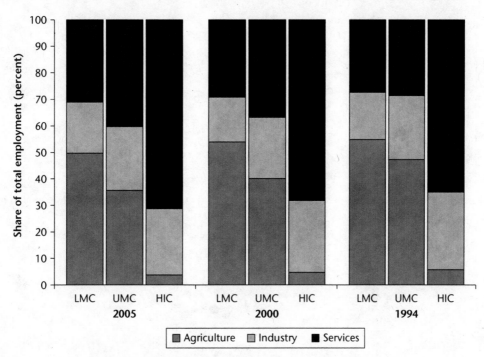

Source: World Development Indicators, accessed in February 2013.
Note: LMC = lower-middle-income country; UMC = upper-middle-income country; HIC = high-income country.

Figure 2.8. Employment in Agriculture, Industry, and Services in Selected Low- and Lower-Middle-Income Countries, 2006

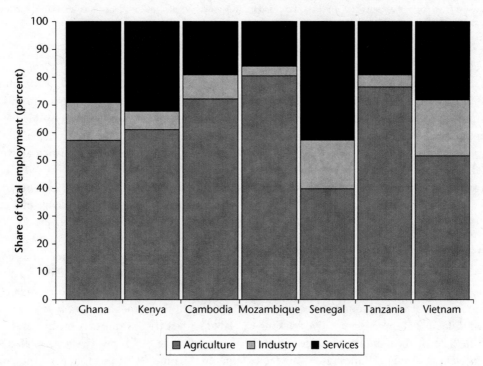

Source: World Development Indicators, accessed in February 2013.
Note: Data for Kenya are for 2005; data for Mozambique are for 2003.

MODULE 2

Figure 2.9. Share of Value Added and Share of Employment in Selected Countries, by Sector, 2008–10

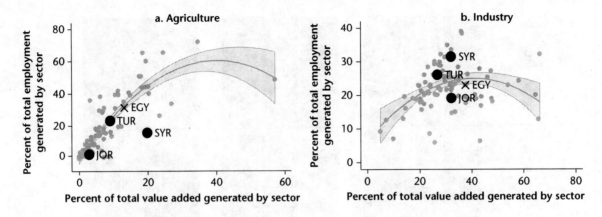

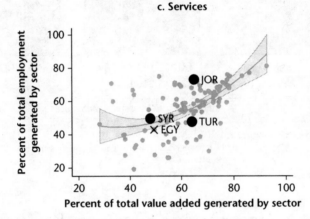

Source: World Development Indicators, accessed in February 2013.
Note: Each panel shows a fitted line of the scatter plot. The lines above and below it are the 95 percent confidence intervals. EGY = Arab Republic of Egypt, JOR = Jordan, SYR= Syrian Arab Republic, TUR = Turkey.

similar levels of value added generated by the services sector. Jordan employs an above-average share (nearly 80 percent) of its workforce in services, with another 18 percent employed in industry. In Syria and Egypt, employment in the services sector is about average for the size of their services sector.

Firm-level data are another source with which to assess the importance of services in the domestic economy (box 2.2).

Domestic Services Sectors in Relation to International Trade

A final measure for assessing the importance of the domestic services sector is its relation to international trade. As shown in table 2.1, there is a positive relationship between the size of the domestic services sector and its competitiveness in trade. Building on this fact, figure 2.10 shows the degree to which value added of services exports (expressed as a percentage of value added

in total exports) is linked with countries' economic complexity. Figure 2.10 plots the Economic Complexity Index (ECI) constructed by Hausmann and others (2014) against the share of services value added exports in total value added exports. The intuition behind the ECI is that making a product requires a particular type and mix of knowledge. Countries that possess more knowledge can produce a more diverse set of products. In other words, the amount of embedded knowledge of a country is represented in the number of distinct products that it makes. In addition, products that are knowledge-intensive are only produced in countries where the required knowledge is available (Hausmann and others 2014). Although the ECI refers essentially to goods trade characteristics, figure 2.10 shows that complexity is also positively correlated with services exports contribution to total exports. Generally, the ECI is positively correlated with development (income per capita), and so the contribution of services exports in total trade either measured in terms of **backward** or **forward linkages** (defined below) will be

Box 2.2. What Is the Structure of the Services Sector? Evidence from Romania

Firm-level data provide insights into the structure of the services sector. Figure B2.2.1 shows the shares of employment, value added, output, and exports of goods, traditional services, modern services, and professional services in Romania.

Figure B2.2.1. Concentration of Employment, Value Added, Output, and Exports in Romania, by Sector, 2008

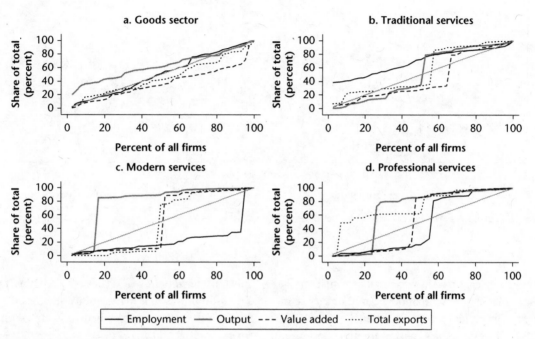

Source: World Bank Structural Business Survey.

The structure of the sectors varies substantially. For goods, most of the indicators are distributed in a uniform manner: all four lines are close to the 45-degree line. To some extent, this is also the case for the traditional services sector, although a small number of firms accounts for a substantial share of employment (almost 40 percent). In the modern services sectors, however, less than 20 percent of firms account for almost 80 percent of output, and about 50 percent of firms account for almost 80 percent of exports. For professional services exports, about 5 percent of firms account for almost 50 percent of exports.

higher. In other words, the ability to successfully participate in services exports is linked to the existing type and mix of knowledge available in a country.

Linkages to the Rest of the Economy

Assessing the Value Added of Services
Several indicators are critical to assessing the value added of services and their linakges to other economic activities. Assessing the importance of the services sector for the overall economy is based on the value added content that is generated by services and goes into downstream exported sectors. This methodology helps appraise the relevance of specific services inputs for the overall competitiveness of a country and for particular types of production.

Assessment of the services content of goods is based on methodologies proposed by Francois, Manchin, and Tomberger (2013) and Francois and Woerz (2008).

They include the value added versus direct share, the share of a country's value added in world value added, and forward and backward linkages of a region or country. Data on these indicators should be collected for specific years for all countries. Useful sources of information include the following:

- OECD's Database for Structural Analysis (input-output tables)
- OECD-WTO's Trade in Value Added (TiVA) or Global Trade Analysis Project (GTAP) databases
- World Bank's Export of Value Added Database (see appendix A).

Figure 2.10. Knowledge and Services Exports Contribution to Total Exports, 2007

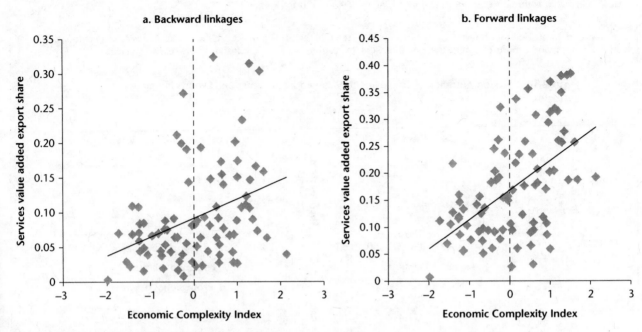

Sources: Hausmann and others 2014; Export of Value Added Database.

Services can be exported in two ways: as a final service or as an intermediate input in another good or service by any downstream industry. Most trade analysis examines gross values. However, policy makers are more and more interested in what a country produces and exports in net terms, because goods and services cross borders many times. Net or value added analysis therefore avoids double counting.

Methodologies assessing the relevance of services as inputs to downstream exports also present challenges. These methodologies are based on value added and input-output data. Combined with trade data, they provide an indication of the reliance on domestic versus foreign inputs of production destined for domestic and foreign markets.

The OECD-WTO's Trade in Value Added (TiVA) Database provides net and gross value added figures for exports of goods and services. Most countries in the database are Organisation for Economic Co-operation and Development (OECD) countries; most developing countries are left out.

This section uses the World Bank's **Export of Value Added Database** of gross and net production and export figures based on input-output tables provided by the Global Trade Analysis Project (GTAP) Database. GTAP tables provide a more aggregated picture than other sources, but they include many developing countries and are available

only for intermittent years. They are also subject to restrictive assumptions that may significantly bias the quantification of the technology coefficients assumed for different types of production.

Disentangling value added from gross figures is important because it provides insights into the importance of the domestic content of trade (appendix A explains the methodology employed to calculate trade in value-added terms). Figure 2.11 breaks down gross and net exports of machinery and business services by income groups. (Business services were selected because this sector has been the most dynamic services subsector in recent years.)

Across income groups, the share of value added in exports is much larger than the gross share for services compared to goods. For both machinery and business services, high-income countries export the most value added, although lower-middle-income countries are not far behind. For both machinery and business services, lower-middle-income countries export more value added than upper-middle-income countries.

Gross versus Net Value-Added Share

A cleaner output measure is therefore the net value produced in a sector. It shows the real importance of a good or service for the economy. A useful indicator that can reveal

Figure 2.11. Gross Exports and Value Added of Exports of Machinery and Business Services, by Income Level, 2007

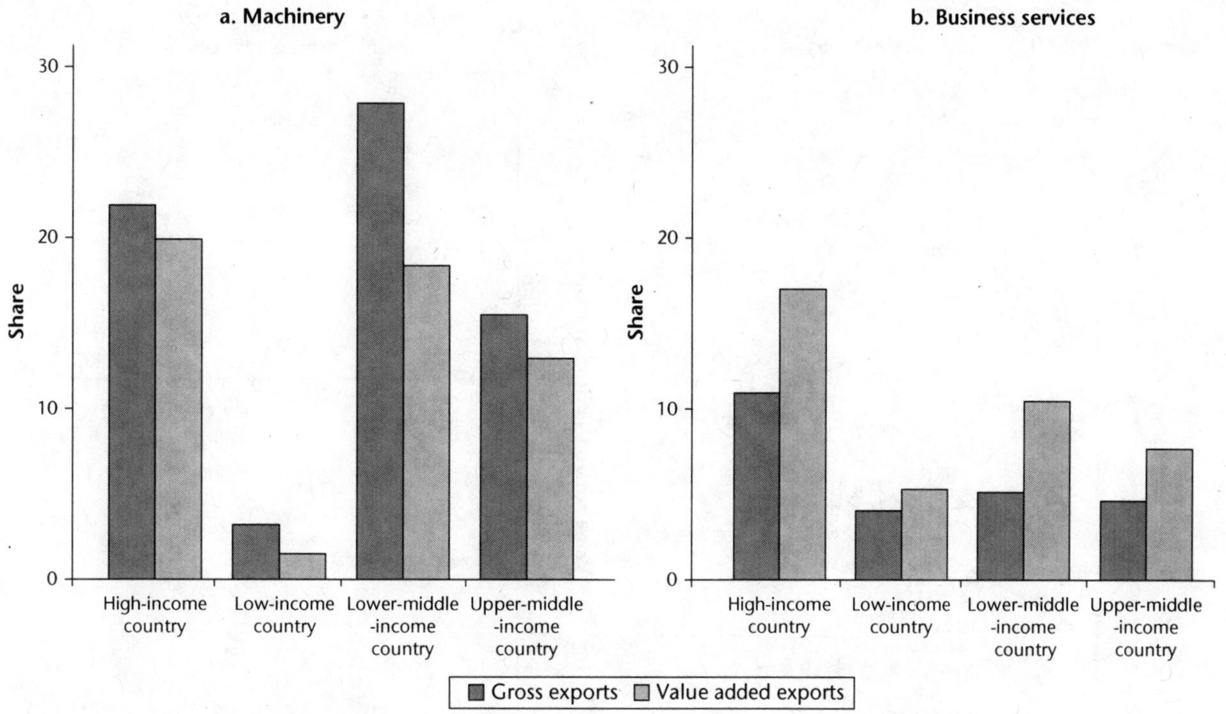

a. Machinery

b. Business services

Gross exports   Value added exports

Source: Export of Value Added Database.

this importance is the ratio of the net share to the gross share of value added:

$$\text{Net-gross ratio} = \frac{\dfrac{VA_{ki}}{VA_i}}{\dfrac{GR_{ki}}{GR_i}}$$

where VA_{ki} is the exported value added in a sector k in country i; VA_i is the total exported value added of country i; GR_{ki} is the gross value of exports in sector k in country i; and GR_i is the total gross value exported of country i. A ratio higher than 1 means that looking at the net value added term is the right way of judging a sector's contribution to the national economy. The indicator also shows how much the sector is underestimated in gross terms. Figure 2.12 plots this ratio for each country against the level of development for a goods and a services sector.

In panel a, this ratio is less than 1 for many countries, indicating that the manufacturing sector tends to have a much higher component of gross exports than value added. Panel a also shows a positive relationship between the net-gross ratio and the level of development. This relationship implies that most of the value added in goods exported by developing countries comes from other sectors, in the

form of intermediate inputs; it is not brought forward by these sectors themselves as they produce relatively little value added. In contrast, higher-income countries seem to export more value added produced by their own goods sector.

This relationship disappears in the services sector (panel b). The fitted value line is flat, indicating that on average, developing countries produce and bring forward as much value added in services as developed countries. The ratio of the shares of value added to gross value is high for most countries, indicating that evaluating services at gross values is a misplaced way of looking at the importance of the sector to the economy as a whole.

Value Added of Production for Domestic and Export Markets

How can exports be calculated in value added terms? How can one estimate how much value added a country carries over from other sectors? How can one estimate how much value added a country brings forward into other sectors?

This section uses input-output information from the Export of Value Added Database to calculate forward and backward linkages of value added. Forward linkages indicate how much value added is carried by other

MODULE 2

Figure 2.12. Ratio of Value Added to Gross Value and Development for Machinery and Business Services in Selected Economies, 2007

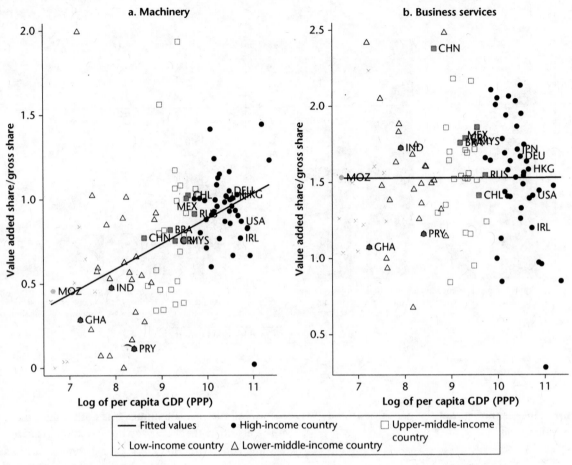

Source: Export of Value Added Database.
Note: BRA = Brazil, CHL = Chile, CHN = China, CRI = Costa Rica, DEU = Germany, GHA = Ghana, HKG = Hong Kong SAR, China, IRL = Ireland, JPN = Japan, MEX = Mexico, MOZ = Mozambique, MYS = Malaysia, PPP = purchasing power parity, PRY = Paraguay, RUS = Russian Federation, USA = United States.

sectors—that is, how important each (services or goods) sector is as an intermediate input for other sectors. Backward linkages show how much value added a sector carries from other sectors—that is, how much the sector embodies inputs that it will further process.

These indicators are usually available as an aggregate for the world or country (the Export of Value Added Database includes about 120 economies). Value added can be calculated for the domestic economic activity and for a country's exports. The value added of exports indicates how much value added a country, income group, or region carries forward through its exports to other countries (forward linkages) or how important a given sector is as a channel of "indirect exports" for its domestic inputs (backward linkages) (see appendix A).

Table 2.3 shows these indicators for Albania, where almost 32 percent of value added production comes from transport and trade services, which are used in

the domestic production of other goods and services. Business services represent about 18 percent of value added production. The figures for backward linkages are similar in the two sectors. For all sectors except dwellings, transport and trade services are the most important source of inputs (after inputs from the sector itself). This pattern is also evident in the value added that is integrated into Albania's exports. Most of this value added stems from or uses transport and distribution services.

The pattern of value added for Albania is not characteristic of all countries. In high-income countries, business services and government services (such as health and education) are the most used and carried forward in domestic production. Value added integrated in exports that are further processed or consumed abroad is done mostly through business services (26 percent); heavy industry goods, such as machinery (20 percent); and machinery equipment (19 percent).

MODULE 2

Table 2.3. Value Added of Domestic Production and Exports in Albania, by Sector, 2007
(percent of total)

Sector	Electricity, gas, and water	Construction	Transport and trade	Business services	Government services	Dwellings	Primary products	Food and beverages	Textiles	Machinery equipment	Other machinery	Forward linkages
Domestic value added												
Electricity, gas, and water	0.99	0.19	0.18	0.31	0.02	0.02	0.04	0.07	0.06	0.00	0.15	2.04
Construction	0.00	7.77	0.09	0.06	0.07	0.09	0.01	0.01	0.00	0.00	0.01	8.12
Transport and trade	0.05	1.98	25.83	0.96	0.23	0.09	0.59	0.80	0.37	0.08	0.84	31.79
Business services	0.07	1.10	3.34	11.76	0.16	0.27	0.39	0.33	0.21	0.05	0.51	18.21
Government services	0.00	0.01	0.04	0.14	8.25	0.00	0.01	0.00	0.00	0.00	0.01	8.47
Dwellings	0.00	0.00	0.00	0.00	0.00	3.94	0.00	0.00	0.00	0.00	0.00	3.94
Primary products	0.04	0.66	2.03	0.82	0.07	0.03	9.33	3.22	0.21	0.01	0.79	17.21
Food and beverages	0.00	0.02	0.16	0.14	0.01	0.00	0.08	2.12	0.01	0.00	0.07	2.62
Textiles	0.00	0.01	0.01	0.01	0.00	0.00	0.00	0.00	1.14	0.00	0.01	1.19
Machinery equipment	0.00	0.02	0.02	0.01	0.00	0.00	0.00	0.00	0.00	0.43	0.00	0.48
Other machinery	0.00	1.88	0.33	0.15	0.05	0.06	0.03	0.05	0.03	0.02	3.31	5.91
Backward linkages	1.17	13.63	32.04	14.36	8.85	4.51	10.49	6.60	2.05	0.59	5.71	100.00
Export value added												
Electricity, gas, and water	0.04	0.01	0.25	0.45	0.01	0.00	0.12	0.02	0.20	0.01	0.45	1.56
Construction	0.00	0.23	0.13	0.09	0.02	0.00	0.02	0.00	0.02	0.00	0.03	0.54
Transport and trade	0.00	0.06	34.75	1.41	0.06	0.00	0.43	0.23	1.27	0.20	2.25	40.66
Business services	0.00	0.03	4.49	17.33	0.04	0.00	0.31	0.11	0.70	0.13	1.35	24.49
Government services	0.00	0.00	0.06	0.21	2.20	0.00	0.02	0.00	0.01	0.00	0.02	2.52
Dwellings	0.00	0.00	0.00	0.00	0.00	0.00	0.00	0.00	0.00	0.00	0.00	0.00
Primary products	0.00	0.02	2.74	1.20	0.02	0.00	6.64	0.95	0.72	0.03	1.89	14.21
Food and beverages	0.00	0.00	0.22	0.20	0.00	0.00	0.03	0.65	0.03	0.00	0.27	1.40
Textiles	0.00	0.00	0.02	0.01	0.00	0.00	0.00	0.00	3.88	0.00	0.04	3.95
Machinery equipment	0.00	0.00	0.02	0.01	0.00	0.00	0.00	0.00	0.00	1.16	0.01	1.21
Other machinery	0.00	0.06	0.44	0.23	0.01	0.00	0.03	0.02	0.12	0.05	8.52	9.46
Backward linkages	0.04	0.40	43.11	21.15	2.36	0.00	7.61	1.98	6.94	1.59	14.81	100.00

Source: Export of Value Added Database.

Box 2.3. Where Do Services Inputs Go? Evidence from Ghana

How important are services as inputs in the domestic economy and as exports? Who are the downstream users of services inputs?

Social accounting matrixes (input-output data) from the Export of Value Added Database developed by the World Bank as a cross-country dataset spanning intermittent years from 1992 to 2007 shed light on these questions. This database contains two tables—a domestic value added table and an export value added table—that identify the value added contribution of particular inputs to sectors that either sell the final good to the domestic market or export it (table B2.3.1). Policy analysts can find use in such tables at a more disaggregated level.

In Ghana, for instance, four services sectors (utilities, construction, transport and trade, and business services) together contributed more than a third to domestic value added and almost 36 percent to export value added. Trade and transport services accounted for a larger share of export value added (23 percent) than domestic value added (14 percent). The same pattern is evident for business services (which contributed 12 percent to export value added and 8 percent to domestic value added) but not manufacturing (which contributed 17 percent to export value added and 28 percent to domestic value added). Construction and agriculture are much more domestically oriented in terms of the value added they produce.

Table B2.3.1. Value Added of Exports and Domestic Production in Ghana, by Sector, 2007
(percent of total value added)

Sector	Manufacturing		Services		Agriculture	
	Domestic	Exports	Domestic	Exports	Domestic	Exports
Agriculture	17.8	11.3	0.0	0.0	85.9	85.8
Manufacturing	59.3	63.6	3.1	0.5	0.6	0.4
Services						
Utilities	1.6	1.8	2.2	1.8	0.3	0.4
Construction	0.4	0.2	46.5	0.9	0.0	0.0
Transport and trade	18.6	20.5	17.5	46.4	10.3	10.0
Business	1.6	1.6	27.6	46.4	1.1	1.8
Other (for example, public services)	0.8	0.7	1.3	3.6	0.6	0.7
Total services	22.1	24.2	93.9	95.5	11.8	12.1

Source: Export of Value Added Database.

Table B2.3.1 shows that most services inputs in Ghana are used for production in other services sectors (93.9 percent for domestic production and 95.5 percent for exports). Within services, construction services are used mostly as inputs in domestic production, whereas transport and trade and business services are used mainly in exports. The downstream manufacturing sector is the second-most important user of services inputs (mainly transport and trade). This pattern may change as Ghana climbs up the supply chain.

A second important sector providing inputs to Ghana's manufacturing industry is agriculture. This pattern reflects Ghana's specialization in the manufacture of products closely connected to agriculture, such as processed cocoa beans.

This structure is visible in figure 2.13, which identifies the forward and backward linkages for machinery and business services for each income group. Middle- and high-income countries carry a substantial share of inputs backward in machinery. For services, this pattern is reversed, so that across all income groups, forward linkages prevail over backward linkages. Box 2.3 illustrates the different roles that services play as inputs in the case of Ghana.

Gross values and backward linkages are more important for goods, whereas net values and forward linkages are more relevant for services. Goods, especially machinery, include inputs from many other sectors, from either the domestic economy or abroad. When the value of a good is recorded at face value, it eventually constitutes an amount of trade measured in gross numbers, amounting to a larger share in total trade each time it crosses the border. The value added to a product or service by each sector is also taken into account,

but the actual value added "produced" by a specific sector is much lower, as indicated by the lower bars for forward linkages of machinery in figure 2.13. For services, the short bars for backward linkages in business services reflect the fact that most services are produced domestically and then exported as inputs for further production elsewhere. The difference between exports of high-income and lower-income country groups is much greater in services than in goods, indicating that high-income countries have a dominant position in services, which they use as inputs for production.

Figure 2.14 plots selected countries' shares of forward and backward linkages in a goods sector (machinery) and a services sector (business services). It shows that services are different from goods for most countries. For goods (panel a), most countries fall above the 45-degree line, indicating that value added is brought backward mainly through goods. In contrast, for services (panel b),

Figure 2.13. Forward and Backward Linkages for Machinery and Business Services, by Income Group, 2007

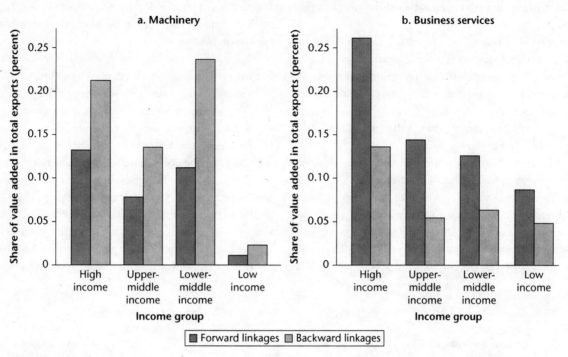

Source: Export of Value Added Database.

Figure 2.14. Backward and Forward Linkages for Goods and Services in Selected Countries, 2007

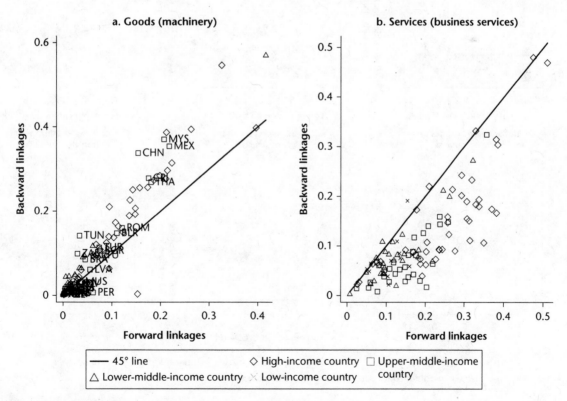

Source: Export of Value Added Database.
Note: For the International Organization for Standardization (ISO) abbreviations, see appendix B.

most countries fall below the 45-degree line, indicating that value added is carried forward mainly through services.

The role of forward and backward linkages can be explored for other services sectors separately. Not all services have the same importance for value added; some services could have a more important direct or gross export component. Not all services have the same role as inputs, either backward or forward. These values may also differ across countries or income groups.

To shed some light on the differences among services, the direct value added shares of a sector plus its forward and backward linkages is separately divided by the gross share of trade of the relevant sector. Figure 2.15 shows the outcome of such an exercise for business, construction, and transport and trade services. This measure is related to the level of development of a country. Panels a–c show each sector's direct value added share plus its forward linkages divided by the gross share of exports of that same sector. Panels d–f show the same ratio for backward linkages.

Figure 2.15 shows considerable variation across sectors. For forward linkages, both business and construction services show a flat relationship with per capita GDP, meaning that the value added component is as important as the gross share of exports across the level of development. For transport and trade services, the relationship is negative, meaning that the gross share of exports is more important the richer a country becomes. Put differently, value added in this sector is carried forward in larger part by lower-income countries. For backward linkages, figure 2.15 shows a slight positive relationship for both business services and construction and a negative relationship for transport and trade. Thus, apart from transport and

Figure 2.15. Direct Value Added plus Linkages/Gross Share and Per Capita GDP in Selected Economies, 2007

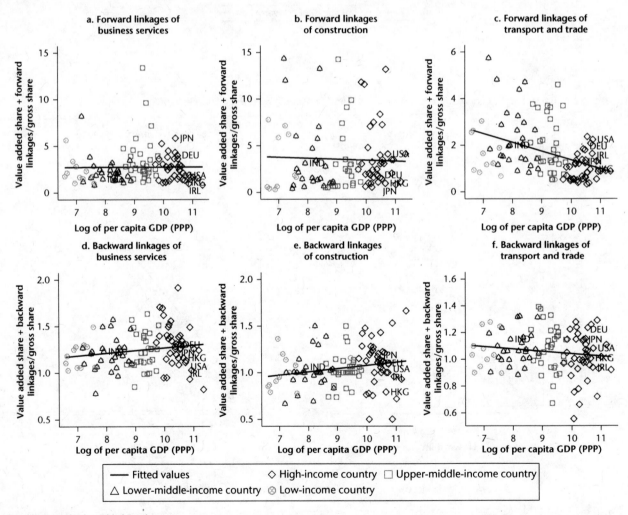

Source: Export of Value Added Database.

Note: DEU = Germany; HKG = Hong Kong SAR, China; IND = India; IRL = Ireland; PPP = purchasing power parity; USA = United States.

trade, there is no clear-cut relationship between value added and the gross value component and a country's level of development. Figure 2.16 shows the importance of value added versus gross shares for the transport and trade sector for several economies over time. Panel a shows that for value added plus forward linkages, most developing countries except India (after 1995) show an upward trend. India and the United Kingdom reduced their presence as forward carriers for inputs of transport and trade services. This pattern is in line with figure 2.15, which shows that on the whole, higher-income countries show a similar pattern. An upward trend is also evident for Argentina, Thailand, and Turkey in panel b, meaning that these countries bring forward value added from the transport and trade sector.

A ratio can be calculated that shows whether a product is used predominantly as an intermediate input or carries value added from other sectors. This ratio is calculated by taking the direct value added share plus each of the linkages and dividing it by the direct value added share without linkages. Figure 2.17 replicates the exercise in Figure 2.15 but uses the direct value added share as the denominator. Panels a–c show the ratio of forward linkages to value added. Panels d–f show the ratio of backward linkages to value added.

No clear pattern emerges for either business services or construction (see figure 2.17, panels a, b, d, and e). These results seem to suggest that forward or backward linkages are as important for high-income countries as they are for developing countries.

In the transport and trade sector, forward linkages are somewhat less important the more developed a country becomes, although the relationship is not very strong. Backward linkages are more important for higher-income countries. These results suggest that value added brought forward in the transport and trade sector is contributed largely by lower-income countries.

The lack of a clear pattern in other sectors may reflect the fact that developing countries export value added in services as easily as developed countries (an example is the well-developed computer sector in India). Another reason could be the high regulatory burdens for both business and construction services, which inhibits tradability.

MODULE 2

Figure 2.16. Direct Value Added plus Linkages/Gross Share for Transport and Trade Services in Selected Economies, 1992–2007

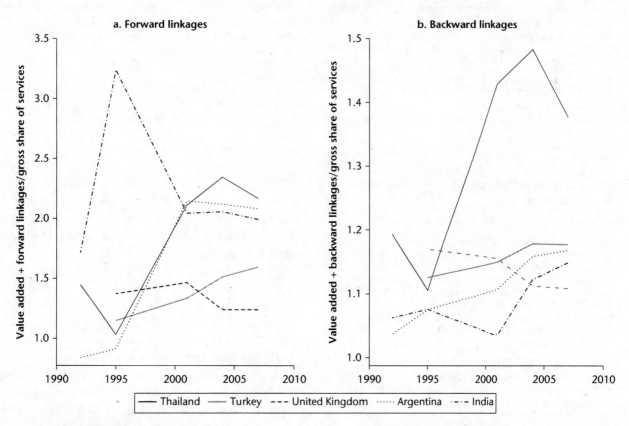

Source: Export of Value Added Database.

Figure 2.17. Relationship between Value-Added Linkages and Development in Selected Economies, 2007

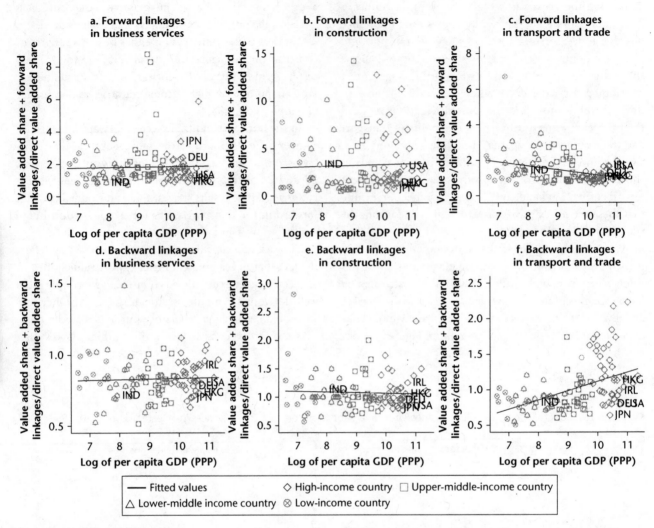

Source: Export of Value Added Database.
Note: DEU = Germany; HKG = Hong Kong SAR, China; IND = India; IRL = Ireland; JPN = Japan; PPP = purchasing power parity; USA = United States.

Domestic or Imported Services Content of Exported Goods and Services

Several indicators are critical to assessing the domestic services content of exported goods and services. They include forward and backward linkages; total exports through Modes 1 and 2; the Revealed Comparative Advantage (RCA) Index; and firm-level customs, firm-level census data, and balance sheet data. Data on these indicators should be collected for specific years for all countries. Useful sources of information include the following:

- OECD-WTO's TiVA or GTAP databases
- World Bank's Trade in Services Database (see appendix B)
- World Bank's Export of Value Added Database (see appendix A)

The diagnostic requires a deep understanding of the country context, based on discussions with government authorities, experts, private sector representatives, and other stakeholders. Table 2.4 indicates some of the questions that need to be addressed.

Services are used as inputs in the production of many goods. They are an essential part of the production process because they increase the productivity of the goods firms (Arnold and others 2012; Arnold, Javorcik, and Mattoo 2011). These services can be produced and provided by domestic firms or imported. The presence of foreign firms providing services inputs tends to increase the productivity of domestic goods firms to an even greater degree than the presence of domestic firms (Arnold and

Table 2.4. Domestic Services Content of Exported Goods and Services: Issues for Discussion

Interviewee	Issue
Senior policy makers at the ministry of trade or foreign affairs	• In which goods sectors is the country specialized? • In which goods sectors does the country have a comparative advantage? • What services do these goods sectors require? • What sectors in which the country has a comparative advantage carry forward and backward value added? • Which services sectors are necessary to capitalize on that value added? • Is the country well connected to global supply chains (that is, does it trade parts and components of goods as opposed to services)? • Are services domestically produced and exported, or does the country import many services as well?
Officials at export promotion agencies	• Have firms encountered any difficulties in obtaining services for their production and exports? If so, what goods sectors do these firms provide? • Are firms forced to specialize in lower-value-added products because they encounter problems obtaining services inputs?
Major goods exporters	• Which services are required for optimal production of the goods you produce? • Which services are essential for exporting the goods you produce? • Are these services easily obtainable? Do you purchase these services from domestic or foreign suppliers? • Are there substantial barriers to importing services that are essential for production and export? • Is your firm inhibited from climbing the value chain by highly regulated services markets? • Would easier access to imported inputs allow your firm to specialize in products with higher value added?

Table 2.5. Impact of Broad Categories of Foreign Services Inputs on Manufacturing Exports

Nature of manufacturing sector	Services inputs				
	Business	Communication	Finance	Insurance	FDI inflow
Technology intensive	Positive***				
Labor intensive	Negative**				
Resource intensive					

Source: Francois and Woerz 2008.
Note: ** $p < 0.05$; *** $p < 0.01$. Blank cells indicate that the relationship is not statistically significant. FDI = foreign direct investment.

others 2012). It is therefore essential that firms have good access to services markets. Such access is especially important when firms are part of global supply chains, because services increase specialization and concentration of the manufacturing firms providing goods further downstream in the chain.

Different industries require different types of services inputs. Sophisticated information technology (IT) services, for example, may be more important in automobiles than in food processing. Industries that are closely tied to global supply chains are more likely to be dependent on a well-functioning domestic transport and logistics services sector than firms that are not. The downstream effects of services supply thus depend on the "depth" of the intermediate linkages of each goods sector.

This section focuses on the knock-on effect of higher levels of services imports on the tradability of the downstream manufacturing or services sector. Francois and Woerz (2008) note that it is important to distinguish between individual manufacturing industries, because they are qualitatively different; looking at the aggregate picture could mask essential features of the effects of foreign services input. At the same time, an aggregate manufacturing classification can be thought of based on factor inputs. Francois and Woerz (2008) estimate the effects of a larger import share on exports of technology-, labor-, and resource-intensive industries.

Table 2.5 summarizes their aggregate findings. It shows that imported business services have a clear and strong positive effect on the exports of manufacturing sectors that are technology intensive. In contrast, a higher level of imported business services is negatively associated with labor-intensive industries. Other services do not seem to have a statistically significant association with a particular type of industry.

This division of sectors may be too broad. Table 2.6 therefore displays a finer degree of disaggregation based on the factor intensities of various manufacturing sectors.

MODULE 2

Table 2.6. Impact of Disaggregated Foreign Services Inputs on Manufacturing Exports

Sector	Services inputs				
	Business	Communication	Finance	Insurance	FDI inflow
Technology intensive					
Chemicals	Positive***			Positive**	
Electrical equipment	Positive**		Positive**	Negative**	
Machinery	Positive**			Negative**	
Motor vehicles			Positive**	Negative**	
Labor intensive					
Textiles	Negative***	Positive***			Negative**
Clothing	Negative***	Positive***			
Leather	Negative***	Positive***		Negative**	
Food					
Other transport equipment	Positive***				
Resource intensive					
Coke		Positive***	Negative**	Negative**	
Minerals					
Metals					
Paper					
Wood					

Source: Francois and Woerz 2008.
Note: *** $p < 0.01$, ** $p < 0.05$. Blank cells indicate that the relationship is not statistically significant. FDI = foreign direct investment.

It shows that most linkages between services imports and manufacturing exports take place in sectors that are intensive in technology or labor, with varying effects. Imported business services are positively correlated with most sectors that are technology (and skill) intensive (exceptions are motor vehicles and food). Insurance services have a negative relationship with technology-intensive manufacturing. Financial services appear to have a positive effect on expansion of some technology-intensive manufacturing exports, including electrical equipment and motor vehicles.

Business services are negatively associated with expansion of trade in light manufacturing, a labor-intensive sector. Communication services appear to be a lever for expansion of light manufacturing: whereas exports in the textiles, clothing, and leather manufacturing industries suffer from having more imported business services inputs, light manufacturing is boosted by imports of communication services. As light manufacturing is a sector in which many developing countries specialize, exploring this relationship through field analysis and country-specific evidence is recommended.

This methodology of tradability provides several insights. It suggests that openness to business services from abroad is highly correlated with the competitiveness of skilled-labor- and technology-intensive manufacturing industries. However, before making any decisions on opening up to

foreign services suppliers, policy makers need to assess which industries a country specializes in and where the value added of particular exports lies.

Services Indirect Linkages

This section examines more closely indirect linkages through exports. Such linkages provide valuable information on how much value added a country, income group, or geographical region carries forward as inputs in exports.

By analyzing value added at the individual-country level, one can investigate the validity for specific cases of the relationship identified by Francois and Woerz (2008) and summarized in figures 2.18 and 2.19. This information can shed light on two important questions:

- To what extent does services value added carried over in a sector increase the value of the sector's exports?
- To what extent is a services sector a component of exports in downstream goods sectors?

Figure 2.18 shows the extent to which business services are a component of value-added exports in other sectors in Malaysia, Romania, and the United States.

The business services sector carries forward more value added in the United States than in Malaysia or Romania. The importance of services value added embodied in other

Figure 2.18. Ratio of Exported Forward to Backward Linkages of Business Services in Other Sectors in Romania, Malaysia, and the United States, 2001 and 2007

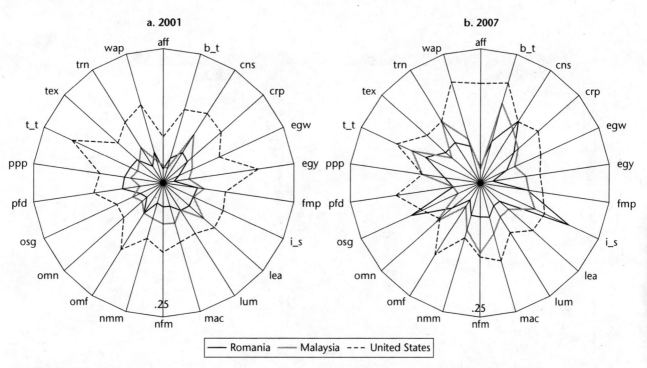

Source: Export of Value Added Database.
Note: Center indicates no value added. The larger the circle, the greater the role of forward linkages relative to backward linkages. aff = agriculture, forestry and fisheries; b_t = beverages and tobacco products; cns = construction; crp = chemical, rubber, and plastic products; egw = electricity, gas, and water; egy = energy extraction; fmp = metal products; i_s = ferrous metals; lea = leather products; lum = wood products; mac = machinery and equipment not elsewhere classified; nfm = metals not elsewhere classified; nmm = mineral products; omf = manufactures not elsewhere classified; omn = minerals not elsewhere classified; osg = public services; pfd = processed foods; ppp = paper products and printing; t_t = transport and trade; tex = textiles; trn = transport equipment; wap = wearing apparel.

sectors increased in both Malaysia and Romania (even in basic sectors such as agriculture, forestry, and fisheries) between 2001 and 2007, reducing the gap relative to the United States. Both Malaysia and Romania also expanded the use of imported services (data are available but not reported in figure 2.18). An alternative way to identify a country's position regarding the value added of services is to analyze complementarity based on each sector's forward linkages. Figure 2.19 shows how important business services are as an input for other sectors' exports (that is, value added carried forward), expressed as a share of business services total exported value added by all other sectors.

In both Mexico and the United States, the machinery and equipment sector uses a relatively large share of business services. Other manufacturing sectors that account for large shares of business services as inputs in both countries are chemicals, rubber and plastic products, and transport equipment. This pattern is consistent with the notion that business services inputs are an important

way to expand exports in technology- and skill-intensive goods sectors. The analytical framework outlined earlier also shows a correlation between performance in these sectors and imported business services inputs, underlying the importance of facilitating the sourcing of the best services, whether they are produced domestically or abroad.

There are also notable differences between Mexico and the United States. Business services, for example, account for a larger share of inputs in Mexico than in the United States. Policy makers have to determine the reasons for such a pattern. Another difference between the two countries is the extent that business services are used in the machinery and equipment sector, which is much higher in Mexico than in the United States. Examination of differences in **RCA Indexes** based on gross flows, forward linkages, and backward linkages can enrich the analysis.

Box 2.4 provides an example of how firm-level data can be used to conduct the analysis. Data on Romania identify additional trends in specific sectors.

Figure 2.19. Sectors Exporting Business Services Value Added as Share of Total Exported Business Services Value Added based on Forward Linkages in Mexico and the United States, 2007

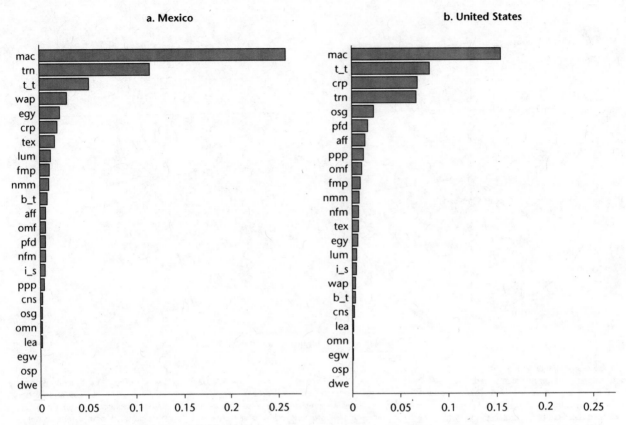

Source: Export of Value Added Database.
Note: aff = agriculture, forestry and fisheries; b_t = beverages and tobacco products; cns = construction; crp = chemical, rubber and plastic products; dwe = dwellings; egw = electricity, gas, and water; egy = energy extraction; fmp = metal products; i_s = ferrous metals; lea = leather products; lum = wood products; mac = machinery and equipment not elsewhere classified; nfm = metals not elsewhere classified; nmm = mineral products; omf = manufactures not elsewhere classified; omn = minerals not elsewhere classified; osg = public services; osp = other private services; pfd = processed foods; ppp = paper products and printing; t_t = transport and trade; tex = textiles; trn = transport equipment; wap = wearing apparel.

Box 2.4. Output, Value Added, and the Importance of the Wholesale Sector for Exports of Downstream Goods: Evidence from Romania

National input-output tables—and the forward and backward linkages they reveal—provide a good overview of where value added is produced in a country. Firm-level data can help identify trends and developments. Such data can help determine whether the assertion that value added is mostly produced in services but exported through goods holds in specific countries and sectors.

In Romania, the goods sector accounts for a larger share of output exported than value added carried abroad (figure B2.4.1). The opposite is true for most services activities. The share of value added is substantially larger than exported output in the computer and modern communications and computer repair sectors.

However, some variation between output and value added is evident across services. In sectors such as construction, accommodation, transport, and traditional communication, exported output is greater than value added. This finding is largely in line with the results in Module 1 on the **export sophistication** of modern services. Modern services, which have higher value added, are more likely to be exported by developed countries than lower-income countries. Yet Romania exports computer and modern communications and professional services. Ideally, policy would enable Romania to take advantage of sectors that export larger shares of value added, helping these sectors expand.

Firm-level data also highlight the importance of the wholesaling sector to other sectors. Firms can export either directly or through wholesalers. New exporters often use intermediaries, because it saves them the cost and effort associated with learning about foreign markets and export procedures or finding customers abroad.

An increasing share of Romanian exports goes through wholesalers. In 2005, 7 percent of exports from Romania were sold by wholesalers. By 2011, the share had reached 12 percent. Intermediaries play the most prominent role in the export of food and beverages, chemicals, and wood. They do not appear to be important in sectors in which a lead firm (buyer or supplier) dominates the value chain production networks, such as apparel; motor vehicles; electrical machinery; and radio, TV, and communications equipment.

(continued on next page)

MODULE 2

Box 2.4. *(continued)*

Figure B2.4.1. Exports and Value-Added Shares of Selected Services Subsectors in Romania

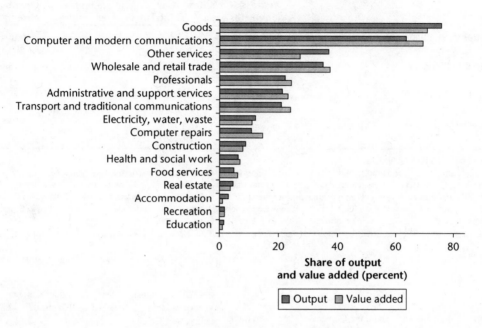

Share of output and value added (percent)

Output   Value added

Table B2.4.1 indicates that export unit values (a proxy for quality) are higher for exporters that use wholesalers. This relationship is driven by the food and beverages, chemicals, plastics, and wood and furniture sectors.

More experienced and sophisticated exporters prefer to deal directly with foreign customers. Although initiating such business relationships may be costly, direct interactions with foreign customers allow producers to tailor their products better to the needs of the market. Such relationships also increase margins and establish long-term relationships.

Table B2.4.1. Unit Values of Direct Exports versus Exports through Intermediaries

Sector	Regression coefficients of log unit values on dummy for exports by intermediary exporters	Number of observations
All	0.0530**	362,822
	(−2.16)	
Food products and beverages	0.199***	69,672
	(−5.08)	
Chemicals	0.244***	66,255
	(−4.81)	
Wood	0.173***	73,622
	(−6.91)	
Coke	−0.202	61,631
	(−1.35)	
Leather	−0.0870**	82,995
	(−2.23)	
Basic metals	0.261***	64,541
	(−4.41)	
Furniture	0.0963**	86,979
	(−2.5)	
Radio, TV, and communications equipment	−0.106	67,043
	(−1.25)	
Apparel	0.0257	164,327
	(−0.42)	
Machinery and equipment	0.0903**	83,941
	(−2.54)	

(continued on next page)

MODULE 2

Box 2.4. *(continued)*

Table B2.4.1. *(continued)*

Sector	Regression coefficients of log unit values on dummy for exports by intermediary exporters	Number of observations
Other transport equipment	−0.102 (−1.45)	64,010
Rubber and plastic	0.175*** (−4.87)	74,007
Electrical machinery	0.0236 (−0.6)	77,728
Motor vehicles	−0.233** (−2.34)	77,696

Source: Romanian Structural Business Survey.
Note: Only manufacturing and wholesale firms are included. Intermediary exporters are exporters whose primary activity is wholesale (code 51 in NACE rev. 1.1). Regressions are run separately for several two-digit NACE (rev. 1.1) industries. Observations are defined on firm-product-destination-year level and include product-destination-year fixed effects. Standard errors are clustered on firm level. *t*-statistics are in parentheses. ** $p < 0.05$, *** $p < 0.01$. NACE = *Nomenclature statistique des activités économiques dans la Communauté européenne* (Statistical Classification of Economic Activities in the European Community).

Note

1. For example, both Baldwin and Lopez-Gonzalez (2013) and Feenstra and Jensen (2012) find that the proportionality assumption in the use of intermediates and by different industries leads to nontrivial errors in some cases.

References

Amin, Mohammad, and Aaditya Mattoo. 2006. "Do Institutions Matter More for Services?" Policy Research Working Paper 4032, World Bank, Washington, DC.

———. 2008. "Human Capital and the Changing Structure of the Indian Economy." Policy Research Working Paper 4576, World Bank, Washington, DC.

Arnold, Jens Matthias, Beata Javorcik, Molly Lipscomb, and Aaditya Mattoo. 2012. "Services Reform and Manufacturing Performance: Evidence from India." Policy Research Working Paper Series 5948, World Bank, Washington, DC.

Arnold, Jens M., Beata S. Javorcik, and Aaditya Mattoo. 2011. "Does Services Liberalization Benefit Manufacturing Firms? Evidence from the Czech Republic." *Journal of International Economics* 85 (1):136–46.

Baldwin, Richard, and Javier Lopez-Gonzalez. 2013. "Supply-Chain Trade: A Portrait of Global Patterns and Several Testable Hypotheses." NBER Working Paper 18957, National Bureau of Economic Research, Cambridge, MA.

Clark, Colin, 1940. *The Conditions of Economic Progress.* London: Macmillan and Company.

Eichengreen, Barry, and Poonam Gupta. 2011. "The Service Sector as India's Road to Economic Growth." NBER Working Paper 16757, National Bureau of Economic Research, Cambridge MA.

———. 2012. "Exports of Services: Indian Experience in Perspective." Working Paper 12/102, National Institute of Public Finance and Policy, New Delhi.

Feenstra, Robert C., and J. Bradford Jensen. 2012. "Evaluating Estimates of Materials Offshoring from US Manufacturing." *Economics Letters* 117 (1): 170–73.

Fisher, Alan G. B. 1939. "Production, Primary, Secondary and Tertiary." *Economic Record* 15 (1): 24–38.

———. 1952. "A Note on Tertiary Production." *Economic Journal* 62 (248): 820–34.

Francois Joseph, Miriam Manchin, and Patrick Tomberger. 2013. "Services Linkages and the Value Added Content of Trade." Policy Research Working Paper 6432, World Bank, Washington, DC.

Francois, Joseph, and Julia Woerz. 2008. "Producer Services, Manufacturing Linkages, and Trade." *Journal of Industry, Competition and Trade* 8 (3): 199–229.

Global Trade Analysis Project (GTAP) Database. Purdue University, Lafayette, IN. https://www.gtap.agecon.purdue.edu/databases.

Hausmann, Ricardo, César A. Hidalgo, Sebastián Bustos, Michele Coscia, Sarah Chung, Juan Jimenez, Alexander Simoes, and Muhammed A. Yıldırım. 2014. *The Atlas of Economic Complexity: Mapping Paths to Prosperity* (Revised edition). Cambridge, MA: The MIT Press.

Liping, Zahang, and Simon Evenett. 2010. "The Growth of China's Services Sector and Associated Trade: Complementarities between Structural Change and Sustainability." International Institute for Sustainable Development, Winnipeg, Canada.

Trade in Services Database. World Bank, Washington, DC.

World Development Indicators (database). World Bank, Washington, DC. http://data.worldbank.org/data-catalog/world-development-indicators.

ASSESSING THE POTENTIAL
FOR TRADE IN SERVICES

This module explores how countries can assess their services trade potential and identify untapped opportunities. It does so by:

- examining alternative modes of supply
- identifying the geographical pattern of production and demand of services
- identifying services sectors in which a country has a comparative advantage
- using **gravity models** to determine trade potential.

These steps can help identify "low-hanging fruit"— underexploited sectors that can easily become sources of exports.

Assessing Tradability by Modes

Several indicators are critical to assessing tradability by modes. They include the volume of trade and the share of trade through Modes 1, 2, and 3; the most dominant mode of trade for each sector; and the ratio of Modes 1 and 2 trade to Mode 3 trade. Data on these indicators should be collected for specific years for all countries. Useful sources of information include the following:

- World Development Indicators (services flows for Modes 1 and 2)
- World Bank's Trade in Services Database (see appendix B)
- Organisation for Economic Co-operation and Development (OECD), United Nations Conference on Trade and Development (UNCTAD), Eurostat, and national sources (such as the Bureau of Economic Analysis for statistics on the United States and Foreign Affiliates Trade Statistics [FATS])
- UNCTAD (foreign direct investment statistics).

The diagnostic requires a deep understanding of the country context, based on discussions with government authorities, experts, private sector representatives, and other stakeholders. Table 3.1 indicates some of the questions that need to be addressed.

Analytical Approach

Services are tradable through various modes. Many services require face-to-face contact (simultaneous consumption and production) between producer and consumer. For example, many medical services can be provided only if the doctor and patient are in the same place. Other services, such as telecommunication services, are delivered over the Internet or by a foreign affiliate that invests in the domestic market.

The General Agreement on Trade in Services (GATS) of the World Trade Organization (WTO) and other trade agreements define four modes of supply (figure 3.1):

- **Mode 1:** Supply of a service from the territory of one country to another country. Supplier and consumer interact across a distance (cross-border trade or trade over the Internet).
- **Mode 2:** Consumption of a service by consumers of one country who visit or move temporarily to another country, which supplies the service (consumption abroad).
- **Mode 3:** Services provided by a foreign affiliate that has established a commercial presence in another country (commercial presence).
- **Mode 4:** Services supplied by a foreign natural person, employed or self-employed, who at the moment the service is provided stays temporarily in the territory of the consuming country (presence of natural persons).

Table 3.2 provides examples of activities traded through each mode of supply, estimates the importance of each mode in total trade in services, and describes some of the data inadequacies that the study of services trade still confronts.

Table 3.1. Assessing Tradability by Modes: Issues for Discussion

Interviewee	Issue
Senior policy makers at the ministry of trade or foreign affairs	• Do exporters export mainly through Mode 1 and Mode 2 or through Mode 3? • Which mode accounts for a larger share of trade in this sector, Mode 1 or Mode 3? • In which mode is growth highest? • Has there been a slowdown in a particular mode in recent years? • Has policy changed with reference to a mode in recent years? • Are companies allowed to hire foreign nationals?
Major exporters	• Is your company using both Mode 1 and Mode 3 for exports? • Are Mode 1 and Mode 3 complements or substitutes in your company's business strategies? • Does the choice of mode depend on the characteristic of the service, or do other factors such as endowments, transportation costs, demand, and the regulatory environment play a role in determining the mode of export? • Which of the following are important in choosing an export mode: regulatory barriers or cost of supplying reliable and quality services? • Has trade in services changed from one mode to another over time? What evolution is likely? • Are payment systems in place that allow your company to export through your preferred mode of supply? Are there different problems depending on the destination?
Chamber of Commerce	• How large are services exporters? Does the size of the company affect the mode through which it exports? • Which sectors are most likely to export through Mode 1? Mode 3? • Are services exports through Mode 3 concentrated in one sector?

Note: For a description and examples of the modes of trade in services, see figure 3.1 and table 3.2.

Figure 3.1. The Four Modes of Trade in Services

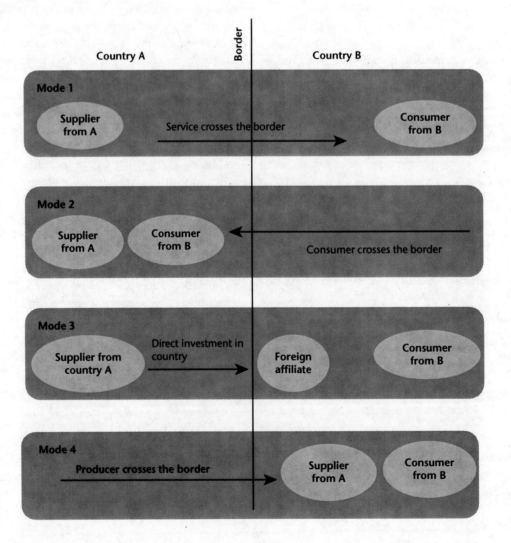

Table 3.2. Examples of Services Trade by Mode

Mode of supply	Examples	Challenges	Estimated share of total services trade (percent)
Mode 1: Cross-border trade	• International phone calls • Telemedicine • Online courses • International transportation services	Balance of payments does not distinguish between cross-border supply and presence of natural persons	25–30
Mode 2: Consumption abroad	• Tourism • Education • Health tourism	Tourism includes goods and is not subdivided into categories of services consumed by tourists. Some transactions are in other balance of payments categories.	10–15
Mode 3: Commercial presence	• Financial services • Distribution services • Construction services	Foreign Affiliates Trade Statistics (FATS) are available for only a limited number of countries (largely OECD countries). Foreign direct investment (FDI) statistics cover a larger set of countries, not only majority-controlled companies. Statistics do not distinguish between Modes 3 and 4.	55–60
Mode 4: Presence of natural persons	• Professional services • Entertainment services	Balance of payments does not distinguish between cross-border supply and presence of natural persons or between modes.	Less than 5

Sources: Maurer and others 2008; Magdeleine and Maurer 2008.
Note: OECD = Organisation for Economic Co-operation and Development.

Services in a sector can be provided through several modes of supply. In the tourism sector, for example, Mode 2 is the main mode of supply, but exports of travel agency services fall under Mode 1, investment in hotels and restaurants under Mode 3, and the movement of managers and chefs under Mode 4. Table 3.3 identifies the dominant modes of services exports for various sectors.

Trade through the four modes is recorded in various sources. International organizations such as the Organisation for Economic Co-operation and Development (OECD), the United Nations Conference on Trade and Development (UNCTAD), and Eurostat, report internationally comparable trade data across countries and sectors through Modes 1 and 2 using the Extended Balance of Payments Services (EBOPS) classification system. Sources for trade flows also include the **Trade in Services Database, World Development Indicators**, and the International Monetary Fund's Balance of Payment Statistics.

Comparable and comprehensive cross-country data for Mode 3 can be accessed through the **Foreign Affiliates Trade Statistics (FATS)**, available from the OECD, UNCTAD, and Eurostat. FATS provides a range of indicators on the activities of foreign affiliates, including exports and imports, sales, expenditures, profits, value added, inter- and intrafirm trade, and employment, with a focus on services. **Inward FATS** cover the operations of foreign-owned (a minimum of 10 percent of book value) firms in the host economy. **Outward FATS** report statistics on foreign affiliates of domestic companies (a minimum of 10 percent of

Table 3.3. Dominant Modes of Services Exports by Sector

Type of service	Mode			
	1	2	3	4
Business	x		x	x
Communications	x		x	
Computer and information	x		x	
Construction	x		x	x
Distribution			x	
Education		x	x	x
Financial	x		x	
Health		x	x	x
Insurance	x		x	
Personal, cultural, and recreational		x	x	
Transportation	x		x	
Travel		x		

book value). Construction services are the only Mode 3 category that use the EBOPS classification system.

These data can also be constructed using firm-level balance sheet and census data. Doing so is cumbersome and time consuming, however. Firm-level information includes sales; output; employment; value added; exports and imports of goods and services; the number of enterprises; and the source of ownership, imports, and exports. Many countries collect foreign direct investment (FDI) flows, but few provide geographical and activity breakdowns. Moreover, these data stand as a very rough proxy for sales by foreign affiliates.

Data for Mode 4 are even scarcer, and there is no centralized source of data. Although some Mode 4 trade is recorded in the balance of payments under compensation

---

Box 3.1. How Are Remittances Classified?

For many countries, remittances exceed official aid flows or foreign direct investment (FDI). The two standard items that relate to remittances, as defined in *Balance of Payments and International Investment Position Manual*, Sixth Edition (BPM6), are compensation of employees and personal transfers. Compensation of employees represents "remuneration in return for the labour input to the production process contributed by an individual in an employer-employee relationship with the enterprise" (BPM6, para. 11.10). It refers to the income of border, seasonal, and other short-term workers who are in an employer-employee relationship in a country where they are not resident and residents in an employer-employee relationship with a nonresident entity.

Personal transfers consist of "all current transfers in cash or in kind, made or received, by resident households to or from non-resident households" (BPM6, para. 12.21). Such transfers include all current transfers from resident to nonresident households, independent of (a) the sources of income of the sender (whether he or she receives income from labor, entrepreneurial or property income, social benefits, or any other types of transfers or disposes of assets); (b) the relationship between the households (whether they include related or unrelated members); and (c) the purpose for which the transfer is made (inheritance, alimony, lottery, and so forth). BPM6 recommends recording a supplementary item entitled "workers' remittances," which covers current transfers made by employees to residents of another economy.

Data on compensation of employees and personal transfers broken down by relevant categories (for example, intracorporate transferees or people directly employed by a foreign affiliate in services) could provide additional information on Mode 4. However, these flows will not reflect the value of the service contract (or sales of services) and cannot therefore be used to measure the international supply of services. Based on the definition of compensation of employees and personal transfers, as well as other remittances indicators, a majority of contractual service suppliers do not belong to the set of people to whom these balance of payments items refer.

In addition, in the (rare) cases where some Mode 4 persons are covered, double counting would occur, because the value of the services would be included implicitly, either within the value of trade in services statistics (between residents and nonresidents) for Mode 4 or in Foreign Affiliates Trade Statistics (FATS) for Mode 3. In some instances, however, compilers might use this information to extract a Mode 4 estimate for some contractual service suppliers from appropriate balance of payments services items. Although this additional information could not be tracked to specific transactions, it could be used as a check. However, it is often difficult to identify specific compensation of employees/personal transfers for categories of interest for Mode 4 (that is, people who become residents of the host economy), because related transactions often represent a small proportion of the relevant income and transfer transactions.

Source: Manual on Statistics of International Trade in Services 2010, Department of Economic and Social Affairs of the United Nations Secretariat, Statistics Division, © (2011) United Nations. Reprinted with permission of the United Nations.

---

of employees, workers' remittances, or migrants' transfers, it is difficult to distinguish Mode 4 trade from other modes of supply (Magdeleine and Maurer 2008; box 3.1).

Implementation

The importance of trade in a particular service through a particular mode can be checked with country-specific data. It is particularly important to assess the relevance of Mode 3, which represents a sizable and growing share of services trade. Data for Modes 1 and 2 can be verified through the Trade in Services Database or other readily available cross-country sources. Trade data for Mode 3 are more difficult to locate.

The preferred alternative is to complement cross-country resources with country-specific information. Sources for these data can be accessed with permission from national authorities and statistical offices. Identification of access points to obtain these data should be a key component of a services trade diagnostics exercise.

Table 3.4 illustrates the analysis of tradability of services in the United States. Data on Mode 3 come from the Bureau of Economic Analysis (BEA) of the U.S. Department of Commerce (under the heading "Data on Direct Investment and Multinational Company Activities"). Data on Modes 1

and 2 come from the Trade in Services Database. The table shows the volume of exports through Modes 1 and 2 and compares it to the volume of exports through Mode 3. Sales of foreign affiliates include only companies that are majority owned by U.S. companies.

With the exceptions of travel and transport services, tradable U.S. services exports are concentrated in Mode 3. Mode 2 dominates travel, because it includes consumption in the United States by foreign tourists. Transport services are traded though both Modes 1 and 3, but Mode 1 dominates.

Exports through Mode 1 are nevertheless important for a range of services, including construction; business services; personal, cultural, and recreational services; and, to a lesser extent, communications. This mode accounts for almost 30 percent of exports for business services; personal, cultural, and recreational services; and construction (and about 15 percent of communications services). These services sectors indicate that although most U.S. services exports are Mode 3 transactions, Mode 1 still accounts for a significant share of exports in these sectors. It forms a sizable part and therefore remains important for U.S. competitiveness.

Other services sectors in the United States, such as finance, insurance, and to a lesser extent computer

Table 3.4. Tradability of U.S. Services through Modes 1, 2, and 3, 2009

Service	Exports (millions of dollars)		Ratio Mode 1/2:3
	Mode 1/2	Mode 3	
Travel	121,153	8,315	14.57
Transportation	61,841	38,761	1.60
Business services	91,650	232,679	0.39
Personal, cultural, and recreation (including motion picture and sound-recording industries)	13,710	35,264	0.39
Construction	6,792	17,970	0.38
Communications	9,549	51,884	0.18
Financial	55,456	335,099	0.17
Computer and information	13,380	119,665	0.11
Insurance	14,654	145,198	0.10
Education	76	2,940	0.03
Health	25	2,493	0.01
Distribution	2,854	1,375,403	0.00

Sources: Trade in Services Database and U.S. Bureau of Economic Analysis.

Figure 3.2. Number of Exporting Firms in Romania, by Sector, 2009

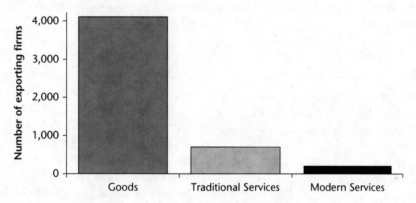

Source: Romanian Structural Business Survey.

and information services, have very high absolute trade figures for Mode 1. However, the likely mode of tradability nonetheless appears to be Mode 3 where exports are even higher, so that the ratio remains low. Distribution, health, and education services are also traded largely through Mode 3. Although exports through Mode 1 exist in these sectors, trade potential within this mode is weak.

Another option is to use firm-level data. Figure 3.2 shows that in Romania in 2009, the number of firms exporting goods was more than 4 times the number of firms exporting traditional services and more than 16 times the number of firms exporting modern services. Traditional services such as trade and transport were the dominant subsectors within the services sector. Although the number of firms exporting modern services is small, their importance should not be underestimated, as expansion of this sector offers an alternative

growth path, as explained in Ghani (2010) and Mishra, Lundstrom, and Anand (2011).

Assessing Tradability Based on Production

Several indicators are critical to assessing tradability through production. They include employment and GDP data by region, the share of inputs used in final production by downstream industries, the share of employment in a particular industry in a region, the Tradability Index developed by Jensen and Kletzer (2006), and the Gini coefficient. Data on these indicators should be collected for specific years for all countries. Useful sources of information include the following:

- World Development Indicators (services flows for Modes 1 and 2)
- World Bank's Trade in Services Database (see appendix B)
- National sources measuring Mode 3 trade (FATS)
- National sources (input-output matrixes, employment statistics).

MODULE 3

Table 3.5. Assessing Tradability Based on Production: Issues for Discussion

Interviewee	Issue
Senior policy makers at the ministry of trade and other relevant ministries (infrastructure, transport, health)	• Is production of some services sectors centralized within a region or other geographical unit? • Which services sectors have a tendency to agglomerate? • Do the centralized and agglomerated sectors correlate with the Tradability Index? • Are there strong employment effects in sectors that are considered tradable? • How much growth in employment have tradable sectors experienced in recent years?
Major exporters	• Are all relevant ministries aware that the concentration of production is a good indicator of tradability? • Is production in your sector largely local, or does it take place in a particular place within the country? • How does your industry compare with others in terms of centralization or agglomeration? • Are economies of scale the main reason for concentration, or are other factors, such as regulation or concentrated demand, at work? • Does the reason for concentrating production in a particular location say anything about the tradability of the services produced in your sector?

The diagnostic requires a deep understanding of the country context, based on discussions with government authorities, experts, private sector representatives, and other stakeholders. Table 3.5 indicates some of the questions that need to be addressed.

Analytical Approach

Like goods, some services are produced in particular locations. Production may be concentrated for a variety of reasons, including increasing returns to scale, proximity to inputs, the high cost of trade, and regulation. Goods and services that are tradable usually show a higher level of geographical concentration of production than goods and services that are not. Firm-level data can reveal tradability and the characteristics of the traded activities.

The methodology of Jensen and Kletzer (2006) combines insights from the literature on agglomeration and revealed comparative advantage, which are closely linked. Implicit in both concepts is the notion that the place of production of a service is not related to the place of consumption. When production is concentrated in an area, some of it is consumed there; what is not consumed is sent to another area of the country, exported for consumption, or incorporated as an input in a final good or service produced abroad. Therefore, if production does not match demand in a geographical area, the sector is probably tradable. Lower transportation costs or greater production economies induce this concentration of production.

Jensen and Kletzer (2006) use a **Gini coefficient** (G) to measure the difference between production and demand within a country. Their index is different from other pure agglomeration indexes, because it is unaffected by the number of firms that produce in the same location. To measure G, one needs empirical indicators of demand and production. Jensen and Kletzer (2006) use employment data for both measures, so that

$$G_i = \left| 1 - \sum_r (\sigma Y_{i,\,r-1} + \sigma Y_{i,\,r}) * (\sigma X_{i,\,r-1} - \sigma X_{i,\,r}) \right|$$

where r stands for region (or any other geographical unit), which must be sorted by the region's share of industry employment; i for industry; $\sigma Y_{i,\,r}$ for the region's cumulative share of industry i's employment; $\sigma Y_{i,\,r-1}$ the cumulative share of each industry's employment in the region with the next-lowest share of industry employment; $\sigma X_{i,\,r}$ the region's cumulative share of total employment; and $\sigma X_{i,\,r-1}$ the cumulative share of total employment in the region with the next-lowest share of industry employment. In this equation, similar employment data are used for both the Y's and X's, but they need to be adjusted for the fact that services are often used as inputs for further production. If a services industry is geographically concentrated and has high demand for the nontraded services that are used as inputs, this nontradable service will also be geographically concentrated. The sector would be incorrectly identified as tradable.

To correct such miscalculation, one needs to determine how much of industry i's output is used in any other industry, j, for each region. This region-specific measure of demand (IDS_{ir}) is calculated as follows:

$$\mathrm{IDS}_{ir} = \sum_j \left(\frac{Y_{i,j}}{Y_i} * \frac{\mathrm{EMP}_{jr}}{\mathrm{EMP}_j} \right).$$

This measure corrects for the value of services used as inputs. The first term is the share of industry i's output used in industry j, multiplied by industry j's employment share in region r. IDS$_{ir}$ adjusts for the concentration of the downstream industry and corrects the X's. Data on how much a particular service or good is used as an input in another industry are available from national input-output tables. Each country should have a detailed record of its output structure to trace back how much industries produce and use inputs from one another. Cross-country input-output tables are also available (from the World Bank or OECD), albeit at a more aggregated level.

The last step in constructing the true Gini coefficient for production concentration for each service is to plug in the region-specific demand measures for the X's in the previous equation to obtain:

$$G_i = \left| 1 - \sum_r (\sigma Y_{i,r-1} + \sigma Y_{i,r}) * (\sigma IDS_{i,r-1} - \sigma IDS_{i,r}) \right|.$$

The Gini coefficient measures the absolute difference between production and demand in a region for specific industries in a country. The greater the difference between these two variables, and hence the higher the index, the more production of the sector is concentrated in a particular region. Such concentration is a good indicator of international tradability.

Data on employment are available from national databases. For instance, employment data for the United States are available from the Place of Work Consolidated Metropolitan Area (POWCMA) field on the Decennial Census Public-Use Microdata Samples (PUMS).

Implementation

Jensen and Kletzer (2006) calculate Gini coefficients for the United States. These data serve as rough proxies for other developed countries and give a sense of which services are most likely to be tradable if an economy reaches a high level of development.

Analysis of the tradability of services for a country consists of two steps. The first is to identify the tradability of sectors based on the estimates for the United States by Jensen and Kletzer (2006). The second is to connect the **Tradability Indexes** with trade data from the country under analysis. Field interviews and other qualitative information are also necessary.

Table 3.6. Gini Classes

Gini class	Gini coefficient
1	<0.1
2	0.1–0.3
3	>0.3

Source: Jensen and Kletzer 2006.

Gini coefficients range from 0 to 1, with higher values indicating a greater likelihood of tradability. Jensen and Kletzer (2006) distinguish three classes of coefficients (table 3.6). The classes should not always be interpreted on a strictly ordinal basis: a sector in a higher Gini class may not have greater export potential than a sector in a lower class. Higher Gini coefficients may indicate that forces other than production economies or transportation costs are at stake. Sometimes the nature of a service is such that it cannot be produced everywhere (one example is mining).

This module follows Jensen and Kletzer (2006) in using 0.1 as the threshold for tradability. Sectors that fall into Gini classes 2 or 3 are thus considered tradable.

Annex table 3A.1 shows the Gini class for various services sectors, as classified by the North American Industry Classification System (NAICS). Only about half of all services subsectors are assessed as tradable. Within financial and insurance services, for example, activities performed by banks and savings institutions are not tradable, whereas activities related to securities and commodities or financial investment are highly tradable. About 46 subsectors (half of all subsectors) appear to be tradable (that is, in Gini class 2 or 3). This figure varies widely across sectors (figure 3.3).

The next step is to connect the trade figures with the Tradability Indexes. This can be done by adding trade data to subsectors that are tradable.

Table 3.7 assesses the distribution of exports across sectors. It is based on benchmarking Modes 1 and 2 data in Malaysia against the United States from the Trade in Services Database. It shows that Malaysia's export basket is heavily skewed toward tourism, exports of which represent about 95 percent of total services exports. This share is very high, particularly given that only one subsector of the sector (travel accommodation) is tradable. Malaysia also shows export potential in professional, scientific, and technical services and management services.

The export patterns of services in the United States and Malaysia differ greatly. In the United States,

MODULE 3

Figure 3.3. Tradable versus Nontradable Services Subsectors

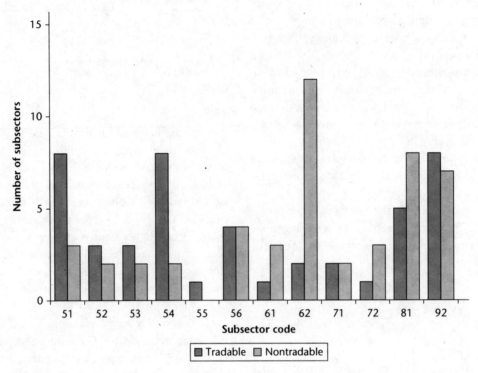

Source: Jensen and Kletzer 2006.
Note: Subsectors are defined by the North American Industry Classification System (NAICS): 51 = information; 52 = finance and insurance; 53 = real estate and rental; 54 = professional, scientific, and technical services; 55 = management; 56 = administrative support; 61 = education; 62 = health care and social services; 71 = arts, entertainment, and recreational services; 72 = accommodation; 81 = other services; 92 = public administration.

Table 3.7. Share of Trade and Tradability Index by Services Sector in Malaysia and the United States, 2009

Sector	Number of tradable/number of nontradable subsectors	Percent of total services trade	
		Malaysia	United States
Tourism	1/3	94.64	33.86
Professional, scientific, and technical	8/2	2.12	8.95
Management	1/0	1.97	2.03
Finance and insurance	3/2	0.52	15.78
Information	8/3	0.45	7.84
Administrative support	4/4	0.20	25.05
Public administration	8/7	0.06	5.82
Real estate and rental	3/2	0.02	0.57
Arts, entertainment, and recreation	2/2	0.02	0.06
Education	1/3	0.00	0.02
Health care and social services	2/12	0.00	0.01
Other services	5/8	0.00	0.00

Source: Trade in Services Database and Jensen and Kletzer 2006.

tourism represents only 34 percent of total services trade; in Malaysia it accounts for 95 percent. Other important services exports by the United States are administrative support (25 percent); finance and insurance (16 percent); professional, scientific, and technical (9 percent); and information (8 percent) services. Geographical concentration ratios show that many sectors in the information, professional, and public administration sectors are tradable. These figures suggest that the United States could exploit its trade potential in these sectors even more than it has.

Box 3.2. Quantifying Tradability Potential: Evidence from Romania

Panel a of figure B3.2.1 shows the number of firms in the goods sector and in 15 services sectors in Romania. The number of firms in the largest services sector (wholesale and retail trade) is slightly higher than the number of firms in the goods sector. This pattern is observed in most countries.

Panel b shows that almost 30 percent of Romanian goods producers export. This figure is much lower for services: even in the sector with the largest percentage of exporters (computer and modern communications), just 10 percent of firms export. Romania's retail sector has the second-highest share of exporters. This finding is interesting, as the tradability list of Jensen and Kletzer (2006) excludes retail sales (see annex table 3A.1).

Exporting is a measure of firm performance. Comparing the rankings of the number of firms and the percentage of exporting firms helps identify the scope for efficiency gains in different sectors. For example, wholesale and retail trade and construction services appear to be populated largely by nonexporters. Policy interventions might be able to increase the export potential of these sectors.

Firm-level data also allow the computation of Jensen and Kletzer–like indexes at the country level.

U.S. industry data reveal that about 37 percent of industries are classified as Gini class 1, 37 percent as Gini class 2, and 27 percent as Gini class 3. The final classification for all industries by two-digit NAICS is shown below.

Table B3.2.1 lists all services sectors for Romainia in which the Tradability Index was high (Gini class = 3 or Gini coefficient > 0.2) or moderate (Gini class = 2, Gini coefficient = 0.1–0.2).

Figure B3.2.1. Number of Firms and Percentage of Exporters in Romania, by Sector, 2009

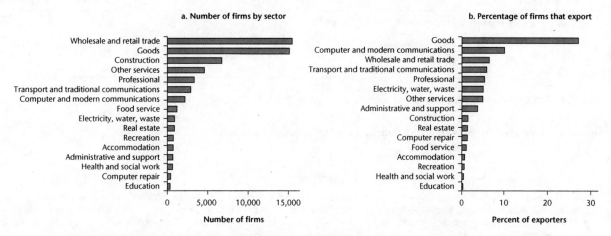

Table B3.2.1. Services Tradability Index for Romania, 2008

Sector	Gini class	Gini coefficient
Wholesale trade, except of motor vehicles and motorcycles	3	0.62
Land transport and transport via pipelines	3	0.36
Air transport	3	0.34
Computer programming, consulting, and related activities	3	0.31
Waste collection, treatment, and disposal activities, materials recovery	2	0.28
Activities of head offices, management consulting	2	0.26
Electricity, gas, steam, and air conditioning supply	2	0.25
Architectural and engineering activities, technical testing and analysis	2	0.22
Water transport	2	0.21
Telecommunications	2	0.21
Repair and installation of machinery and equipment	2	0.20
Real estate	2	0.18
Wholesale and retail trade and repair of motor vehicles and motorcycles	2	0.17
Publishing	2	0.17
Other professional, scientific, and technical activities	2	0.17
Office administrative, office support, and business support activities	2	0.16
Building construction	2	0.15
Warehousing and support activities for transportation	2	0.13
Rental and leasing	2	0.10
All other services sector	1	> 0.1

Note: Two-digit sectors are defined by the North American Industry Classification System (NAICS). For Gini classes, see table 3.6.

(continued on next page)

Box 3.2. *(continued)*

The availability of a wide range of firm-level indicators helps analysts identify the relationship between the tradability of a sector and the underlying characteristics of the firm. Table B3.2.2 does so for goods and services, testing the explanatory power of tradability for firm wages, turnover, investment in information technology (IT), and investment in research and development (R&D). It shows that firms whose goods are more tradable pay higher wages, have higher turnover, and invest more in IT. In contrast, for services only turnover seems correlated with exporting.

Table B3.2.2. Correlation between Sectoral Tradability and Firm Characteristics in Romania, 2009

	Goods				Services			
	(1)	(2)	(3)	(4)	(1)	(2)	(3)	(4)
Item	ln(wage)	ln(turnover)	ln(IT)	ln(R&D)	ln(wage)	ln(turnover)	ln(IT)	ln(R&D)
Gini coefficient	5.26***	6.93**	7.37**	4.38	1.87	3.95**	2.71	1.68
	(1.35)	(2.97)	(3.39)	(4.370)	(1.67)	(1.48)	(2.33)	(2.06)
Observations	23	23	23	23	45	45	41	45
R-squared	0.364	0.255	0.168	0.057	0.038	0.156	0.037	0.012
Root mean square deviation	0.785	1.336	1.850	2.007	1.279	1.238	1.899	2.027

Note: Robust standard errors are in parentheses. ***$p < 0.01$, **$p < 0.05$.

Box 3.3. The Updated Tradability Index of Gervais and Jensen

Gervais and Jensen (2013) define an industry's geographic concentration index as follows:

$$G = \sum_{i=1}^{M} (s_i - x_i)^2$$

where s_i represents the share of industry employment in region i, and x_i represents the share of total employment in region i. A high index indicates that production of the good or service in a region greatly exceeds consumption. This mismatch indicates the tradability of a good between regions. The authors show that manufacturing has the highest G-score, followed by business services, wholesale and retail services, and personal services. However, there is considerable variation within each sector.

Box 3.2 expands the application of the Jensen and Kletzer (2006) methodology using firm-level data for Romania.

The Jensen and Kletzer (2006) methodology provides an intuitive and straightforward way to determine the tradability of particular services sectors. It has limitations, however. The method was developed in order to circumvent the often poor quality of services trade data; it therefore does not use any trade indicators. For instance, according to the Tradability Index, accounting and bookkeeping services are considered nontradable (Gini class 1). However, these services have proven to be highly tradable and an important source of services exports for many countries: in 2009, Malaysia exported about $3.5 million and the United States about $567 million of these services.

Gervais and Jensen (2013) have updated the methodology of Jensen and Kletzer (2006) (box 3.3). Their methodology uses the geographical distribution of production based on data from the U.S. Bureau of Economic Analysis' Labor Market Area.

Assessing Tradability Based on Comparative Advantage

Several indicators are critical to assessing tradability based on comparative advantage. They include standard trade cost proxies (as used in gravity equations, described below); factor intensities; factor endowments; Costinot's Complexity Index (described below); and measures of the strength of legal institutions. Data on these indicators should be collected for specific years for all countries. Useful sources of information include the following:

- World Bank's Trade in Services Database (see appendix B)
- Panel Study of Income Dynamics (PSID) survey data (services sectors)
- EU KLEMS (factor intensities in services)
- The Conference Board
- World Development Indicators (number of Internet users per 100 people)
- Barro and Lee (2012) data set (educational attainment)
- Fraser Institute
- World Bank governance indicators (rules of law and regulatory quality).

Table 3.8. Assessing Tradability Based on Comparative Advantage: Issues for Discussion

Interviewee	Issue
Senior policy makers at the ministries of trade, tourism, telecommunications, transports, and relevant services (infrastructure, transport, health care)	• What is the current state of physical infrastructure? How does it affect the export of services? • In which services sectors does your country specialize in terms of exports? • Do these services use much high-skilled labor? Do they use much ICT-related capital? • How available are high-skilled labor and ICT-related capital? • How strong is contract enforcement?
Major exporters	• How do transportation costs affect the supply of services to foreign markets? • Is good physical infrastructure necessary to export your services? • What is the main endowment factor used to produce your services? • What kind of institutional climate would help your company export? • Is a strong rule of law an important factor for exporting your company's services? • How much training is required at your company? • Is it difficult to find workers with the right qualifications? • What type of capital is critical to produce and export your company's services? Is it easy to obtain?

The diagnostic requires a deep understanding of the country context, based on discussions with government authorities, experts, private sector representatives, and other stakeholders. Table 3.8 indicates some of the questions that need to be addressed.

Analytical Approach

This section introduces a methodology that uses comparative advantage to identify prospective export sectors. Unlike the Tradability Index of Jensen and Kletzer (2006), this methodology is applicable to a wide set of countries using trade in services data that are commonly available.

The methodology consists of two steps. The first is the identification of the drivers of comparative advantage in services. The second is the computation of an index of services tradability, following the methodology in van der Marel (2011) and van der Marel and Shepherd (2013).

The literature on the factors influencing tradability relates largely to goods. It uses the foundational Ricardo model of comparative advantage (which attributes trade to differences in technology) to assess variations in industry productivity across countries.

One set of factors that influences a country's ability to trade in services is its "endowments." In early trade literature, it was typical to view endowments as primarily encompassing different types of labor and capital. Recent literature has developed a broader set of endowments, which includes such factors as institutional quality and a strong rule of law to enforce contracts. This type of institutional factor is an important source for trade in goods. These factors probably play an important role for services.

Figure 3.4 shows that both the amount of high-skilled labor supply and the strength of the domestic legal system and property rights are strong predictors of higher levels of services exports. These factors can affect a country's competitiveness in the world market for services, but countrywide characteristics such as the availability of high-skilled labor or the Internet and a strong rule of law cannot alone increase the productivity of a service or allow a company to export. At a sectoral level, what matters are not just relative endowments but their interaction with sector-specific factor intensities. Chor (2010) proposes a relative endowments framework in which specialization by comparative advantage implies that countries tend to produce and trade services that are relatively intensive in the endowments in which they are relatively abundant.

To export, different services sectors require different shares of skilled labor. The tourism sector, for example, uses much less high-skilled labor than the financial services sector. Some sectors require more information and communication technology (ICT) equipment than others to facilitate production and export. Factor intensities thus range widely across sectors. Many service sectors need more mid-skilled labor and capital than highly sophisticated factors of production.

Table 3.9 shows the intensities of high-skilled labor, ICT-capital, and service complexity for selected services sectors at the most disaggregated level available (three-digit EBOPS). It ranks sectors by the median value of these factor intensities. Box 3.4 explains how factor intensities are computed.

Computer and information services rank highest in the use of high-skilled labor, followed by business services and financial services. Travel and construction rank last. ICT-capital intensity is highest for "other business services," finance, and transportation. The production and supply of these services appear to rely heavily on investment in ICT equipment. Financial services appear to be the most complex and travel and transportation the least complex sectors.

MODULE 3

Figure 3.4. Services Trade, High-Skilled Labor Supply, and the Rule of Law in Selected Countries, 2009

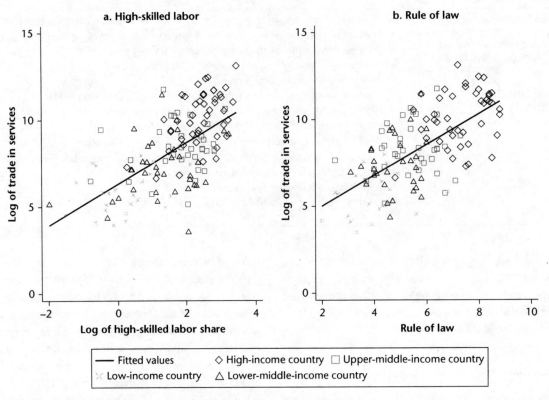

Sources: Trade in Services Database; Barro and Lee 2012; and World Bank Governance Indicators.

Table 3.9. Rank of Factor Intensities for High-Skilled Labor, Information and Communications Technology (ICT) Capital, and Complexity

Sector	High-skilled labor intensity	ICT-capital intensity	Complexity
Computer and information services	1	8	5
Other business services	2	1	7
Financial services	3	2	1
Communications services	4	9	4
Insurance services	5	6	3
Personal, cultural, and recreation services	6	5	6
Transportation	7	3	8
Travel	8	4	9
Construction services	9	7	2

Sources: EU KLEMS and van der Marel and Shepherd 2013.

Box 3.4. How Are Factor Intensities Computed?

Factor intensity for high-skilled labor is calculated as the ratio of the hours worked by high-skilled labor to the total number of hours worked by all types of workers in a sector, multiplied by the total share of high-skilled labor in value added.

Information and communication technology (ICT) capital intensity is measured as the ratio of ICT compensation to total capital compensation, multiplied by the total share of ICT capital in value added for each sector. The same procedure can be performed for non–ICT capital intensity.

The production complexity of a service is computed from responses in the Panel Study on Income Dynamics (PSID) survey to the question, "How long does it take for each employee to be fully educated and qualified for the job in each service sector?" This methodology, borrowed from Costinot (2009), provides a measure of the magnitude of fixed training costs. It proxies the intensity of sectors in the use of good institutions. Complex sectors usually depend on good domestic institutions in order to produce efficiently.

MODULE 3

Implementation

These sectoral features are to a large extent dependent on country characteristics. An empirical exercise to assess the tradability of a service should therefore include both country and industry dimensions. Such an approach builds on Eaton and Kortum (2002) and Chor (2010), which explains the observed pattern of specialization for industries by a productivity term that contains a systemic component. Empirically, this pattern is driven by interaction effects between country and industry variables. Sectors vary in the factor and institutional conditions needed for production, and countries differ in their ability to provide these requirements. Comparative advantage stems from the interaction between the two components. Therefore, one needs to find the country supply factors that best match the factor intensities described above.

The recent empirical literature on comparative advantage has developed variables that measure country endowments in terms of high-skilled labor, ICT capital supply per worker, and institutional quality. The supply of high-skilled labor is measured by the proportion of high-skilled (tertiary-educated) employees in the population over 24. These data come from the Barro and Lee (2012)

data set. The supply of ICT-capital intensity is measured by the number of Internet users per 100 people. These data come from the World Development Indicators. A proxy for institutional quality is a standard measure of the strength of the domestic legal system and enforcement of property rights. These data come from Gwartney and Lawson (2012).

Figure 3.5 displays the country supply measures rescaled from 0 to 10, with increasing values indicating a higher endowment. There is significant variation across countries for all three types of factor inputs. The United States is well endowed with all three factors. Indonesia has substantially lower levels of high-skilled labor and Internet supply, but its institutional quality is fairly good. Haiti is better endowed in skills than ICT, and its legal systems lag far behind most countries. Romania scores well in terms of legal institutions and skill supply.

The next step is to compute the index of tradability, which can be done by examining the relation between the interaction terms of comparative advantage and the effect on exports. Van der Marel and Shepherd (2013) perform such an analysis within a gravity model (see below) by applying standard trade cost proxies, such

Figure 3.5. Index of Supply of High-Skilled Labor, Legal Institutions, and Internet in Selected Countries, 2009

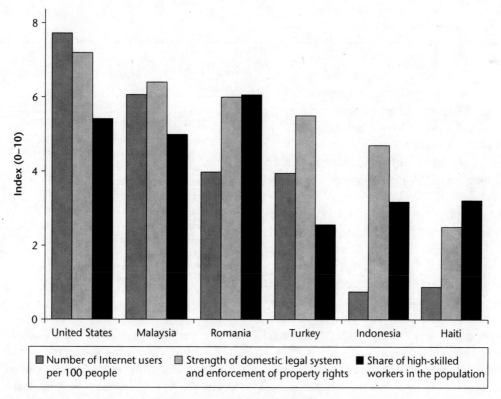

Sources: World Development Inicators; Gwartney and Lawson 2012; and Barro and Lee 2012.

MODULE 3

Box 3.5. What Does Firm Productivity Say about the Likelihood of Exporting? Evidence from Romania

As the basis of the Tradability Index is the productivity "shock" observed in a pattern, it explains the extent to which firms in a typical services sector can capitalize on the endowments in an economy. The match between these endowments and factor intensity for a service explains productivity, as explained by the comparative advantage model (see Chor 2010 and van der Marel and Shepherd 2013).

Firm-level data can help determine whether this productivity match is observable. Romania's position on the index of factor supply is relatively high for legal institutions and high-skilled labor supply (as shown in figure 3.5), suggesting that Romania should specialize, or have a comparative advantage, in sectors that use these factors intensively.

One should therefore observe above-average productivity for these sectors. Figure B3.5.1 indicates that productivity is above average for education, computer repair, and other services. Romania's relatively high-skilled-labor endowments may explain the high productivity of education and computer repair services. The figure also suggests that there is unexploited export potential for construction and communications services, as both types of services are complex and Romania scores relatively high on institutions.

Figure B3.5.1. Relative Productivity of Selected Export Sectors in Romania, 2009

Source: Romanian Structural Business Survey.

as distance, common language, colony, and a regional trade agreement, together with the comparative advantage terms for each exporter. They use a probit estimator (of which the results are given in annex table 3A.2) to propose a Tradability Index for services based on trade through Modes 1 and 2 by country and industry. Box 3.5 provides an extension of this analysis by using firm-level data for Romania.

This index is displayed in table 3.10 for sectors at the most aggregated (one-digit) level. Higher values indicate greater trade potential. In principle, all services listed are tradable, as even personal, cultural, and recreational services have positive indexes. Business services have the highest index, followed by travel and communication services. Both insurance and financial services score relatively low, possibly because both sectors are still highly restricted in most parts of the world for Mode 1.

This Tradability Index can be extended to a sector classification that is more disaggregated or includes indexes by exporters or importers. Policy makers can use these

Table 3.10. World Tradability Index for Selected Services Sectors

Rank	Sector	Index
1	Other business services	0.725
2	Travel	0.649
3	Personal, cultural, and recreational services	0.480
4	Communications services	0.442
5	Computer and information services	0.421
6	Insurance services	0.372
7	Government services	0.364
8	Financial services	0.348
9	Construction services	0.337
10	Transportation	0.187

Source: van der Marel and Shepherd 2013.
Note: Index ranges from 0 to 1.

data to verify their country's relative position. The index of tradability can also be connected to trade patterns of countries along the **intensive margin**, as Jensen and Kletzer (2006) do. Information on the factor and institutional intensities for each sector yields additional policy insights regarding which country characteristics can be improved to increase tradability.

Assessing Tradability through Gravity Models

A gravity model can be used to assess whether a country is currently fully exploiting its trade potential with selected partners or whether country-specific barriers could be removed to enhance integration. This section provides an example in which there is scope to increase services trade integration between Association of Southeast Asian Nations (ASEAN) countries at the aggregate level. The analysis is based on an estimated gravity model of trade in services that is founded in microeconomic theory. The gravity model of trade relates countries' bilateral trade flows to structural determinants of gross domestic product (GDP), geographic distance, and other factors. The model has been extensively used in international trade because of its intuitive empirical and theoretical appeal. (Anderson and van Wincoop 2003, Feenstra 2004, and Baldwin and Taglioni 2006, among others, present exhaustive literature reviews on the **gravity equation** as applied to international trade.)

The structural determinants for each pair of countries together with the estimated regression coefficients are used to compute bilateral trade potential. Subsequently, the level of bilateral trade between a pair of countries relative to trade potential is estimated to categorize bilateral exports as "overtraded" or "undertraded." The regression includes a country's Services Trade Restrictions Index from the World Bank Services Trade Restrictions Database to assess whether these determinants are important in explaining the level of bilateral services trade (see Module 4 for an explanation of the database). Bilateral trade flows are from the Trade in Services Database (described in appendix B), which covers bilateral services flows for about 200 countries across a multitude of sectors.[1]

The average 2008–09 bilateral exports flows for 102 countries are regressed on the following country-specific and bilateral characteristics: the log of distance, dummy variables for contiguity, common language, a common colonial power, the Services Trade Restrictiveness Index of exporter and importer, and the log of GDP of exporter and importer (to proxy economic mass). The results are presented in the middle column of table 3.11.

The right column of table 3.11 shows the results of an alternative specification for the gravity equation in which the economic mass variable is picked up not by GDP but by importer and exporter fixed effects (referred to as a **dyadic gravity equation**).[2] It shows the results of

Table 3.11. Regression Results of Gravity Model of Trade in Services, 2008–09
Dependent variable: Log(export value)

Item	Coefficient estimate	Dyadic coefficient estimate
Log(distance)	−0.8526***	−0.9059***
	(0.037)	(0.029)
Contiguity	0.3454**	0.4285***
	(0.168)	(0.110)
Common language	0.9000***	0.4314***
	(0.124)	(0.082)
Common colonial power	0.3089	0.6241***
	(0.217)	(0.109)
Importer Services Trade Restrictiveness Index	0.0012	
	(0.003)	
Exporter Services Trade Restrictiveness Index	−0.0141***	
	(0.003)	
Log(importer GDP)	1.0866***	
	(0.021)	
Log(exporter GDP)	1.0808***	
	(0.021)	
Observations	2,533	4,925
Adjusted *R*-squared	0.700	0.813

Sources: World Development Indicators, Trade in Services Database, and Services Trade Restrictions Database (all from the World Bank) and Centre d'Etudes Prospectives et d'Informations Internationales (CEPII).
Note: Coefficients on the fixed effects are not shown. Robust standard errors are in parentheses. ***$p < 0.01$, **$p < 0.05$.

MODULE 3

regressing bilateral exports for 198 countries on the log of distance and dummy variables for contiguity, common language, and common colonial power. Only bilateral characteristics can be included in a dyadic model, because the nation dummies prevent the inclusion of country-specific variables such as GDP and the Services Trade Restrictions Index. Fixed effects (dyadic) estimations control for a wide variety of country-specific factors that affect bilateral trade flows, including omitted variables that are too difficult to measure directly. These variables include all country-specific (nonbilateral) trade policy barriers that cannot be measured by, for example, the Services Trade Restrictiveness Index. These nonmeasurable country-specific characteristics fall in the residual in the specification in which GDP proxies economic mass (potentially biasing the estimates).

The results of the gravity model seem to suggest that the Services Trade Restrictiveness Index of the exporting country matters in determining the bilateral exports of that country. Countries with more restrictive services regulatory environments are significantly less likely to export services. The relationship between the level of restrictions in the importing country and that country's bilateral services imports is not statistically significant. However, the data set included only data on cross-border trade (Mode 1) and consumption abroad (Mode 2). Had FDI (commercial presence or Mode 3) or the temporary movement of people (Mode 4) been included, the coefficients may have been significant.

Figure 3.6 plots the residuals against the model's fitted values for the dyadic specification as well as a specification that does not correctly control for such barriers. The Services Trade Restrictiveness Index was removed from the specification in order to focus on what happens when these barriers are not accounted for. Fitted values perform better once these other obstacles in the specification with fixed effects are properly controlled for.

Figure 3.7 plots the predicted bilateral trade levels from the specification with GDP on the x-axis and the predicted levels from the specification with fixed effects on the y-axis. The dots represent Indonesia's bilateral exports with other countries. Observations below the 45-degree line show that the predicted levels from the specification with fixed effects are lower than they are for the specification with GDP. Because the specification with fixed effects properly controls for country-specific barriers to trade, this result suggests that barriers to trade at the national level are preventing Indonesia

Figure 3.6. Residuals and Fitted Values of Gravity Model, Estimated with GDP and Fixed Effects, 2008–09

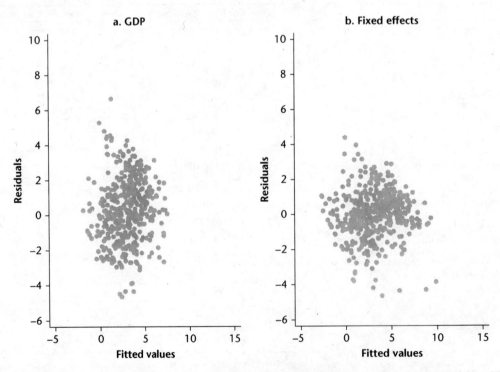

Sources: World Development Indicators, Trade in Services Database, and Services Trade Restrictions Database (all from the World Bank) and Centre d'Etudes Prospectives et d'Informations Internationales (CEPII).

MODULE 3

Figure 3.7. Predicted Trade between Indonesia and Other Countries, Estimated with GDP and Fixed Effects, 2008–09

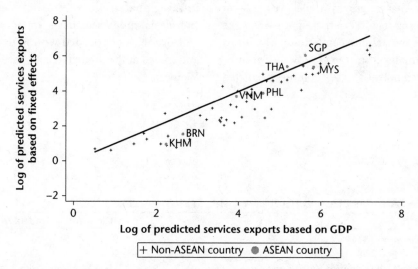

Sources: World Development Indicators, Trade in Services Database, and Services Trade Restrictions Database (all from the World Bank) and Centre d'Etudes Prospectives et d'Informations Internationales (CEPII).
Note: ASEAN = Association of Southeast Asian Nations. For the International Organization for Standardization (ISO) abbreviations, see appendix B.

Figure 3.8. Actual Trade and Predicted Trade of Gravity Model, Estimated with Fixed Effects, 2008–09

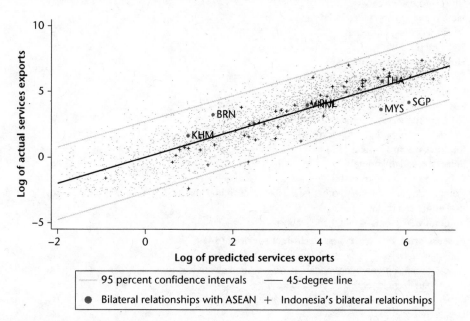

Sources: World Development Indicators, Trade in Services Database, and Services Trade Restrictions Database (all from the World Bank) and the Centre d'Etudes Prospectives et d'Informations Internationales (CEPII).
Note: ASEAN = Association of Southeast Asian Nations, BRN = Brunei Darussalam, KHM = Cambodia, MYS = Malaysia, PHL = Philippines, SGP = Singapore, THA = Thailand, VNM = Vietnam.

from reaching its full trade potential with a particular country. Lower potential trade after properly controlling for country-specific obstacles suggests that barriers are deterring services trade with ASEAN and non-ASEAN countries. This result could suggest that a high level of regulatory restrictions (as captured by the Services

Trade Restrictiveness Index, for example) and a low level of regulatory governance may be dampening trade potential.

Figure 3.8 shows actual and predicted bilateral export relationships with Indonesia (given by the dyadic gravity equation). If an observation is above (below) the 45-degree line, the average observed export relationship in 2008–09 was more (less) than what the gravity model predicts—on the basis of countries' structural determinants—and the exporter is said to be overtrading (undertrading) with its trading partner. Estimates from the gravity model indicate that the estimated potential trade volumes predicted by structural trade determinants differed from the actual intraregional trade values between 2008 and 2009. Indonesia appears to have overtraded with Cambodia and Brunei, undertraded with Malaysia and Singapore, and traded at the predicted level with the Philippines and Vietnam.

Annex

Table 3A.1. Gini Class and Tradability of Selected Services Sectors

Industry	Gini class	Tradable?
Information (51)		
Newspaper publishers	1	No
Radio and television broadcasting and cable	1	No
Libraries and archives	1	No
Wired telecommunication carriers	2	Yes
Data processing services	2	Yes
Other telecommunication services	2	Yes
Publishing except newspapers and software	2	Yes
Other information services	3	Yes
Motion pictures and video industries	3	Yes
Sound recording industries	3	Yes
Software publishing	3	Yes
Finance and insurance (52)		
Saving institutions, including unions	1	No
Banking and related activities	1	No
Insurance carriers and related activities	2	Yes
Nondepository credit and related activities	2	Yes
Securities, commodities, funds, trusts, and other financial investment	3	Yes
Real estate and rental (53)		
Videotape and disk rental	1	No
Other consumer goods rental	1	No
Commercial, industrial, and other intangible assets rental and leasing	2	Yes
Real estate and rental	2	Yes
Automotive equipment rental and leasing	2	Yes
Professional, scientific, and technical services (54)		
Veterinary services	1	No
Accounting, tax preparation, bookkeeping, and payroll services	1	No
Architectural, engineering, and related services	2	Yes
Other professional, scientific, and technical services	2	Yes
Legal services	2	Yes
Specialized design services	2	Yes
Computer systems design and related services	2	Yes
Advertising and related services	2	Yes
Management, scientific, and technical consulting services	2	Yes
Scientific research and development services	3	Yes
Management (55)		
Management of companies and enterprises	2	Yes
Administrative support (56)		
Waste management and remediation services	1	No

(continued on next page)

Table 3A.1. *(continued)*

Industry	Gini class	Tradable?
Business support services	1	No
Services to buildings and dwellings	1	No
Landscaping services	1	No
Employment services	2	Yes
Other administrative and support services	2	Yes
Investigation and security services	2	Yes
Travel arrangement and reservation services	2	Yes
Education (61)		
Elementary and secondary schools	1	No
Colleges and universities, including junior colleges	1	No
Other schools, instruction, and educational services	1	No
Business, technical, and trade schools and training	2	Yes
Health care and social services (62)		
Hospitals	1	No
Nursing care facilities	1	No
Vocational rehabilitation services	1	No
Offices of physicians	1	No
Outpatient care centers	1	No
Offices of dentists	1	No
Offices of optometrists	1	No
Residential care facilities, without nursing	1	No
Child day care services	1	No
Home health care services	1	No
Other health care services	1	No
Office of chiropractors	1	No
Community food and housing, and emergency services	2	Yes
Offices of other health practitioners	2	Yes
Arts, entertainment, and recreation (71)		
Bowling centers	1	No
Other amusement, gambling, and recreation industries	1	No
Museum, art galleries, historical sites, and similar institutions	2	Yes
Independent artists, performing arts, spectator sports, and related	2	Yes
Accommodation (72)		
Drinking places, alcoholic beverages	1	No
Restaurants and other food services	1	No
Recreational vehicle parks and camps, and rooming and boarding houses	1	No
Traveller accommodation	2	Yes
Other services (81)		
Automotive repair and maintenance	1	No
Barber shops	1	No
Religious organizations	1	No
Commercial and industrial machinery and equipment repair and maintenance	1	No
Dry cleaning and laundry services	1	No
Car washes	1	No
Electronic and precision equipment repair and maintenance	1	No
Civil, social, advocacy organizations, and grant making and giving	1	No
Nail salons and other personal care services	2	Yes
Other personal services	2	Yes
Business, professional, political, and similar organizations	2	Yes

(continued on next page)

MODULE 3

Table 3A.1. *(continued)*

Industry	Gini class	Tradable?
Labour unions	3	Yes
Footwear and leather goods repair	3	Yes
Public administration (92)		
Justice, public order, and safety activities	1	No
Administration of human resource programs	1	No
Other general government and support	1	No
Elective offices and legislative bodies	1	No
Military reserves or national guard	1	No
Administration of economic programs and space research	1	No
Administration of environmental quality and housing programs	1	No
Public finance activities	2	Yes
National security and international affairs	3	Yes
U.S. armed forces, branch not specified	3	Yes
U.S. Coast Guard	3	Yes
U.S. Air Force	3	Yes
U.S. Army	3	Yes
U.S. Navy	3	Yes
U.S. Marines	3	Yes

Source: Jensen and Kletzer 2006.
Note: Figures in parentheses are two-digit North American Industry Classification System (NAICS) codes.

Table 3A.2. Probability Results from Comparative Advantage Regressions
Dependent variable: observed exports

Item	(1) Trade costs	(2) Endowments	(3) Institutions
log($distance_{ij}$)	−0.202***	−0.214***	−0.221***
	(0.000)	(0.000)	(0.000)
$contiguous_{ij}$	0.026	−0.004	−0.003
	(0.534)	(0.928)	(0.952)
common official $language_{ij}$	0.027	0.049	0.048
	(0.331)	(0.120)	(0.129)
$colony_{ij}$	0.168***	0.135***	0.125***
	(0.000)	(0.004)	(0.010)
RTA_{ij}	0.132***	0.146***	0.142***
	(0.000)	(0.000)	(0.000)
log($high$-$skill\ labor_i$) * log($high$-$skill\ intensity_k$)		0.020***	0.018**
		(0.006)	(0.017)
log(non-$ICT\ capital\ stock_i$) * log(non-$ICT\ capital\ intensity_k$)		0.041***	0.039***
		(0.001)	(0.002)
log($internet\ users\ per$ 100 $people_i$) * log($ICT\ capital\ intensity_k$)		0.021	0.065**
		(0.407)	(0.018)
$legal_i$ * $complexity_k$			0.115***
			(0.000)
$legal_i$ * $Herfindahl_k$			0.061***
			(0.000)
Observations	39879	32008	31524
Pseudo-R-squared	0.389	0.379	0.380

Source: van der Marel and Shepherd 2013.
Note: Estimation is by logit with fixed effects by exporter, importer, and sector. Probability values based on standard errors corrected for clustering by country pair are indicated in parentheses below the coefficient estimates. Coefficients are reported as marginal effects at the mean. RTA = Regional Trade Agreement.
*$p < 0.10$, **$p < 0.05$, ***$p < 0.01$.

MODULE 3

Notes

1. The Trade in Services Database is currently the best source of data on global trade flows in services, but the quality of trade data for services is far from comparable to trade data for goods. Because of the long tradition of tariff revenues, trade data for goods are of high quality; because of the intangibility and nonstorability of services, at-the-border duties cannot be applied, which has led to much less accurate data.

2. Broadly, a fixed-effects regression model aims at capturing omitted variables by creating a different intercept for the regression using a dummy variable.

References

Anderson, James E., and Eric van Wincoop. 2003. "Gravity with Gravitas: A Solution to the Border Puzzle." *American Economic Review* 93 (1): 170–92.

Baldwin, Richard, and Daria Taglioni. 2006. "Gravity for Dummies and Dummies for Gravity Equations." NBER Working Paper 12516, National Bureau of Economic Research, Cambridge, MA.

Barro, Robert J., and Jong-Wha Lee. 2012. "A New Dataset of Educational Attainment in the World, 1950–2010." NBER Working Paper 15902, National Bureau of Economic Research, Cambridge, MA.

Chor, Davin. 2010. "Unpacking Sources of Comparative Advantage: A Quantitative Approach." *Journal of International Economics* 82 (2): 152–67.

Costinot, Arnaud. 2009. "On the Origins of Comparative Advantage." *Journal of International Economics* 77 (2): 255–64.

Eaton, Jonathan, and Samuel Kortum. 2002. "Technology, Geography, and Trade." *Econometrica* 70 (5): 1741–79.

Feenstra, R. C. 2004. *Advanced International Trade: Theory and Evidence.* Princeton, NJ: Princeton University Press.

Francois, Joseph, and Bernard Hoekman. 2010. "Services Trade and Policy." *Journal of Economic Literature* 48 (3): 642–92.

Gervais, Antoine, and J. Bradford Jensen. 2013. "Are Services Tradable? Evidence from US Micro Data." NBER Working Paper 19759, National Bureau of Economic Research, Cambridge, MA.

Ghani, Ejaz, ed. 2010. *The Service Revolution in South Asia.* Oxford: Oxford University Press.

Gwartney, James, and Robert Lawson. 2012. *Economics Freedom of the World 2012 Annual Report.* Economic Freedom of the World Network, Fraser Institute, Vancouver, Canada.

IMF (International Monetary Fund). *Balance of Payment Statistics.* Washington, DC: IMF.

Jensen, J. Bradford, and Lori G. Kletzer, 2006. "Tradable Services: Understanding the Scope and Impact of Services Offshoring." In *Brookings Trade Forum 2005: Offshoring While-Collar Work*, edited by Susan M. Collins and Lael Brainard, 75–134. Washington, DC: Brookings Institution.

Magdeleine, Joscelyn, and Andreas Maurer. 2008. "Measuring GATS Mode 4 Trade Flows." WTO Staff Working Paper ERSD-2008-05, World Trade Organization, Geneva.

Maurer, Andreas, Yann Marcus, Joscelyn Magdeleine, and Barbara d'Andrea. 2008. "Measuring Trade in Services." In *Handbook of International Trade in Services*, edited by Aaditya Mattoo, Robert M. Stern, and Gianni Zanini, 169–220. Washington, DC: World Bank and New York: Oxford University.

Mishra, Saurabh, Susanna Lundstrom, and Rahul Anand. 2011. "Service Export Sophistication and Economic Growth." Policy Research Working Paper 5606, World Bank, Washington, Washington, DC.

Trade in Services Database. World Bank, Washington, DC.

UN (United Nations). 2012. *Manual on Statistics of International.* Trade in Services 2010 (MSITS 2010) New York.

van der Marel, Erik. 2011. "Determinants of Comparative Advantage in Services." GEM Working Paper, Groupe d'Economie Mondiale, Paris.

van der Marel, E., and B. Shepherd. 2013. "International Tradability of Services." World Bank Policy Research Working Paper 6712, Washington, DC.

World Development Indicators (database). World Bank, Washington, DC. http://data.worldbank.org/data-catalog/world-development -indicators.

MODULE 4

POLICY OPTIONS FOR INCREASING COMPETITIVENESS AND TRADE IN THE SERVICES SECTOR

This module examines broad policy areas and options for addressing the constraints identified in Modules 1, 2, and 3. It distinguishes between sectoral policies that can be implemented in the short to medium term (mostly regulations and barriers to trade) and **horizontal measures** and strategies related to the domestic economy and institutions, which can be implemented only over a longer time horizon. The module addresses policies that affect trade in services, including investment policies, temporary migration policies, and domestic policies that may have unintentional negative impacts on trade. It does not provide prescriptive advice on specific policies that should be adopted. It does include case studies illustrating good and bad policy practices.

The focus is on identifying regulations that affect or can facilitate the importation of input services that are determinants of a country's competitiveness, including regulations that may affect the competitiveness of services exports. For example, regulations that limit the participation of foreign direct investment (FDI) in a sector affect the export of services. A liberal policy toward FDI has helped turn the Philippines into the world's third-largest exporter of **business process outsourcing (BPO)**. In Malaysia, the establishment of branches of foreign universities has boosted exports of education services.

Domestic enabling factors reflect a country's endowments. They include human capital, natural resources (such as sights that attract tourists), infrastructure (such as a telecommunications network that facilitates the delivery of services), and institutions (such as the quality of a country's rule of law or regulatory environment). These factors are an important complement to good trade policies and regulations.

This module examines two sets of policy options that drive the performance of services competitiveness.[1]

Regulatory policy barriers affecting trade, investment, and labor mobility include the entire range of policies affecting cross-border trade, consumption abroad, foreign investment, the participation of multinationals, and the movement of individual services providers. These policy barriers are common across services sectors. They seek to address market failure problems. They are not explicitly targeted to trade in services, but they nevertheless affect trade.

Trade barriers explicitly affecting trade, investment, and labor mobility in services include barriers related to accessing a market or the differential treatment of foreign and incumbent domestic firms. Barriers in this category include indirect barriers, such as domestic regulation or wider regulatory measures that affect trade.

Reasons for Regulatory Policies

Analyzing the determinants of competitiveness is more complex for services than for goods because of the broad definition of trade in services, which encompasses factors of production; the complicated links between modes, inputs, and outputs; policies stemming from different areas and having different social objectives; and new trade patterns emerging as part of technological change. Trade can take various forms other than cross-border trade, including the movement of services and the movement of FDI and skills transferred through temporary labor mobility schemes.

For some type of services, modes of supply may be substitutes or complements. If modes are perfect substitutes, the liberalization of one mode would be enough to fully reap the gains from liberalization. If modes are imperfect substitutes, or complements, their provision normally requires a mix of cross-border trade through Mode 1,

Mode 2, or both and locally supplied services through Modes 3 or 4. Services provision may require complementary inputs. Delivery of one service may thus depend on the use of another. Financial services, for instance, cannot be provided without telecommunications and professional services.

Regulations affecting trade in services are linked to policies in a wide range of areas beyond the sector itself. Exporting health care services, for example, requires addressing migration and labor market regulations that prescribe wage payments to services providers, taxation requirements and social security regulations, and recognition of professional titles and experience.

Technical changes have made services trade more interlinked with other areas and affected trade patterns. Changes in information and communication technology (ICT) reduce the need for proximity between producer and consumer. They also allow for the fragmentation of production into tasks that may be performed in different locations (see, for instance, Jones 2000, Grossman and Rossi-Hansberg 2008, Feenstra 2010, and Helpman 2011 for the theoretical underpinnings). Fragmentation, which affects the production of both goods and services, means that a vertically connected production process that takes place in one location can now be undertaken in different regions or countries.

These trends have increased the interdependence among trade, FDI, and the temporary mobility of both high-skilled and low-skilled workers, complicating policy. New trade patterns are emerging as a result of these technological changes. Baldwin (2011) suggests that whereas trade in the 20th century was mainly about selling goods made in factories in one country to customers in another country, trade in the 21st century is characterized by the trade-investment-services nexus that reflects the intertwining of trade in parts and components; the international movement of investment in production facilities, people, technology, and long-term business relationships; and services that coordinate dispersed production in different locations. Miroudot, Lanz, and Ragoussis (2009) find that intermediate inputs represent 56 percent of goods trade and 73 percent of services trade. Trade flows are thus dominated by products and services that are not consumed but instead used in the production of other goods and services.

Trade costs are higher for services than for goods—as much as twice as high, according to Miroudot, Sauvage, and Shepherd (2010). Policies can raise these costs and restrict the growth and expansion of trade in services, as illustrated by countries that have liberalized the telecommunications sector but have not put in place an adequate regulatory framework (box 4.1).

Measures designed to reserve a market for domestic incumbents explicitly insulate them from foreign competition. Other measures, such as policies implemented in the pursuit of social objectives, may not be protectionist in intent but often unintentionally restrict trade in services.

The difference between explicit and unintentional policy measures can be grasped by comparing tariffs with regulatory barriers. Tariffs are almost always protectionist in intent and effect. In contrast, regulations affecting services sectors often promote other objectives such as equal access or universal service provision. An antiexport bias on trade in services arises if these regulations are implemented in a way that is economically inefficient and increases cost, by restricting free trade in services.

Services regulation intended to achieve legitimate policy objectives—in health, education, and the environment, for example—may become regulatory barriers to trade in services. Because services trade invades areas traditionally reserved to domestic constituencies (such as education and health), removing regulatory barriers is politically difficult. In addition, such measures are often technically complex

---

Box 4.1. Weak Policies, Weak Investment Climate, and Weak Integration into World Markets in the Middle East and North Africa

The countries of the Middle East and North Africa are still poorly integrated into world markets, and they have joined global production chains at a lower level than other developing countries. These countries receive only a small share of global foreign direct investment (FDI) flows, and their participation in world trade is below its potential. The share of components in manufactured exports, for instance, remains far below that of Malaysia or Taiwan, China (Ng and Yeats 2000).

The weak investment climate and the poor quality of backbone services have also contributed to poor performance in several strategic sectors and dampened the competitiveness boost of other measures, including trade liberalization initiatives and the signing of association agreements with the European Union. Quantitative studies find that the quality of procompetitive regulation in the telecommunications sector increases trade in manufacturing goods and helps countries join global production chains, reducing the regulatory risk perceived by investors.

Source: Rossotto, Sekkat, and Varoudakis 2003.

and difficult to understand. They are complex because of the wide range of policy barriers that affect services and the many types of market failures that characterize services markets.

Market failures that need to be addressed through policy include the following (figure 4.1):[2]

- failures that limit competition
- failures related to the **public good** characteristics of a service and divergence with important and necessary noneconomic social goals
- failures caused by **asymmetric information**
- failures caused by divergent private and social utility functions.

Although there are good reasons to develop regulatory policies to correct domestic market failure, these policies have potential economic risks, as table 4.1 shows. Regulatory policies can also impede trade because countries differ in the choice and stringency of instruments, because regulations are deliberately designed to protect domestic service providers, or because the administration and enforcement of regulations is inadequate.

When regulations are designed to protect domestic incumbents or safeguard local interest groups, they are often accompanied by inadequate regulatory planning, weak administration, and poor public oversight. The risk of regulatory failures related to capture by interest groups is especially high when regulatory policies are motivated by noneconomic purposes. Such policies are often based on instruments whose economic rationale is void of analytical or empirical support.

Regulation to correct market failures may lead to market distortions and welfare losses, even when government or regulatory bodies lack the capacity and means to regulate effectively. This problem is most likely to arise as a result of laws and regulations that are not aimed at the

services sectors directly. Market interventions affecting services sectors can be justified on welfare grounds if they correct a market failure. Market failures are often linked to social objectives. In the health care sector, for instance, governments often enjoy a mandate to regulate with the goal of achieving equal access by all.

Regulations should correct market failures in the most efficient and effective way, where "efficient" means that they achieve their goals at the minimum cost in terms of economic welfare and "effective" means that they achieve the goal in question. Policy makers must achieve social objectives in the least restrictive manner when designing, implementing, and applying regulations, so that optimal allocation of goods and services production is guaranteed.

One way to help overcome regulatory failures is to create strong, transparent, and accountable regulatory bodies. Good regulatory policies can be designed through a process that reflects the main principles of good governance. Ideally, these processes and procedures should increase transparency, through consultation that increases the accountability of regulators. Transparency and accountability reduce regulatory capture while contributing to informed and well-designed regulations that are adequately implemented. Expert advice and interagency coordination mechanisms increase efficiency and enhance analytical support for the measures, reducing the scope for regulatory failures (caused by bounded rationality, for example) (Molinuevo and Sáez 2014). A case of good practice is illustrated by the Asia-Pacific Economic Cooperation (APEC) legal service website initiative, discussed in box 4.2.

Natural Monopoly or Oligopoly

Because a monopoly can restrict supply and keep prices high, consumers suffer and economic welfare is reduced. Oligopolies can result in similar effects, through price

Figure 4.1. Types of Market Failures

Limited competition	Asymmetric information	Services with public good characteristics that achieve noneconomic goals	Divergence between private and social utility functions
• Natural monopoly • Oligopoly • Exclusive or controlled access to natural resources	• Between consumer and producer • Between consumer and financial services provider	• Education, health, finance, telecom, public good features • Health and safety protection • Environmental safety and protection • Equal service access • Unemployment reduction	• Underdeveloped domestic services sector • Lack of technological upgrading

MODULE 4

Table 4.1. Instruments for Addressing Market Failures Affecting Trade in Services

Type of market failure or policy goal	Policy objective	Instruments	Affected sectors	Economic risk
Market failure				
Natural monopoly or oligopoly	• Avoid duplicating fixed costs. • Create optimal environment given limited competition.	• Information on price setting • Cross-subsidies • Splitting of networks from service provision	Network industries, such as water, electricity, and telecommunications	• Prices set so low that monopolist unable to recoup fixed costs • Costly to obtain perfect information
Necessity of exclusive or controlled access to natural resources	• Optimally allocate exclusive access. • Ensure competition without regulation. • Avoid negative externality through spectrum signal interference.	• Licensing for usage, through auctioning	Radio transmission, mobile telephony, and other utilities	• Negative spillover effects because of overuse of bandwidth • Insufficient number of firms given license
Public goods characteristics of service	• Achieve social objectives (benefits to society at large).	• Cross-subsidies • Prudential regulation	Health care, education, utilities, and financial services	• Underproduction of positive spillover effects • Underproduction of the service • Free-riding
Asymmetric information between consumer and producer	• Protect consumers. • Reduce consumer safety concerns. • Guarantee quality of service.	• Licensing • Education, including demonstration of work experience • Minimum skill requirements for services providers • Quality control • Compulsory insurance schemes	Financial, insurance, and professional services	• Overregulation • Moral hazard • Strict licensing requirements, which may restrict supply
Asymmetric information between consumer and financial services provider	• Increase stability of financial sector.	• Financial information transparency • Licensing • Minimum standards or capital requirements • Strong central bank • Capital adequacy tests	Investment banking, retail banking, private equity firms, hedge funds, insurance services	• Overregulation • Moral hazard
No market failure	• Achieve other legitimate policy objectives, such as equal services access or reduction of unemployment.	• Promotion of universal access in remote areas • Measures to improve redistribution • Job creation	Network industries; services provided through Mode 3 (investment)	• Increased costs because of higher factor costs or inefficient organization
Policy goal				
Environmental protection	• Promote social welfare rationale • Reduce negative environmental externalities. • Conserve the environment.	• Effective rural and urban planning	Tourism, retail, transportation sectors	• Regulations that are more burdensome than necessary to achieve desired goals
Development of domestic services sector; upgrading of technology	• Generate positive spillover effects for firms in rest of sector.	• Restrictions on legal form of firms • Rules on local employment of personnel/ directors	All services sectors	• Overregulation of FDI • Risk aversion of foreign investors • Barriers to trade in services

---

Box 4.2. Good Policy Practice: Increasing the Transparency of Regulations Governing Lawyers Working in Asia-Pacific Economic Cooperation (APEC) Member Economies

A website of the Asia-Pacific Economic Cooperation (APEC) (http://www.legalservices.apec.org/) enhances the transparency of regulation of legal services. It explains the requirements and procedures for practicing foreign law in the organization's 21 member economies. The site provides information on the licensing and rights of foreign lawyers providing foreign and international legal services. It also provides information for foreign lawyers who work in association with host economy lawyers. The website provides information about APEC members' regulatory regimes for foreign lawyers, compares regulatory arrangements, and helps develop best practice for the regulation of foreign lawyers.

Figure 4.2. Options, Constraints, Levers, and Risks Associated with Regulating Natural Monopoly or Oligopoly

Issues for policy makers	Responses/policy options	Constraints	Levers	Risks
Efficiency costs	Regulation of monopolist to ensure pricing close to economic value	Costly to eliminate information gap between monopolist/oligopolist and regulator	Technological progress to expand information, competition, and unbundling opportunities	Profitability of operator
Rents				Costly to monitor the quality of service
Supply restrictions		Need to ensure profitability of operator		
High prices	Universal access through universal service obligation, tolerance for cross-subsidization, or both			
Welfare costs				
Price fixing				
Collusion				
Lack of incentive to innovate				

fixing or collusion. Both setups can have negative effects on the economy, because they reduce the incentive to innovate, dampening long-run growth prospects.

In some industries, competition is "naturally" limited. In network industries, such as gas, electricity, and telecommunications, the fixed costs of creating a network are enormous. In such cases, it is often efficient for a single firm to create the network, so that the economy avoids paying for more than one network. This situation is referred to as a **natural monopoly**. Figure 4.2 summarizes the options for regulating this type of market failure.

Policy responses to natural monopolies cover two important areas. One is regulation to ensure that pricing remains as close as possible to competitive levels. In a situation of perfect information, it is possible for the government to implement regulated pricing. However, prices still need to be high enough for the monopolist to recoup its initial investment in setting up the network. In practice,

given governments' imperfect information on incumbents' cost structures, natural monopolists charge more than competitive firms.

A second policy response to a natural monopoly has been to try to ensure universal access to the network in question (box 4.3). One way of doing so is to impose a universal service obligation on the supplier. Such an obligation is generally combined with tolerance of cross-subsidized pricing to support the extension of the network to remote areas. Under this model, consumers in urban areas, where network construction is relatively inexpensive, pay somewhat higher prices than they otherwise would in order to subsidize network construction in rural areas. Some consumers therefore end up paying somewhat less than they would if they had to fully cover the costs of network construction themselves.

The regulatory response to natural monopolies has changed over time, at least in developed countries,

MODULE 4

Box 4.3. Good Policy Practice: Achieving Universal Postal Coverage in Trinidad and Tobago

Before reform, the postal service sector in Trinidad and Tobago was characterized by weak financial results, low investment, declining mail volumes, and poor service. On average, mail delivery took 7–10 days, and services reached only half of all households.

The government's reform strategy was to outsource management of TT Post, in the hope of transforming the company into a viable supplier. As part of a two-phased reform process, a delegated management arrangement was set up for five years with the goals of increasing customer satisfaction, achieving universal delivery, improving the quality of service, and raising total revenue and net income. All targets except net income were achieved or nearly achieved (daily coverage rose from 50 percent to 94 percent).

To provide the legislative and regulatory framework needed to support a management contract, the Postal Act of 1999 was established. It provides the new public postal corporation with more management autonomy and commercial flexibility. By engaging stakeholders, including major mailers, labor unions, customer groups, and private postal operators, the government built a broad consensus for reform.

Source: Guislain 2004.

---

primarily as a result of technological progress. The domain of natural monopolies has narrowed, as activities such as network creation and maintenance have been split off from activities such as the provision of services to end-users. Electricity markets were traditionally considered local natural monopolies, but the activities of generation and distribution can now be technically separated, with distribution based on a competitive service delivery model. Even the local monopoly of generation services has come into question, as national or regional grids and "smart" grids have made it possible for generators to compete for market share over a wider area.

Regulation has kept pace with these technological changes by focusing on the need to expand competition wherever possible, in particular through the division of activities. The crucial role for policymakers and regulators once competitive activities have been divested from historical operators is to regulate network access. The goal is to create equal access to all competitors on conditions that are neutral, even if some local monopolies remain.

Exclusive Access to Natural Resources

Limited competition necessarily arises when firms require exclusive access to a scarce resource in order to do business (figure 4.3). Sectors such as radio transmission or mobile telephony are good examples: both require exclusive access to parts of the electromagnetic spectrum. If two firms use the same part of the spectrum, they will be unable to do business, because interference will make signal transmission impossible. It is therefore in the public interest that scarce resources such as the electromagnetic spectrum be allocated so that each firm has exclusive rights to a particular part of the resource.

The policy response to this kind of limited competition is different from the response to a natural monopoly

or oligopoly. The problem in this case is not how to regulate an environment with limited competition but how to ensure that competition without regulation does not impose negative externalities on consumers through signal interference.

Licensing is a common solution to this problem. The spectrum is broken up into bands, each of which is given to a single service provider, which is granted a license to use that particular bandwidth. A regulator decides how much bandwidth is necessary for commercial operations and then allocates it in a way that prevents signal interference. The main economic question is how best to allocate licenses to ensure effective competition among licensees (this issue is discussed below in the context of regulatory strategies). One model involves identifying a fixed number of licenses based on bandwidth requirements and then auctioning them to firms. The regulator can use the auction to ensure that a sufficient number of firms enters the market to ensure a reasonable level of competition.

Public Good Characteristics

Only a few services have a pure public good characteristic. Many services have strong public good characteristics, however. Public goods are defined in terms of nonexcludability (the fact that consumers cannot be individually charged based on their consumption) and nonrivalry (the fact that one person's use of a good does not diminish the ability of another to consume it). Public goods create **positive externalities,** which entail a social benefit.

Many services have public characteristics in some situations. Health services, for example, have public good characteristics only in limited cases, such as vaccinations or control of epidemics. For most types of health care services, the consumer is the primary beneficiary. Many countries nevertheless treat health care services as a public good,

Figure 4.3. Options, Constraints, Levers, and Risks Associated with Regulating Exclusive or Controlled Access to Natural Resources

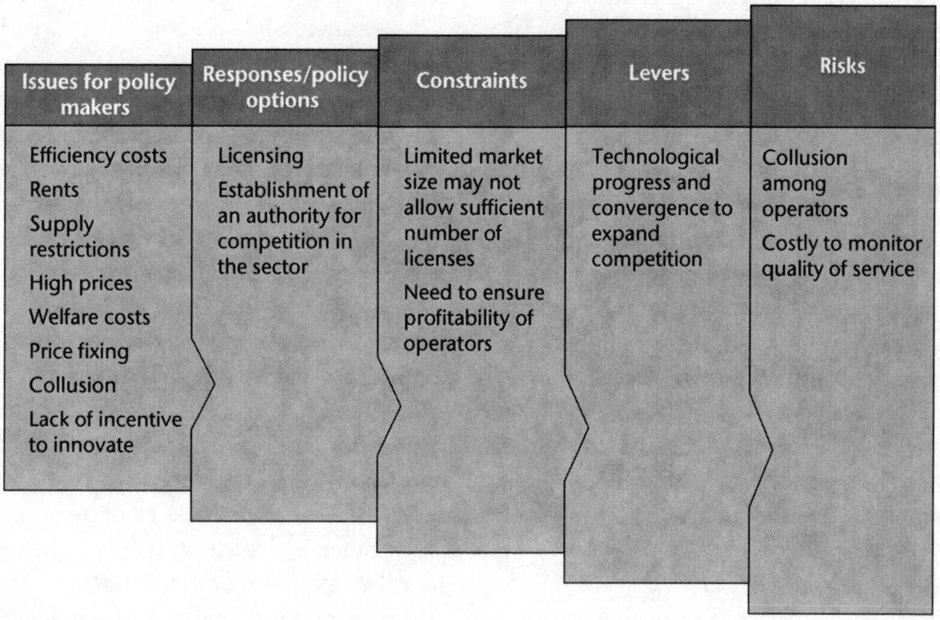

Issues for policy makers	Responses/policy options	Constraints	Levers	Risks
Efficiency costs	Licensing	Limited market size may not allow sufficient number of licenses	Technological progress and convergence to expand competition	Collusion among operators
Rents	Establishment of an authority for competition in the sector			Costly to monitor quality of service
Supply restrictions		Need to ensure profitability of operators		
High prices				
Welfare costs				
Price fixing				
Collusion				
Lack of incentive to innovate				

Box 4.4. Good Policy Practice: Increasing Access to Health Services in Thailand through Regulation Rather Than Provision

In Thailand, the government's role has changed from providing health services to regulating the health services market. During the last two to three decades, the government has moved toward a policy of contractual arrangements in which independent public and private institutions provide services. The shift happened against the background of economic growth during the 1990s.

The introduction of the Social Security Scheme in 1990, medical benefits provided by employers, and rising household demand spurred the rapid growth of private hospitals. In response, the government adopted policies regulating entry and quality control. Although problems—such as oversupply in urban areas—remain, Thailand seems to have moved in the right direction, giving more and more people access to health services.

Regulation is divided into regulation of health care institutions and regulation of professionals. The Ministry of Public Health is responsible for health institutions, controlling the licensing and renewals of private clinics and hospitals. The Social Security Scheme plays an active role through the price system: providers are paid a flat rate per registered worker regardless of the services they require. Professional organizations play a key role in granting certification and licensing for health professionals. The government created strong regulatory rules that require professionals to work a minimum number of years in community hospitals. Price controls for fees, especially for doctors in private hospitals, are weaker than they are for institutions. Quality performance and enforcement seem to require improvements for both health institutions and professionals.

Source: Teerawattananon and others 2003.

---

even though the real justification for regulating them is to ensure the social objective of caring for sick people (box 4.4).

Education, which is widely regarded as a public good, is actually only partially a public good, as a large share of the benefits accrue to the individual being educated (as wage differentials by level of education indicate). Society at large also benefits from education, however, making it a public good as well.

Regulation of pure or partial public goods is necessary because of two problems. The first is that the difference between private and social costs and benefits can result in underproduction of the good. The high costs of higher education, for instance, dampen demand, reducing the positive externalities created. The second is the **free-rider problem** (the fact that some people will consume a good without paying for it). For example, some neighbors may not be willing to pay for garbage collection, assuming that others will. This problem removes the incentive to produce the service. Regulation that aims to create adequate incentives to correct these market failures is therefore necessary to ensure that public goods are produced in socially

MODULE 4

optimal quantities. To do so, developing countries have adopted various policies over the last decade, including **public-private partnerships** (such as the contracting out of selected services or facilities), the development of purchasing arrangements, franchising, and the use of vouchers (figure 4.4).

Consumer Protection

In professions such as law and medicine, failure to provide adequate services can have serious consequences for consumers. Low-quality services in the transport sector also pose safety problems.

The problem can be analyzed through the lens of asymmetric information: consumers want to use "good" services providers but have no way of assessing quality until after they consume the service. Regulation has a role to play in establishing mechanisms that allow only "good" providers to operate.

Licensing is one way of dealing with this market failure. Only people who meet certain standards of education and training are authorized to practice law or medicine in most countries (figure 4.5). Commercial drivers are required to be licensed in most countries. Regulation can never eliminate information asymmetries: service providers of varying skill levels will always be present in the market. Licensing requirements can help exclude providers that fail to meet certain standards, however.

Dealing with information asymmetries is a strong economic rationale for licensing restrictions in some services sectors. The question is how strict these restrictions should be. A related concern is the extent to which regulatory procedures should prescribe particular activities, such as completion of training programs or demonstration of certain competencies. Many licensing regimes impose both sets of requirements. Aspiring lawyers in the United States, for example, must demonstrate that they have completed a period of study at a U.S. or foreign law school and then pass an exam to demonstrate competency. The nature and scope of these types of requirements is crucial in assessing the extent to which they achieve the social objective of minimizing information asymmetries in an economically efficient way.

Assessing the quality of a service is even more difficult than assessing the skills of a provider. Even highly trained surgeons occasionally make errors of judgment or perform an operation in a suboptimal way. Some countries and sectors deal with this problem through compulsory insurance schemes. In professions such as law, for example, services providers are often required to purchase liability insurance to ensure that if the service is provided in an unsatisfactory manner, the consumer has financial recourse against the provider and can be compensated for any losses caused as a result.

Governments can also require providers to be nationals or residents of the country in which the consumer is located.

Figure 4.4. Options, Constraints, Levers, and Risks Associated with Regulating Public Goods

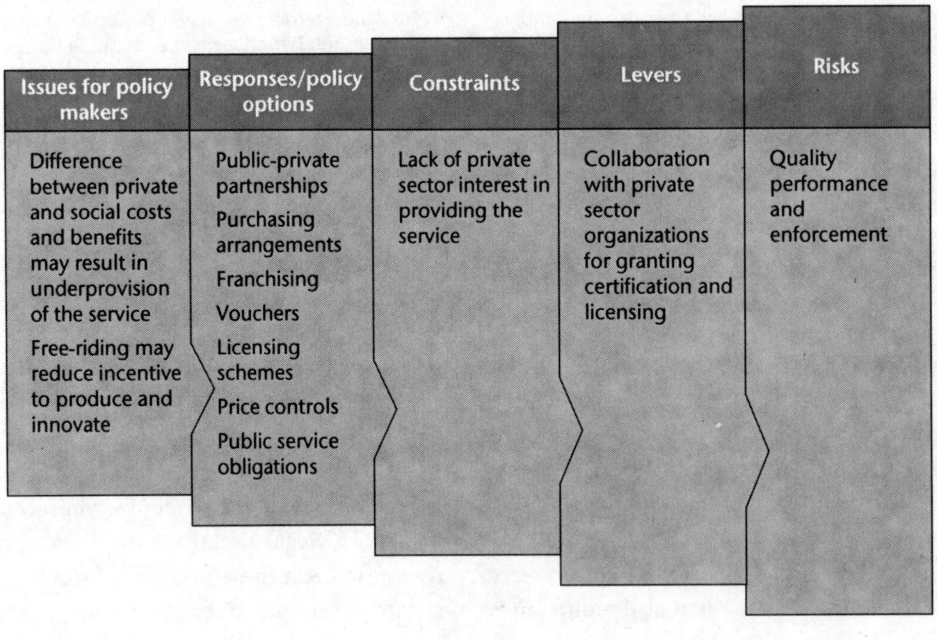

Issues for policy makers	Responses/policy options	Constraints	Levers	Risks
Difference between private and social costs and benefits may result in underprovision of the service Free-riding may reduce incentive to produce and innovate	Public-private partnerships Purchasing arrangements Franchising Vouchers Licensing schemes Price controls Public service obligations	Lack of private sector interest in providing the service	Collaboration with private sector organizations for granting certification and licensing	Quality performance and enforcement

Figure 4.5. Options, Constraints, Levers, and Risks Associated with Addressing Health and Safety Concerns in the Presence of Asymmetric Information

Issues for policy makers	Responses/policy options	Constraints	Levers	Risks
Asymmetric information between provider and user Risk of moral hazard	Licensing schemes Certification requirements Compulsory insurance schemes Nationality restrictions or residency obligations	Impossibility of obtaining perfect information	Increasing quality competition by liberalizing market to foreign providers	Reducing market contestability Creating a closed profession

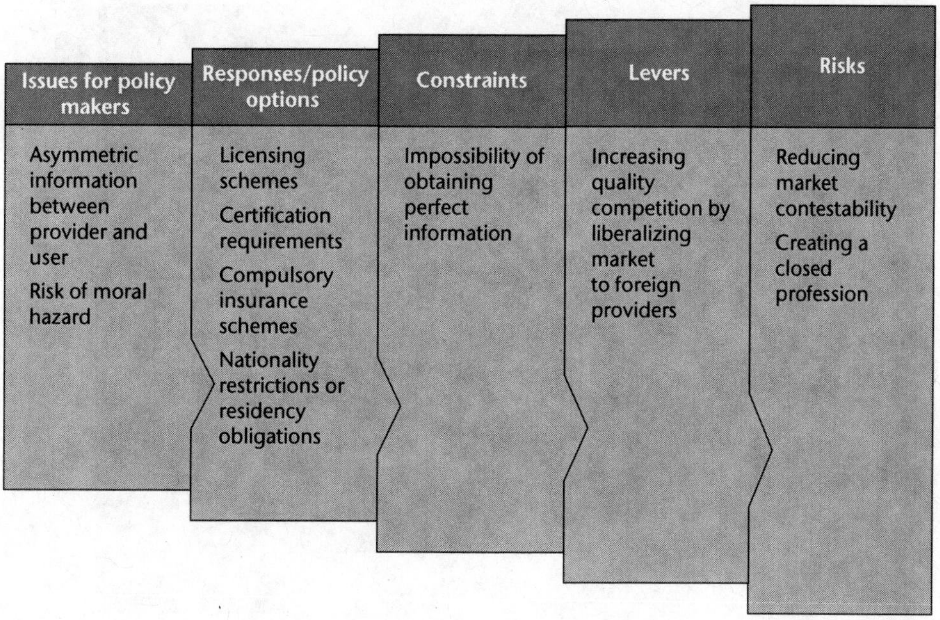

This type of restriction helps ensure that the consumer can sue the services provider for inadequate service (the cost and complexity of suing a defendant abroad make doing so very difficult). Alternatively, governments can require foreign providers to keep a minimum level of assets within the jurisdiction (capital requirement). Doing so provides consumers with an asset pool that can be drawn from if necessary.

Financial Sector Stability

Financial services are a topic of special public policy interest because of their centrality in the economic system. The importance of this sector was made clear during and after the global financial crisis of 2008–09. One justification for special policy intervention in the financial sector has to do with information asymmetry, which is particularly great in retail banking. Consumers want to invest their money in good banks and good financial instruments, but they cannot judge for themselves whether a bank is financially stable. The flip side of this problem is that sudden distrust of a bank can create a run that could lead to the failing of the bank, even if it was healthy.

A variety of policy responses address this problem. Publicly listed banks can be required to disclose substantial financial information. Even with such disclosures, however, which are usually difficult to understand,

consumers may not be able to identify good banks. Most governments therefore also establish a licensing system for the banking sector (figure 4.6). This kind of regulation forces banks that accept deposits from the public to meet minimum standards of capital adequacy. To limit the possibility of bank runs, most economies also require banks to participate in a deposit insurance scheme. Banks are usually also subject to a sectoral regulator, which can be the central bank or an independent body. This body needs to have wide powers of oversight and intervention in order to force banks to remain financially sound.

Outside banking, particularly the retail banking sector, regulation is also required. Insurance companies are generally subject to licensing requirements with capital adequacy tests. They are also supervised by regulators with broad powers. Other financial services providers are sometimes subject to licensing requirements, particularly when they deal with small retail investors or engage directly in market transactions. Wholesale financial institutions, such as investment banks, private equity firms, and hedge funds, are less heavily regulated than retail banking, because the problem of information asymmetry is assumed to be less severe. Unlike retail consumers, wholesale investors are assumed to have sophisticated knowledge of finance. They are expected to calculate risks they take. From a **moral hazard** vantage point, it is

MODULE 4

Figure 4.6. Options, Constraints, Levers, and Risks Associated with Dealing with Asymmetric Information between Providers and Consumers of Financial Services

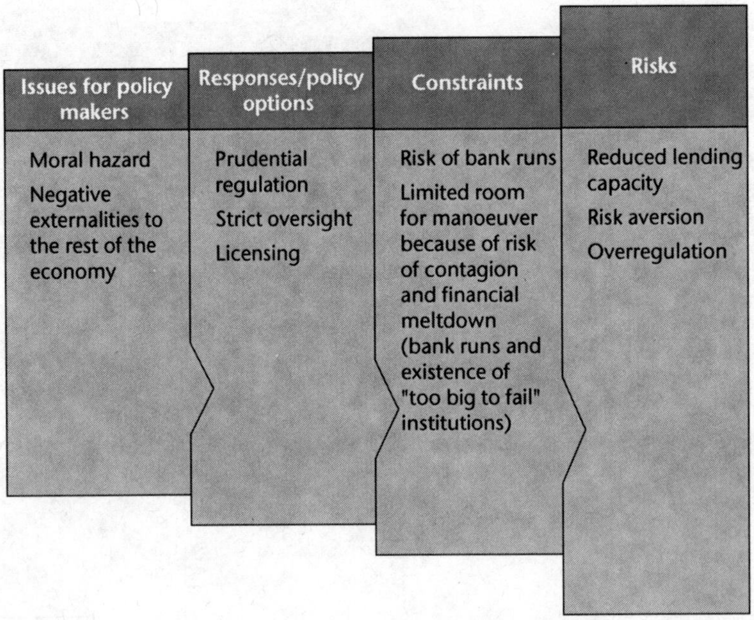

Issues for policy makers	Responses/policy options	Constraints	Risks
Moral hazard Negative externalities to the rest of the economy	Prudential regulation Strict oversight Licensing	Risk of bank runs Limited room for manoeuver because of risk of contagion and financial meltdown (bank runs and existence of "too big to fail" institutions)	Reduced lending capacity Risk aversion Overregulation

---

Box 4.5. What Are the Effects of Planning and Zoning Regulations?

Many studies have been conducted on the effects of regulation related to planning and zoning of the retail sector, most of them on developed countries. After reviewing these studies, the Australian Productivity Commission concluded that land use regulation that centralizes retail activity can either enhance or reduce competition. The effects depend on how regulatory policies are designed and implemented. Research on the impact of regulations that restrict the establishment of large-format stores suggests that such regulations reduce retail productivity and retail employment and raise consumer prices. Other evidence suggests that land use regulations raise residential and commercial property prices. The Productivity Commission concluded that in order to reduce the anticompetitive effects of zoning, policy makers need to make sure that sufficient floor space is allocated to retailers and that there are larger zones. These measures can increase productivity and eventually welfare by allowing new and innovative firms to enter the local market while allowing existing firms to expand.

Source: Australian Productivity Commission 2011.

---

appropriate that they be left to bear the consequences of their decisions.

Environmental Protection

Environmental protection is frequently used to justify regulation of products and packaging. Although it is a less obvious reason for restricting trade in services, it plays an important role in some situations. One is town planning. Many localities impose restrictions on the types of businesses that can establish facilities in particular areas. Other examples include regulations affecting tourism and transport services.

Planning restrictions are particularly important in the retail sector. Many jurisdictions limit the urban areas in which supermarkets and other large retailers can be established, in an attempt to reduce environmental externalities. Restrictions that prescribe the use of roads at specific hours of the day or the size of the vehicle affect market participants who need to establish transportation and distribution centers, which are necessary for supermarkets and large retailers. Another rationale for regulation is the desire to protect small retailers from competition (box 4.5). On economic grounds, this rationale is weaker, because there is no market failure that needs to be corrected. Indeed, such regulation can have negative consequences on consumer welfare. The question, therefore, is not how to implement these regulatory restrictions in the most efficient way but how regulators can put the interests of the majority (consumers) ahead of the interests of an organized minority (store owners).

Technology Transfer

The presence of foreign investors can generate positive spillover effects or externalities for domestic firms in the same sector, particularly through technology upgrading and the development of workforce capabilities. Some developing countries believe that multinational corporations create such spillovers.

For services, the term *production technology* needs to be understood in terms that include all means by which a firm produces its services, including management competence, improvement of organization structures, and the methods used to produce a tailored service for consumers. Some types of "technology" increase productivity within the firm and, in the longer run, the sector. Triplett and Bosworth (2004) find that services sectors accounted for most of the improvements in labor productivity and total factor productivity in the United States after 1995. They note that especially in the financial and distribution sectors, productivity accelerated, in large part because of managerial innovations such as outsourcing and specialization, as well new concepts of retailing.

To stimulate technology spillover, governments often impose an obligation that a foreign investor work with a local firm, through a **joint venture** or similar arrangement (figure 4.7). A joint venture is a business agreement in which the foreign and local firm agree to develop a new product, service, or production procedure. Restrictions on the legal form of foreign investment that stimulate cooperation with local firms can increase technology spillover.

Another way of ensuring that firm-specific technological factors of a foreign company become embedded in the local economy is to require that the foreign firm hires local workers, who learn from exposure to foreign technologies and practices. Restrictions can also be imposed that require foreign firms to employ some local directors or managers (box 4.6). These regulations are usually considered to be barriers to services trade. Trade agreements aim at eliminating them.

Trade Policy Barriers

Limitations or restrictions on trade in services take many different forms, discriminatory and nondiscriminatory, direct and indirect. These measures are usually more complex than trade restrictions on goods.

Barriers may be aimed to the service itself or the services provider. If, for example, credit cards can be provided only by established institutions in a particular country, the credit card

Figure 4.7. Options, Constraints, Levers, and Risks Associated with Promoting Technology Transfer

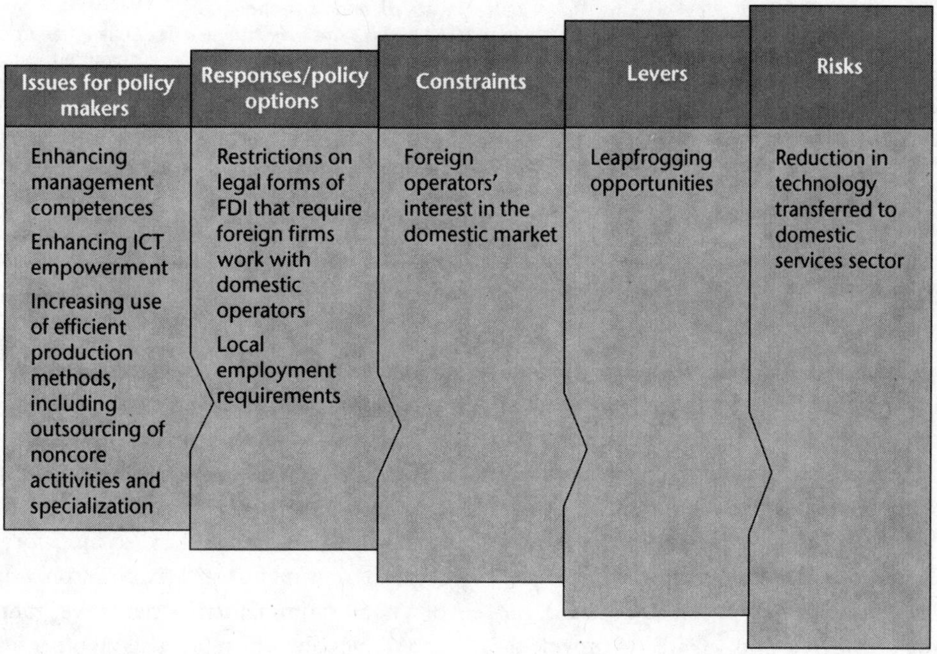

Issues for policy makers	Responses/policy options	Constraints	Levers	Risks
Enhancing management competences Enhancing ICT empowerment Increasing use of efficient production methods, including outsourcing of noncore actitivities and specialization	Restrictions on legal forms of FDI that require foreign firms work with domestic operators Local employment requirements	Foreign operators' interest in the domestic market	Leapfrogging opportunities	Reduction in technology transferred to domestic services sector

Note: FDI = foreign direct investment, ICT = information and communication technology.

MODULE 4

Box 4.6 How Can Developing Countries Increase the Technological Capabilities of Their Services Sector?

Several routes can increase technological capabilities in the host country:

- encouraging trade and providing aid to strengthen production by domestic firms
- providing FDI and contracting with domestic firms to build local export-oriented companies
- developing local subcontracting capacity.

Sector development, and eventually higher productivity and growth, increase only slowly, especially for slow and very late industrializers. Slow industrializers are countries in which the manufacturing sector accounts for no more than 15 percent of GDP (examples include Algeria, India, and South Africa). Very late industrializers are low-income countries with even smaller manufacturing bases. Experience in East Asia suggests that acquiring established technologies and building up technological capabilities based on their application can spur growth.

For some very late industrializers, the conventional route of industrial development may not be appropriate. Low-income countries often lack an industrial base or have an agriculture sector that contributes only marginally to economic output. Some developing countries, therefore, have adopted the strategy of **leapfrogging**—skipping more "traditional" development paths. Firms in China, for example, have moved from producing products for the domestic market to production activities through joint ventures that are organized around global supply chains.

Leapfrogging often takes place in services sectors. Low-tech leapfrogging is found in the tourism industry. Developing countries have capitalized on their good weather and labor resources. Governments have invested in and imported management skills. Recent examples of leapfrogging include software development and lower-tech back office functions, such as call centers. What is needed in such cases are good technological infrastructure and telecommunication systems, which can be obtained through foreign participation.

A crucial difference between goods and services is that for services, countries need only to adapt the technology to provide the service; they do not need to replicate or develop technologies. Adapting the technology requires good-quality infrastructure, the ability to add value, and the availability of technically trained labor.

Source: Bennet 2002.

Table 4.2. Examples of Restriction on Trade in Services, by Mode

Mode 1 (cross-border trade)	Mode 2 (consumption abroad)	Mode 3 (commercial presence)	Mode 4 (movement of natural persons)
• Local registration; local agent; local presence; and authorization, license, or permit required to market or supply services.	• Local registration of offshore provider—applied on a transparent, readily accessible, and nondiscriminatory basis—required to market services. • Transfer of capital, payments, or use of credit cards for transactions subject to authorization. • Trade permitted only through firms with commercial presence in country or specific "brand-name" entities.	• Full or partial acquisition of existing businesses not permitted. • Restrictions on establishment of new businesses. • Reservation of some sectors or activities, state-owned enterprises to be privatized, and government-contracted services, for investment only by nationals or permanent residents. • Requirement that providers established in one part of a country have a minimum number of resident providers of their agents for provision in another part of a country.	• Permission for specific categories of personnel subject to approval and labor market tests. • Approval for intercorporate transferees and specialists subject to general economic needs test. • Only intracorporate transferees permitted, subject to a limit of two foreign transferees per operation and mandatory training of local staff. • Provision of services by self-employed persons not permitted.

Source: Adapted from Thomson and Nielson 2001.

service is affected. If instead a regulatory policy prescribes that credit card services can be provided only by financial institutions owned or controlled by nationals, the restriction affects both the service and providers of credit card services.

The provision and trade of a service can be limited through specific modes of supply. When, for example, the national government is the sole provider of a service (as in the case of education and health care services in some countries), foreign and domestic providers are not allowed to provide the service through any mode of supply. This measure affects

market access through all modes of supply. Table 4.2 provides other examples of some restrictions by mode.

Barriers to trade can be discriminatory or nondiscriminatory. Discriminatory measures target foreign providers; nondiscriminatory measures affect all firms, foreign and domestic. An example of a discriminatory barrier is a tax imposed only on foreign services or providers. An example of a nondiscriminatory barrier is the granting of a market to a monopoly, which prevents all other firms, foreign and domestic, from accessing the market (table 4.3).

Table 4.3. Policies Affecting Trade in Services

Nature of policy	Policies on entry/ establishment	Policies on ongoing operations
Nondiscriminatory	Licensing requirements	Quality and safety requirements
Discriminatory	Special requirements for foreign operators	Requirement that foreign operators comply with additional requirements such as rules governing technology transfer

Source: Deardorff and Stern 2008.

Barriers affecting trade in services can be explicit (de jure) or implicit (de facto). Explicit measures are clear, known by firms, and comprehensible; they are formulated in a transparent way. When a regulatory barrier is implicit, it may be created by the effect of the regulations on the provider. A language requirement, for example, may prevent a foreign entity from providing a service. Both explicit and implicit regulations increase costs, raising prices for consumers.

Discriminatory enforcement of a trade barrier or regulatory policy may also limit trade. De facto discrimination may also occur when the absence of a regulatory policy may affect a provider's ability to deliver a service. In network industries such as telecommunications, for example, providers must be able to access the infrastructure to provide a service. The absence of a legal requirement requiring access and use of the infrastructure may affect the provision of the service.

Typology of Services Barriers

A wide range of regulations restrict trade in services. Table 4.4 provides a typology of barriers and restrictions that are subject for negotiations in trade agreements. Agreements reflect the international efforts to classify and eliminate restrictions that affect trade in services. The following sections discuss all three types of barriers and provide some empirical findings showing their impact on trade.

Market access

Under the General Agreement on Trade in Services (GATS) and other trade agreements, market access restrictions include barriers that may or may not discriminate against foreign firms. The GATS defines six types of market access limitations, which can affect all modes of supply:

- the number of service suppliers, monopolies, or exclusive service suppliers
- the total value of assets or service transactions

- the total number of service operations or volume of service output
- the total number of natural persons that may be employed in a sector
- restrictions or requirements specific to the type of legal entity through which a service supplier can supply a service
- limits on foreign ownership (participation of foreign capital).

Barriers to services trade distort trade patterns and reduce welfare gains. Based on data from the World Bank's Services Trade Restrictions Index (STRI) Database (box 4.7), Borchert, Gootiiz, and Mattoo (2012a, 2012b) find that merger and acquisition activity by foreign firms is lower in countries that restrict ownership to a minority stake. Other significant barriers include discriminatory licensing criteria, restrictions on the repatriation of earnings, and the inability to appeal licensing decisions. Surprisingly, the authors do not find limits on the number of licenses to be a significant barrier.

Using detailed cross-border data, Shepherd and van der Marel (2013) investigate the role of the STRI barriers on services trade by sector. They find that restrictions in Mode 1 have a detrimental effect on total services (when all services are taken together) and on transportation services specifically, but surprisingly not on other specific services sectors. In contrast, regulatory restrictions on Mode 3 have a greater negative effect than Mode 1 restrictions on services trade flows for business, financial, and insurance services. The authors provide evidence of cross-modal substitution effects in total services trade but complementarity effects in business, financial, and insurance services.

National treatment

National treatment measures are domestic regulations that discriminate, in a de jure or de facto manner, against foreign services and services providers. GATS Article XVII requires that once foreign services providers enter the domestic market, they should not face less favorable terms than domestic providers. The GATS does not contain an exhaustive list of measures that may limit national treatment. Measures that fall within national treatment restrictions include prior residency requirements for the issuance of a license to supply a service; subsidies or tax rules that discriminate against foreign providers; and restrictions on the purchase, lease, or use of real estate. Market access and national treatment limitations are the main focus of services negotiations at the multilateral level.

Empirical studies explicitly measuring the role of national treatment are rare. Some studies analyze the

MODULE 4

Table 4.4. Typology of Barriers to Trade in Services

Type of barrier	Type of effect (direct or indirect)	Examples	Sources of information on restrictions
Restricted market access	Direct: Restrictions (usually quantitative) on foreign entry into domestic markets	• Number of service suppliers, monopolies, or exclusive service suppliers' total value of assets or service transactions • Total number of service operations or volume of service output • Total number of natural persons that may be employed in a sector • Restrictions or requirements specific to the type of legal entity through which a service supplier can supply a service • Limits on foreign ownership (participation of foreign capital) • Restrictions on the movement of people	• WTO/GATS (http://i-tip.wto.org/services/) • World Bank Services Trade Restrictiveness Index (STRI)
National treatment requirements	Direct: De jure discrimination against foreign firms or de facto discriminatory impact	• Discriminatory requirements • Discriminatory taxes or limiting of subsidies to nationals only • Restrictions related to competition • Restrictions on property or land use • Residency requirement for obtaining license to provide a service • Domestic preference on the allocation of bandwidth frequencies for transmission within the national territory	• WTO/GATS (http://i-tip.wto.org/services/) • OECD (http://www.oecd.org/economy/growth/indicatorsofproductmarketregulationhomepage.htm)
Domestic regulation	Indirect: Nondiscriminatory regulations that do not explicitly target foreign firms but have an impact on trade. These measures can be categorized as "entry" or "conduct" measures (measures that affect the operation of the firm).	• Qualification and licensing requirements and (licensing or qualification) procedures that are lengthy, complex, and nontransparent, which discourage foreign service providers from seeking access to markets • Technical standards • Lack of objective and transparent authorization criteria • Public service obligations for quality and social policy reasons • Rules governing conduct and operations, including limits on advertising and store opening hours, regulations on prices and fees, burdensome migration requirements, and regulations on the form of business and interprofessional cooperation • Restrictions on ownership, including barriers to vertical integration	• WTO/GATS (http://i-tip.wto.org/services/) • World Bank Doing Business • OECD Product Market Regulations (http://www.oecd.org/economy/growth/indicatorsofproductmarketregulationhomepage.htm)

Note: GATS = General Agreement on Trade in Services, OECD = Organisation for Economic Co-operation and Development, WTO = World Trade Organization.

discriminatory and nondiscriminatory effects of services policies on the welfare of developing countries using **computable general equilibrium models.**

Jensen and Tarr (2012) estimate the gains to Armenia from creating a deep and comprehensive trade agreement with the European Union that also includes further liberalization of barriers in services. They estimate these barriers (a) using an index in which regulatory barriers impose costs on both domestic and multinational firms in a nondiscriminatory manner and (b) examining discriminatory barriers against multinational services providers only. They find that the gains from nondiscriminatory liberalization

of services plus tariff barriers are about three times the gains from a preferential liberalization of goods and services with the European Union alone. They also find that more than 85 percent of the gains from unilateral liberalization come from liberalization of services rather than tariff liberalization.

Using similar modeling techniques, Jensen, Rutherford, and Tarr (2008) estimate that the welfare gains for Tanzania of full reform of services are equal to 5.3 percent of Tanzanian consumption in the medium run and 16 percent in the long run. The medium-term gains derive primarily from the removal of inefficient

Box 4.7. The World Bank's Services Trade Restrictiveness Index (STRI) Database

The STRI Database includes information from 103 countries, including 79 developing countries and 24 Organisation for Economic Co-operation and Development (OECD) countries. The data were collected during 2007–08. An update using the original methodology and 2012 data did not reveal significant changes.

The database focuses on five sectors: financial services (banking and insurance), telecommunications, retail distribution, transportation, and professional services (accounting and legal services only), with each sector disaggregated into subsectors as applicable. Within each subsector, the database covers the most relevant modes of supply.

The measures affecting commercial presence are classified under the following broad categories:

- requirements regarding the legal form of entry and restrictions on foreign equity
- limits on licenses and discrimination in their allocation
- transparency and accountability of licensing
- restrictions on ongoing operations
- relevant aspects of the regulatory environment.

For some sectors, this information is supplemented with specific issues, such as regulation to ensure access to the market in telecommunications. For cross-border transactions, the focus is on conditions under which trade takes place. The temporary movement of people is covered only in professional services.

Within each subsector and mode, policy regimes are rated using the scale shown in table B4.7.1.

Table B4.7.1. Levels of Trade Openness in the World Bank's Services Trade Restrictiveness Index (STRI) Database

Level of openness	Score
Completely open	0
Virtually open but with minor restrictions	25
Major restrictions	50
Virtually closed, with limited opportunities to enter or operate	75
Completely closed	100

Source: http://iresearch.worldbank.org/servicestrade/.

nondiscriminatory regulatory barriers against service providers and of regulatory barriers against multinational service providers. In a similar study of Kenya, Balistreri, Rutherford, and Tarr (2009) find even larger welfare gains. These gains are explained largely by the liberalization of services policies.

Domestic regulation

In contrast to market access and national treatment, domestic regulatory barriers are not a primary concern of GATS negotiations. However, the GATS does call upon World Trade Organization (WTO) members to develop any necessary disciplines to ensure that measures relating to qualification requirements and procedures, technical standards, and licensing requirements and procedures do not constitute unnecessary barriers to trade in services. For example, excessively lengthy, complex, and nontransparent licensing procedures may discourage foreign firms from entering a market even if there are no explicit discriminatory barriers. Lack of objective and transparent criteria on

which regulators grant access to the domestic market can be viewed as a hidden protectionist barrier. To prevent domestic regulations from reducing trade in services, they should be based on objective and transparent criteria, be no more burdensome than necessary to ensure the quality of the service, and not themselves restrict supply, in the case of licensing procedures (box 4.8).[3]

Restrictiveness of Services Barriers

Triplett and Bosworth (2004) show that in the United States, services are a critical source of labor productivity and total factor productivity (TFP) growth. Inklaar, Timmer, and van Ark (2008) confirm this conclusion across countries by showing that observed differences in productivity growth and levels are explained mainly by services, particularly business services, rather than goods or ICT investments.

Foreign competition in the form of trade in services can increase productivity in the wider economy. This

MODULE 4

Box 4.8. Domestic Regulations and the World Trade Organization's Necessity Test

The General Agreement on Trade in Services (GATS) provides for a "necessity test" in Article VI:4 (domestic regulations) and in the Article XIV exceptions. Broadly speaking, a necessity test examines four issues:

- Legal rulings relating to the objectives of the measure. The Appellate Body has consistently ruled that it is not the necessity of the policy objective that is to be examined but the necessity of the measure to achieve the intended policy objective.
- The level of attainment a member is seeking to achieve with the measure. The Appellate Body has ruled that the choice of a measure can indicate the objective sought by it as well as the level of protection the measure intends to achieve.
- The necessity of the measure.
- The burden of proof.

Necessity figures in three of the exceptions to General Agreement on Tariffs and Trade (GATT) Article XX. Panels have relied on a balancing approach in analyzing necessity. In the leading World Trade Organization (WTO) case on this issue, analyzing a discriminatory Korean regime for imported beef, the Appellate Body noted that claims of necessity must be evaluated in relation to the circumstances and that the evaluation involves a process of weighing and balancing a series of factors. These factors include the actual contribution made by the measure to achieving the stated objective within Article XX, the importance of the common interests or values protected, and the restrictive impact of the measure on trade. In this and other cases, the Appellate Body looked for a relation between the measure and the end pursued that is not just a contribution to accomplishing the objective but is closer to being indispensable to accomplishing that objective. The party must demonstrate that its measures are necessary by providence evidence establishing that the measures contribute to the achievement of the objectives pursued. Evaluation of a measure's necessity also requires evaluation of its restrictive effect on trade (or on the behind-the-border sale or distribution of imports, if the issue is behind-the-border discriminatory regulations). The less restrictive a nontariff measure is, the more likely it is to be deemed "necessary."

In the Korean beef (WTO 2000) and U.S. gambling (WTO 2005) cases, the Appellate Body clarified that as a panel evaluates necessity, it must examine whether the defending party could reasonably be expected to employ an alternative measure that is WTO consistent (or less WTO inconsistent) that would achieve the objectives pursued by the measure at issue. An alternative measure may not be "reasonably available" (that is, it may be relevant only in theory) or it may impose an undue burden on a member (examples include prohibitive costs or technical difficulties in implementation). Moreover, an alternative measure that is "reasonably available" must preserve the defending party's right to achieve its desired level of protection with respect to the objective pursued under Article XX. Where the complaining party identifies an alternative measure, the defending party has the burden of demonstrating that its GATT-inconsistent measure is "necessary."

To determine whether an alternative measure exists, the panel must evaluate whether the measure is economically and technically feasible from an economic and technical point of view, whether the alternative would achieve the same objectives as the original measure, and whether it is less trade restrictive than the measure analyzed. If any of these conditions is not met, the alternative measure is deemed to be incompatible with WTO obligations.

Sources: WTO 2000, 2003, 2005, 2011; Cadot, Maliszewska, and Sáez 2011.

---

finding is reflected in trade studies analyzing the effect of reducing domestic regulatory policies and trade barriers in services on productivity or TFP, particularly in the manufacturing sector.

Arnold, Mattoo, and Narciso (2008) analyze the relationship between communications, financial, and electricity services on firm TFP in the manufacturing sector. They show that countries with competitive and efficient telecom markets can provide new phone line connections in a few days; in countries with inefficient public monopolies, it may take months to establish a new connection. According to the authors, efficient telecom services have had a positive effect on the productivity of firms in Africa.

Other econometric country case studies corroborate evidence that reducing domestic regulatory barriers to foreign competition increases manufacturing TFP. Examining the reform process in the Czech Republic, Arnold, Javorcik, and Mattoo (2011) find a positive and statistically significant relationship between firm performance in manufacturing and policy measures such as overall reform in

services for both domestic and foreign providers, the presence of foreign providers in the services sectors, and the level of privatization. Allowing foreign entry into services industries appears to be the key channel for higher TFP in goods industries.

Arnold and others (2010) assess the effect of services policy reforms in India on TFP in the manufacturing sector. They find that private sector participation, liberalization of decisions on operational activities, and the scope for foreign participation increase downstream productivity.

Barriers that are not explicitly addressed in trade agreements may constitute barriers to trade in services. Migration restrictions that include visa requirements and other administrative necessities may form a barrier to trade. Interdiction of vertical integration of the production process may also act as a barrier for services firms.

The OECD, the World Bank, and the Australian Productivity Commission have each developed methodologies to assess the importance of a variety of regulatory policies (boxes 4.9 and 4.10). This research has attempted

---

Box 4.9. The Australian Productivity Commission's Trade Restrictiveness Index

The Australian Productivity Commission has developed indexes of policy reform in services for economies in Europe, Asia, and North and South America. It defines two broad sets of regulations: establishment (or entry) barriers and barriers on operational activities.

Depending on the sector, establishment barriers normally refer to the form of establishment (foreign partnership or joint venture), nationality or citizenship requirements, residency or local presence, quotas or economic needs test, licensing, and regulations affecting the permanent movement of people. Operational barriers are activities reserved to certain professions or providers. They include limits on advertising and fees and restrictions on the temporary movement of people. For both types of barriers, the Australian Productivity Commission distinguishes between discriminatory and nondiscriminatory measures.

A Services Trade Restrictiveness Index score is calculated for each economy. Scores are assigned to each restriction on the basis of a judgment about how stringent it is. The more stringent the restriction, the higher the score (scores range from 0 to 1). The restriction categories are then weighted based on a judgment about their relative economic cost.

Separate indexes are calculated for domestic and foreign providers. The foreign index measures all restrictions, discriminatory and nondiscriminatory, that hinder foreign firms from entering and operating in an economy. The domestic index includes restrictions applied to domestic firms. It generally covers only nondiscriminatory restrictions. The difference between the foreign and domestic scores is a measure of discrimination against foreigners.

Box 4.10. Static and Dynamic Impact of Restrictions on Entry and Operations

There are important differences between measures restricting market access and measures affecting operations. On a purely static basis, entry barriers tend to create rents for incumbents that might be partly shared with the state if, for example, licenses are sold rather than being given out. Removal of such restrictions increases consumer surplus and reallocates rents away from producers and the state. Measures that increase the cost of doing business "waste" economic resources, in the sense that goods and services must be allocated to paying for activities that produce no gains for the national economy. In a dynamic sense, it is not obvious that the gains from removing cost-creating measures outweigh the gains from removing market entry barriers. Market entry barriers are often associated with dynamic inefficiencies—a waste of economic resources—that are greatly reduced when markets are made more contestable. When a services market with a domestic monopolist is opened up to international competition by the elimination of an unduly strict licensing requirement, for example, there is not just an increase in consumer surplus, there is also a reduction in the cost of doing business because of the need to be more efficient in the face of competition from foreign service providers.

Keeping the dynamic gains in mind suggests the need to sequence reform. In general, market entry barriers should be removed first, because they stimulate competition, at least in markets that are not freely contestable, as is the case in services markets in many developing countries.

An additional reason for preferring market entry barriers as the starting place for reform is that the gains from reducing the costs of doing business are unlikely to be fully passed on to consumers in noncompetitive environments. Dealing effectively and efficiently with measures that restrict market entry is therefore often a necessary prerequisite to reducing the cost of doing business for firms already in the market and ensuring that the benefits are passed on to consumers.

---

to go beyond the classifications employed in trade negotiations by including a wider range of limitations. These studies have tried not to assess the letter of the law but rather whether access is provided in practice.

Little quantitative analysis has been conducted on whether wider policy barriers in services have an effect on performance. Van der Marel (2012) finds that services trade—particularly inward FDI and services imports—has a significant effect on TFP in services. These effects are inhibited by domestic and FDI regulation. Regulation is the main factor explaining cross-country differences in TFP growth over time while domestic and FDI-conduct restrictions are the most important factors explaining TFP growth in services. These regulatory barriers include limits on advertising, regulations on store hours, regulations on prices and fees, and regulation of the form of

business and interprofessional cooperation. Van der Marel (2012) finds that conduct regulation within each services sector is a more robust factor in explaining TFP growth than entry barriers.

Quantifying Regulatory Barriers

The aim of a quantitative assessment is to calculate the benefits and costs of maintaining or implementing services regulations. It is conducted for policy makers in order to choose the most efficient regulatory mix.

Molinuevo and Sáez (2014) review the literature on services trade. They describe some methods used to assess the impact of regulatory frameworks on services, particularly the impact of regulations on the provision, price, and cost of services.

Quantitative methods can be classified according to three not mutually exclusive taxonomies:

- whether they employ direct or indirect measures
- whether they focus on sectoral or economywide impacts
- whether they use a retrospective or prospective approach.

Direct methods gather information on restrictions and policy, to include in econometric analyses in order to assess the impact on outcomes of interest. Researchers lacking direct information on restrictions use **indirect methods**. They estimate or infer the level of openness, restrictiveness, or contestability of a market by comparing countries against a benchmark (a country with no or few restrictions). The main limitations of indirect methods are that the resulting estimated restrictions may well be capturing more than trade barriers and it usually proves difficult to link the estimates to a specific policy measure, making this approach less suitable than direct methods for guiding policy decisions.

Because a wide range of regulations affects the provision of services, comparing the contestability of markets across countries can be difficult. Studies normally deal with this problem by constructing indexes that try to summarize in one indicator a set of policies affecting the provision of a services category in a country. Once the methodology is applied to several countries, the market contestability of a category can be compared across economies (see box 4.7 and Borchet, Gootiiz, and Matoo 2012a for an in-depth discussion of the World Bank's restrictiveness index methodology).

Gravity models can be used to quantify country-specific barriers. Various methodologies can be used to quantify the level of regulatory protection in domestic markets for services of an importing country, including a quantity-based approach that measures barriers by estimating tariff equivalents. The methodology most commonly applied in the literature, as proposed by Park (2002), computes the average protection applied by each importer from the residuals of an estimated gravity model of trade for services. The approach compares actual levels of trade flows with potential levels of trade, given the physical and economic characteristics of countries and their trading partners. As the residuals may be capturing factors other than trade barriers, actual and predicted trade are normalized relative to a theoretical situation considered to be the free-trade benchmark. This benchmark is the country in the sample with the highest level of actual imports relative to predicted imports.

Formally, the tariff equivalent of importing country j, τ_j, is calculated as

$$\ln(1+\tau_j) = \left(\ln\left(\frac{\sum_{i \neq j} M_j^{actual}}{\sum_{i \neq j} M_j^{predicted}} \right) - \ln\left(\frac{\sum_{i \neq j} M_{benchmark}^{actual}}{\sum_{i \neq j} M_{benchmark}^{predicted}} \right) \right)^{1/-\sigma}$$

where $\sum_{i \neq j} M_j$ is the sum of imports over all trading partners, M_j^{actual} and $M_j^{predicted}$ are actual and predicted imports from the gravity model of trade, $M_{benchmark}$ is imports by the free-trade benchmark country (the country with the lowest ratio of actual to predicted imports), and σ is the elasticity of substitution. The same gravity model specification is estimated in table 3.11, except that the STRI variables are excluded, in order to be consistent with the literature in allowing the residuals to fully capture the barriers to services trade. For robustness, two separate values of the elasticity of substitution are assumed, $\sigma = 1.95$ and $\sigma = 5.6$, adopted from the literature.[4]

This method is used to estimate the tariff equivalent of services barriers in selected countries (table 4.5). In general, countries with more restrictive services regulatory environments are much less likely to export services. Undertrading in services may thus suggest untapped potential to increase exports through the removal of trade-related obstacles.

Barriers to trade not only dampen services export potential, they also act as barriers to services imports. Table 4.5 presents the average tariff equivalents for Belarus, the Russian Federation, and each Eurpoean Union (EU) country in the sample over the period 2009–11 for the two values of the elasticity of substitution. Although the magnitudes of the tariff equivalents are quite sensitive to the elasticity of substitution, the country rankings are preserved.

Belarus shows high levels of regulatory protection of its domestic services. Its estimated trade barriers in services—an estimated tariff equivalent of 65 percent assuming the lower elasticity value and 120 percent assuming the higher value—are higher than all EU countries and Russia. Belgium's average protection of 63 percent (118 percent at the higher elasticity) is the highest among the EU countries; Ireland's rate of 48 percent (106 percent) is the lowest. The average EU country's tariff equivalent is 55 percent (112 percent). Russia's tariff equivalent of 54 percent (111 percent) is just below the average for the European Union.

Table 4.5. Tariff Equivalents of Barriers to Services Trade in Selected Countries, 2009–11

Importer	Tariff equivalent (percent)	
	$\sigma = 1.95$	$\sigma = 5.6$
Austria	57.7	113.9
Belarus	65.2	119.6
Belgium	62.9	117.9
Bosnia and Herzegovina	60.6	116.2
Bulgaria	53.8	110.8
Cyprus	49.4	107.1
Czech Republic	56.8	113.2
Denmark	51.4	108.7
Estonia	51.5	108.8
Finland	53.0	110.1
France	60.7	116.3
Germany	59.4	115.3
Greece	54.2	111.1
Hungary	53.3	110.4
Ireland	48.3	106.1
Italy	56.9	113.3
Latvia	54.7	111.5
Lithuania	54.1	111.0
Luxembourg	51.9	109.2
Malta	47.7	105.6
Netherlands	57.8	114.0
Poland	56.5	112.9
Portugal	54.4	111.2
Romania	56.3	112.8
Russian Federation	54.3	111.2
Slovak Republic	58.3	114.4
Slovenia	56.3	112.9
Spain	54.0	111.0
Sweden	53.3	110.4
United Kingdom	56.4	112.9

Sources: World Development Indicators, Trade in Services Database, and Centre d'Etudes Prospectives et d'Informations Internationales (CEPII).
Note: $\sigma =$ is the elasticity of substitution. For robustness, two values, adopted from the literature, were used.

These estimations are based on cross-border trade. They do not capture services trade flows from FDI or the movement of people. These flows remain an important channel through which foreign providers supply services. If restrictions on services affect commercial presence more than cross-border trade, the tariff equivalent will be under-reported. This analysis does not reveal which sectors are more protected or what the underlying causes of these high levels of protection are.

Domestic Factors that Enable Trade in Services

Miroudot, Sauvage, and Shepherd (2010) ask whether and how trade costs can be reduced. They find that some trade barriers, such as geography or cultural barriers,

are difficult to change. Governments can reduce the costs of other measures through good regulatory policies on the domestic economy and institutions. Horizontal measures—measures affecting a wide range of services sectors—complement the specific trade and domestic policies discussed above. These factors are referred to as domestic enabling factors.

Domestic enabling factors (or fundamentals) affect trade in services. None of these factors can be changed in the short run. They reflect a country's endowments of four factors:

- human capital, including skills and entrepreneurial ability
- natural resources, such as sights that attract tourists
- infrastructure, such as a telecommunications network that facilitates the delivery of services
- institutions, such as the quality of a country's rule of law or regulatory environment.

Table 4.6 lists some of the domestic enabling factors governments can target to reduce trade costs. The gains from good regulatory practices can be increased by putting in place the right institutional and economic environment for firms. These domestic enabling factors are as important for goods as they are for services. However, particular features of services may make them more sensitive to these enabling factors. For example, good domestic institutions in the form of a strong rule of law, in particular regarding contract enforcement, affect both services and goods firms. However, some goods are less sensitive to contractual enforcement, simply because there are fewer information asymmetries regarding their inherent characteristics and features. In contrast, many services are differentiated to a very high extent to meet clients' needs. For these services, there are more information asymmetries, and the many tailored inputs and features are harder to write down in a contract.

Some enabling factors are easier to implement than others. It takes years to strengthen the rule of law in a country where corruption is deeply rooted or to improve education enough to create a large pool of skilled workers. Other policies, such as tax breaks for inward FDI, have more immediate effects.

It may be easier for policy makers to improve enabling factors than to adopt regulatory policies that have a direct effect on firms. For instance, government policies encouraging entrepreneurial skills or increasing the number of university graduates are likely to encounter less opposition than reforms aimed at opening up markets. Governments

MODULE 4

Table 4.6. Domestic Factors that Enable Trade in Services

Policy area	Objective	Indicator	Relation to services
Labor skills	Increase capacity to produce sophisticated services exports; climb up ladder of comparative advantage in services (or from goods to services), especially in professional, computer and computer-related, and business services.	• Share of population with tertiary education • Tertiary enrollment • Average level of schooling • Average years of schooling • Share of population with technical education • Number of IT graduates	• On average, services are more skill intensive than goods. • Level of skills of both exporter and importer is related to level of two-way trade in services, which takes place mostly between OECD countries.
Management and entrepreneurial skills	Enhance adoption and use of modern technologies that are essential for producing a service or good.	• Number of management graduates • Average level of management diploma • Ranking of management school of employed managers • Type of management practice (Bloom and van Reenen 2010) • Number of entrepreneurs	• Highly differentiated nature of services makes them particularly sensitive to management competence and organizational structure. • Services firms are generally smaller than manufacturers, which makes it easier for entrepreneurs to start up an enterprise.
Trade-related infrastructure	Reduce costs related to delivery of services (transportation, telecommunications, export, transaction, and search costs).	• Density of telecommunications • Quality of telecommunications infrastructure • Number of computers per 1,000 people • Number of Internet users per 1,000 people	• Cross-border trade (Mode 1) can be conducted over the Internet. Internet access reduces search costs and can reduce asymmetry of information. • Telecommunications services are an essential input for other services.
Institutions	Establish governance arrangements to foster relationships between private parties rather than those between private parties and the government (Acemoglu and Johnson 2005).	• Quality of rule of law (World Bank Governance Indicators) • Quality of legal system and security of property rights (Gwartney, Lawson, and Hall 2012)	• Services are complex, highly differentiated, and relationship specific, requiring strong contract-enforcing institutions.
Governance	Increase ability of governments to formulate and implement sound policies and regulations that allow and promote private sector development.	• Quality of regulation (World Bank Governance Indicators)/independence of regulator • Government efficiency (World Bank Governance Indicators) • Voice and accountability (World Bank Governance Indicators) • Level of corruption (World Bank Governance Indicators)	• Services require strong independent regulators that can implement good policies that open markets for services. • Well-governed regulatory bodies are more likely to resolve market failures in services.
Business environment	Attract FDI and multinational corporations in order to benefit from export expansion and increased domestic competitiveness.	• Tax breaks to attract FDI • Mix of policies to attract FDI (including reducing tariffs on inputs for downstream users)	• Complementarity between outward FDI and services exports. • Inward FDI is positively correlated with exports in the goods sector.

Note: FDI = foreign direct investment, IT = information technology, OECD = Organisation for Economic Co-operation and Development.

need to have the means to address the policies that stimulate services activities (box 4.11).

Institutions

Institutions matter a great deal for economic activity. They relate to the optimal governance of relationships between private parties rather than between private parties and the government, as Acemoglu and Johnson (2005) show. They are essential for free trade.

Differences in institutions are a critical factor determining comparative advantage. Levchenko (2007) shows that sectors with complex input use are more dependent on strong rule of law than other sectors. Costinot (2009) shows that more complex sectors that require a longer training period for employees (fixed training costs) need stronger domestic institutions for optimal production. Nunn (2007) points to the character of business relationships

among firms, which is harder to quantify in contracts and therefore requires strong institutions.

Empirical research finds a robust and significant relationship between institutions and the competitiveness of services. Amin and Mattoo (2006) find that countries with better institutions have larger and more dynamic services sectors. They suggest that because of the complex web of transactions involved in the production of services, regulatory and contract-enforcing institutions (such as the rule of law) play a key role in their development. They hypothesize that services are more relationship-specific than goods because they involve investments in customization, which increase the costs of switching from one supplier or customer to another. Services therefore require stronger contract-enforcing institutions than goods. For example, a firm's willingness to outsource the transcription of confidential client information is much greater if there is confidence in the

---

Box 4.11. Challenges Facing Potential Services Exporters in Kenya

Lack of knowledge about exporting opportunities, markets, and processes and a lack of awareness as how to acquire such knowledge are widespread in Kenya. According to a 2009 survey, 48 percent of Kenyan services exporters do not have a plan for exporting, and 54 percent do not conduct any market research before exporting. These findings suggest that, although Kenyan services firms may be innovative and successful domestically, many do not engage in any systematic attempt to export their services. If nearly half of Kenyan exporters do not have an export business plan, there are likely many other firms that are able to export but do not. This lack of knowledge is an important constraint that must be overcome.

Many services providers in Kenya, especially small ones, lack international networks and find it very difficult to obtain market intelligence on foreign markets. Lack of contacts, knowledge of foreign markets, tax implications, and other market intelligence prevents them from taking advantage of potential export opportunities.

Services firms in Kenya are also unaware of the support services the government provides, the institutions that support trade, and the services they offer. For example, surveyed exporters were unclear about the activities and role of the Kenya Chamber of Commerce.

Another important constraint is the difficulty of penetrating foreign markets. The problem is caused partly by the domestic regulatory restrictions on Kenyan firms in local and foreign markets. But global perceptions of Kenya also act as a disincentive for potential clients to work with Kenyan exporters.

Current and potential services exporters face regulatory barriers that affect their operations and export opportunities. Surveyed firms cite taxation-related restrictions, burdensome procedures, and licensing requirements to operate in Kenya; outdated sector-specific regulatory measures; and sectoral restrictions such as advertising prohibitions in accounting, architectural, engineering, and legal services. Burdensome requirements for academic and professional qualifications and licensing requirements restrict Kenyan firms from entering foreign markets.

Kenya has low international brand equity as a business service provider. In contrast to its counterparts in India or South Africa, the government does not sponsor international conventions or events to showcase the business process outsourcing (BPO) services available in Kenya. The foreign perception of Kenya's government as unstable also deters foreign companies from using Kenyan BPO. However, Kenya does have high visibility as a business service provider in the East African Community region.

Skills mismatches and skills shortages pose a significant challenge to many Kenyan exporters. Kenya is relatively well endowed with graduates who could work in various business services firms, including in the BPO sector. Recent graduates need to receive substantial training to catch up with international standards, however. Such training costs represent a substantial part of BPO contact center costs. Kenyan institutions produce good programmers, but information technology (IT) firms lack exposure to foreign markets, promotional expertise, and skills in exporting their services.

Kenya faces an acute shortage of engineers, particularly mechanical engineers. In the insurance sector, technical skills are weak. It is so difficult to find individuals with the necessary skills that firms devote substantial resources to in-house training and sponsoring staff to attend courses. Kenya has many lawyers, but legal training grasp is very theoretical, and few lawyers are qualified to export their services.

Another frequently cited constraint is the lack of information and communication technology (ICT) infrastructure. It is being overcome by two new undersea fiber optic cables, which have given Kenya access to high-speed Internet.

Source: Dihel and others 2012.

MODULE 4

privacy and data protection laws in the country in which the services are provided.

Figure 4.8 shows the results of a cross-country regression of the relationship between the complexity of services and the rule of law. The horizontal axis shows the rule of law index, taken from the World Bank's Governance Indicators, which the empirical trade literature often uses to capture the strength of domestic institutions. The vertical axis shows the share of trade in "complex" services sectors (professional services such as accounting and legal services, finance, and insurance; see also table 3.9). This measure is based on Costinot's (2009) calculations. The relationship between the two indicators is positive, albeit with extreme outliers. Countries such as the United States, the United Kingdom, and Ireland have large export shares of finance and professional services partly because of historical reasons and similar legal systems. Lebanon and Mexico have large export sectors in complex services given the level of their domestic institutions.

Using a different approach, Lejour and Verheijden (2004) show that differences in institutions can explain

trade within a country or economic union. They contrast the determinants of bilateral services trade within Canadian provinces and within EU member states. Economic institutions and regulations should have no effect on trade within a country (intraprovincial trade in Canada) but should affect trade across countries (within the European Union). Their measure for economic institutions is the overall product market regulations indicator for services sectors. The analysis reveals that exports are very sensitive to economic institutions in the exporting country and to regulations in the importing country. Tentative estimates suggest that intra-EU services trade could be much greater if the internal market functioned like the Canadian market.

Governance

Governance structures are of major importance for economic activity. Undertaking reforms in domestic governance signals to investors and exporters that the business

Figure 4.8. Complexity of Services versus the Rule of Law in Selected Countries, 2010

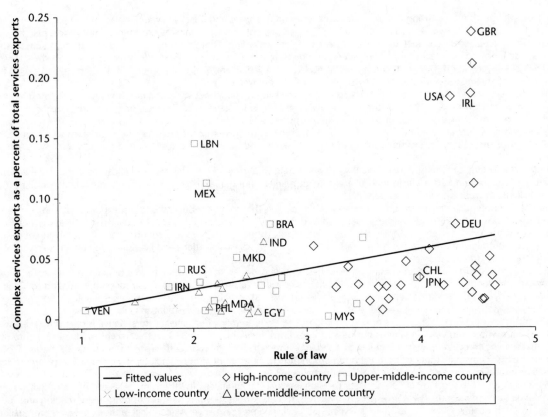

Sources: World Bank Governance Indicators and Trade in Services Database.
Note: The rule of law captures perceptions of the extent to which agents have confidence in and abide by the rules of society. It covers contract enforcement, property rights, the police, the courts, and the likelihood of crime. It is measured on a 1–5 scale, where 5 represents the strongest rule of law. BRA = Brazil, CHL = Chile, DEU = Germany, EGY = Arab Republic of Egypt, GBR = United Kingdom, IND = India, IRL = Ireland, IRN = Islamic Republic of Iran, JPN = Japan, LBN = Lebanon, MDA = Moldova, MEX = Mexico, MKD = Macedonia FYR, MYS = Malaysia, PHL = Philippines, RUS = Russian Federation, USA = United States, VEN = Venezuela, RB.

climate is competitive, reduces the regulatory burden on businesses, and increases transparency.

Governance can be measured in various ways. The World Bank Governance Indicators include the level of corruption, regulatory quality, voice and accountability, and other measures (Kaufman, Kraay, and Mastruzzi 2009). Reform of these policies can best be achieved through simplification and gradualism. Simplification means that the process of governance should avoid complexity and be efficient. Simplifying new policies, regulators have to ensure that the potential for any reintroduction of cumbersome or ineffective changes is minimized. A gradual reform process is more realistic than radical reforms. Partial reform can set off positive feedback experience, which encourages policy makers to reform other elements of the governance structure.

Where private goods markets are functioning, competition serves as a substitute for regulation. With good governance structures in place, government regulators take on the function of enablers of competitiveness and economic growth (Reis and Farole 2012).

To some extent, competition plays this role for services, too. Figure 4.9 shows a negative relationship between the governance index of regulatory quality and the STRI for both services restrictions overall and financial services through Mode 3. Governments with good regulatory policies facilitate well-functioning and competitive services markets.

This relationship suggests that addressing trade restrictiveness is a necessary but not sufficient condition for increasing competitiveness: domestic institutions play a complementary role in creating competitive markets.

Figure 4.9. Services Trade Barriers versus Regulatory Quality in Selected Countries, 2008–10

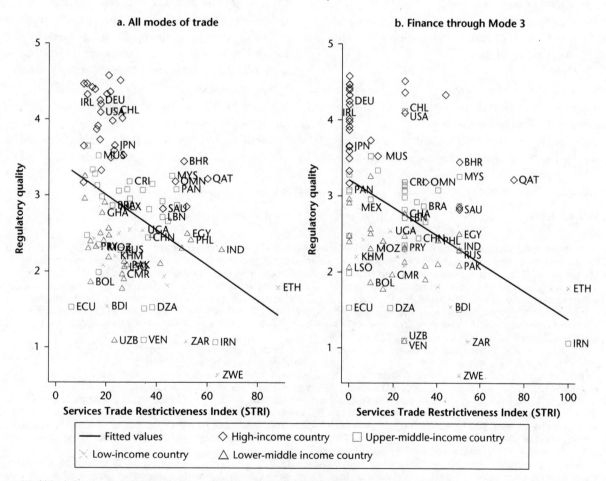

Sources: World Bank Governance Indicators Database and Services Trade Restrictiveness Index.
Note: Regulatory quality reflects perceptions of the ability of the government to formulate and implement sound policies and regulations that permit and promote private sector development. It is measured on a 1–5 scale, where 5 represents the highest value. The STRI is measured on a scale of 0–100, where 100 represents the highest value. For the International Organization for Standardization (ISO) abbreviations, see appendix B.

MODULE 4

Van der Marel (2011) finds that countries with more sophisticated governance frameworks are better able to export services sectors in which behind-the-border barriers are limited.

In the same vein, Molinuevo and Sáez (2014) propose that when assessing the regulatory governance framework for services, policy makers should examine both institutions and their capacity to conduct their regulatory functions. Services markets often suffer from market failures that require regulations. Regulators need to walk a fine line between the need to achieve social objectives and the need to minimize the burden of regulation on market participants. Molinuevo and Sáez (2014) note that a poor regulatory environment may arise from a poor regulatory setting. In this situation, the government bodies and agencies charged with regulating services markets lack a mandate to regulate. They are unable to resist pressures from other government bodies or private stakeholders. Regulatory agencies must have adequate resources to understand and evaluate fully the complexity of the market and the impact of regulatory policy.

An assessment of regulatory governance and its likely impact on services trade must examine at least three aspects of the institutional setting:

- the mandate and independence of the regulatory agency in the broader context of the general institutional framework of the government
- the institutional capacity to fulfill that mandate, which is determined mainly by the regulator's staff, especially

its technical understanding of the regulatory field and services sector
- the financial resources allocated to regulation of the sector.

The Business Environment

Developing countries compete for FDI by offering tax incentives to large multinationals or by reducing barriers to foreign investment (box 4.12). They do so because of the widely held view that multinational corporations are a catalyst for export expansion and improve the competitiveness of the host country. The business environment is also very much influenced by governance, institutions, and overall regulatory policymaking.

FDI promotes exports of a host country by augmenting domestic capital for exports, transferring technology for new products for exports, facilitating access to new and large foreign markets, and training and upgrading the technical and management skills of the local workforce. Empirical evidence suggests that FDI promotes trade in the host country by introducing new technology and management techniques, diffusing market information and increasing market access, and stimulating competition in the host country (Blomström and Kokko 1998; Borzenstein, De Gregorio, and Lee 1998; UNCTAD 1999). As a result of FDI, East Asian economies witnessed tremendous growth before the crisis of 1997–98.

Another area of policy making related to the business environment is the promotion of trade and investment.

Box 4.12. Has the Philippine Economic Zone Authority (PEZA) Boosted Services Exports?

In 2004, the Philippine government formally recognized service exports as one of its top priorities for employment generation and foreign exchange earnings. An executive order issued that year resulted in the formation of a public-private partnership task force. The private sector's proactive involvement seems to be key to the Philippines' successful export performance.

As a result, the business process outsourcing (BPO) sector has performed remarkably well. The Philippines has the world's third-largest market share of BPO. The rapid growth of the sector partly reflects investment incentives provided by the government, which allows 100 percent foreign ownership in a BPO firm. Since 2000, ICT has been one of the Investment Priority Plan sectors. BPO firms registered with the Philippine Economic Zone Authority (PEZA) and located in designated information technology (IT) parks and IT buildings have been eligible for PEZA incentives.

PEZA has created a more business-conducive environment. For companies registering under PEZA, it offers one-stop-shop services for business registration and provides an exemption from local government business permits, licenses, and fees. PEZA issues permits related to building and occupancy, import and export, and environment clearance. Such services reduce business start-up time and costs. In an effort to reduce graft and corruption, PEZA rotates staff members on a regular cycle.

Because data are limited, one cannot conclusively determine whether firms receiving PEZA incentives have generated more BPO exports than non–PEZA firms. PEZA reports that exports by PEZA IT-BPO firms amounted to $4 billion in 2009. This figure seems low, given that planned BPO investment in PEZA areas from 2003 to 2009 was about 85 percent of total planned BPO investment, according to the Board of Investment. A possible underestimation may have occurred because of a discrepancy in the classification of IT-BPO firms by PEZA and the Business Processing Association of the Philippines.

Additional research needs to be conducted to determine how effective PEZA was in boosting BPO exports. The Board of Investment has been building a statistical database on the performance of the BPO industry. Completion of this work would shed some light on this subject.

Source: Yi 2012.

Export and investment promotion agencies are responsible for institutional reform, capacity building, and private sector participation. These agencies need to develop a targeted export promotion or investor strategy to optimally profit from the interaction between modes, especially where complementarities between Mode 1 and Mode 3 trade exist. Domestic firms can be linked to and therefore profit from attracting foreign FDI. Costa Rica attracted foreign FDI, in particular from Intel, in the 1990s that dramatically changed its export and economic structure. Special agencies developed a program to enhance linkages between local small and medium-size enterprises and foreign investors (see Reis and Farole 2012).

Grünfeld and Moxnes (2003) try to identify the determinants of services trade through cross-border (Mode 1) and foreign affiliates (Mode 3). Their study, which focuses on OECD countries, reveals strong links between FDI and cross-border trade in services. It also finds that outward FDI and services exports are complements. Lennon (2009) also finds complementarity between Mode 1 and Mode 3 trade. These findings are policy relevant because a large

proportion of services trade is facilitated through foreign affiliates.

Figure 4.10 illustrates the complementarity between Mode 1 (and 2) services trade and Mode 3 trade barriers. The negative relationship between the STRI and trade in services is evident in both the finance and telecommunications sectors (it is somewhat stronger for telecommunications). Laxer restrictions on Mode 3 services are associated with greater cross-border trade through Mode 1 (and 2), an indication that at least in these sectors, the two modes reinforce each other.

More recent studies using firm-level services trade data examine the determinants for choosing a mode of supply in a deeper manner. Kelle and others (2013) show that firms choose foreign affiliates based on their productivity and that more productive firms are more likely to trade through Mode 3. Other important factors include wages, which are negatively correlated with Mode 3 trade, and costs related to trade through Mode 1. Higher organizational costs for cross-border trade make firms more likely to set up foreign affiliates. It would be useful for investment promotion agencies

Figure 4.10. Mode 3 Barriers versus Modes 1 and 2 Trade, 2008–10

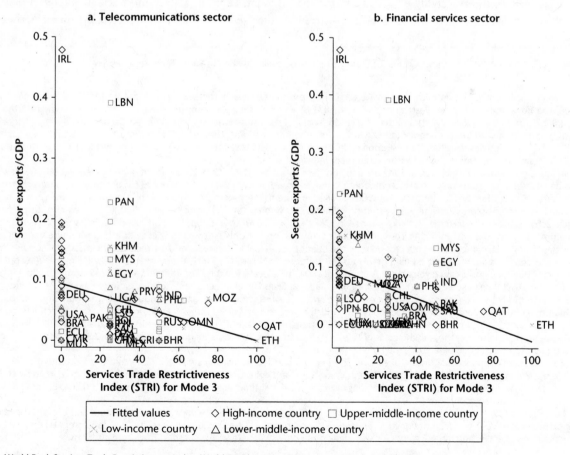

Sources: World Bank Services Trade Restrictiveness Index, World Development Indicators, and Trade in Services Database.
Note: For the International Organization for Standardization (ISO) abbreviations, see appendix B.

to identify services sectors that engage in many small trans-actions rather than a few larger ones, so that policies can be tailored to specific activities.

Labor Skills

High-skilled labor is strongly associated with economic devel-opment (Hall and Jones 1999). This relation is documented in various studies analyzing trade patterns: skill-intensive industries are found in skill-abundant countries that stimu-late productivity; such industries are correlated with higher economic growth (Findlay and Kierzkowski 1983).

Economists debate the causal direction of the relation-ship between trade and labor skills. Depending on the type of labor (skilled, semi-skilled, low-skilled), opening up domestic markets can also have distributional consequences for workers. Many services sectors are significantly more skill intensive than many goods sectors (Nusbaumer 1987; Gibbs 1986; Jensen 2008; van der Marel 2011). Economists believe that skilled labor can help increase the sophistication of exports. In the long run, a skilled labor base will allow countries to climb the **ladder of comparative advantage**.

After access to high-bandwidth telecommunica-tions infrastructure, the availability of skilled labor is the most important determinant of the long-term growth of IT and information technology–enabled services (ITES) sectors. Institutional mechanisms for aligning skills develop-ment with the needs and requirements of the industry are critical (box 4.13).

Figure 4.11 illustrates the relationship between higher education and services exports. The indicator of education measures not merely the number of people with degrees; it also takes into account the qualitative aspects of education and includes information on both the current and future workforce. The figure shows a correlation between the two variables, indicating that countries that are better endowed with high-skilled labor and qualitatively better education export more services (box 4.14).

Shingal (2010) documents the correlation between skills and services exports. Using gross tertiary school enrollment as a proxy for human capital, mainly in OECD countries, he shows that human capital is critical for aggregate services exports. In a study of mostly OECD economies, Lennon (2009) finds that years of schooling, secondary school enrollment, and high school educational attainment in both the importing and exporting country affect services trade.

Through a theoretical model of economic develop-ment, Lennon, Mirza, and Nicoletti (2009) hypothesize that services trade is characterized by tasks that need

---

Box 4.13. What Are Developing Countries Doing to Develop Skilled Labor in High-Tech Services Sectors?

Governments, in collaboration with the private sector, have undertaken a number of initiatives to address skills mismatch. In 2008, the government of Mexico established MexicoFIRST as a partnership between the Asociación Mexicana de la Industria de Tecnologías de Información (AMITI) and the Asociación Nacional de Instituciones de Educación en Tecnologías de la Información (ANIEI). ProSoft, a government agency tasked with promoting information technology (IT) and information technology–enabled services (ITES) industries, facilitated and supported its creation. MexicoFIRST interfaces with industry and Mexican universities to facilitate training programs at the universities that meet industry needs.

In India, the National Association of Software and Services Companies (NASSCOM) assessment of competency (NAC) framework was developed in consultation with ITES companies. It has emerged as India's national standard for generic skills and recruitment of entry-level talent for the ITES industry. NASSCOM rolled out the framework in partnership with a number of state governments in India. Assessment scores indicate areas for improvement, allowing customization of training. NASSCOM has also developed a NAC-Tech certification, which benchmarks engineering skills for the IT industry. It, too, is being rolled out in partnership with state governments. Applying and enforcing common industry certification not only helps align skills with industry requirements, it also provides IT and ITES companies with an estimate of the talent pool available and reduces their recruitment costs.

Several countries are providing training grants for this purpose. In November 2007, the president of the Philippines directed the Technical Education and Skills Development Authority (TESDA) to allocate ₱350 million (about $8 million) to provide scholarships for training 70,000 call center agents. Singapore has a national Skills Development Fund for upgrading worker skills. It launched the Initiatives in New Technology scheme to establish new capabilities within companies or industries by encouraging manpower development in the application of new technologies, industrial research and development, and know-how. South Africa offers up to R 12,000 (about $1,700) per worker for company-specific training and skills acquisition. Under its ICT Capacity Building Program, Sri Lanka funds a portion of the training costs of IT and ITES companies. It also offers grants of up to $10,000 to bring in a special-ized trainer from abroad under a "train the trainer" program.

To address the significant shortage of skills, many large IT and ITES companies have launched skills development initiatives, building training centers, employing hundreds of training staff, and collaborating with academic institutions. Infosys's new Global Education Center in Mysore, India, for example, has more than 300 full-time faculty and is able to train 13,500 employees at a time. The company invested more than $120 million in this 335-acre, 2-million-square-foot facility.

Some governments and universities have used public funding and public-private partnerships to nurture and expand the talent pool. These initiatives have been designed to expand existing university infrastructure and faculty, develop competencies that are benchmarked globally, and forge linkages for skills development with private sector and best-in-class institutions.

Source: Sudan and others 2010.

Figure 4.11. Human Capital versus Services Exports in Selected Countries, 2010

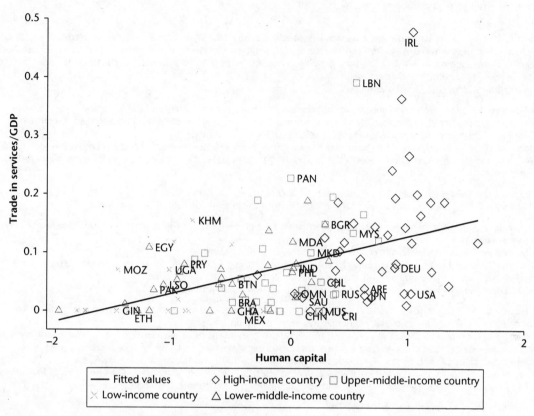

Sources: World Development Indicators and World Economic Forum (WEF 2010).
Note: The horizontal axis shows standard deviations from the mean on the human capital scale of the World Economic Forum 2010. For the International Organization for Standardization (ISO) abbreviations, see appendix B.

to be produced together in order for any of them to be of high value. They emphasize the quality of task performance in the home and host countries for the successful delivery of services. In contrast, for goods, only the exporting country's characteristics seem to affect exports. This model is confirmed by the authors' empirical results, which show that human capital in both the importing and exporting countries are important for services trade. These results suggest that developing countries would do well to focus their services exports on higher-income countries.

Management and Entrepreneurial Skills

Micro-level studies in developing countries suggest that managerial skills play a key role in the adoption of modern technologies, which are critical for producing high-quality goods and services for export. Saxenian (1999, 2000, 2004) and others suggest that transnational entrepreneurial networks have played an essential role in the development of exports from several developing countries. Development of the Indian software industry, for

example, is attributed to entrepreneurs of Indian origin who received world-class management training or worked abroad in well-established multinational firms (Gregory, Nollen, and Tenev 2009). Lall (1999) illustrates the critical role managers played in changing traditional human resource attitudes and policies, allowing these economies to develop and export the products that were in demand in the advanced economies.

Few data are available on the relationship between services exports and management practices. Figure 4.12 shows a positive association between overall management and exports of commercial services. The overall management measure, taken from Bloom and van Reenen (2010), reflects practices such as monitoring management, target management, and incentive management based on firm-level surveys.

Results on the link between management practices and productivity in services are mixed. Wolf (1999) finds that the introduction of ICT or "computerization" decreased TFP in the services sector. O'Mahony and van Ark (2005) provide evidence that productivity in the retail sector in the United Kingdom increased thanks

MODULE 4

Box 4.14. Assessing the Knowledge Economy

The World Bank created the **Knowledge Assessment Methodology (KAM)** to assess a country's preparedness to compete in the **knowledge economy**. It measures 148 structural and qualitative variables of 146 countries, including most OECD and more than 90 developing countries. To allow for cross-country comparisons, KAM provides both absolute and normalized (relative to other countries in the comparison group) values.

The normalization procedure used is as follows:

- Actual data (u) for all variables and countries are collected from World Bank data sets and the literature.
- Countries are ranked based on the absolute values. Countries that perform at the same level are assigned the same rank.
- The number of countries with a higher rank (Nh) is calculated for each country.
- The formula $10 * (1 - Nh/Nc)$ is used to normalize the scores for every country on every variable according to their ranking and in relation to the total number of countries in the sample (Nc) with available data. It yields a normalized score of 0–10 for each country.

The strength of the KAM methodology is its cross-sectoral approach, which allows users to take a holistic view of a wide range of relevant factors. The variables serve as proxies for the four pillars of the knowledge economy framework:

- an economic and institutional regime to provide incentives for the efficient use of existing and new knowledge and the flourishing of entrepreneurship
- an educated and skilled population to create, share, and use knowledge well
- an efficient innovation system of firms, research centers, universities, consultants, and other organizations to tap into the growing stock of global knowledge, assimilate and adapt it to local needs, and create new technology
- ICT to facilitate the effective creation, dissemination, and processing of information.

The methodology includes several variables that track the performance of the economy. These variables indicate how well an economy is using knowledge for its overall economic and social development.

KAM offers several preset display modes for simple visual representations of a country's knowledge economy readiness. A country can be assessed and compared with others on the aggregate performance on each of the knowledge economy pillars or the overall Knowledge Economy and Knowledge Indexes for 1995–2000 and the most recent available year. KAM also makes possible customized country analysis and cross-country comparison on the indicators chosen, allowing users to focus on specific aspects of a country's ability to generate, diffuse, and apply knowledge for economic development.

Source: World Bank (http://go.worldbank.org/39Z6SV9C80).

Figure 4.12. Commercial Services Exports versus Management Score in Selected Countries, 2006–09

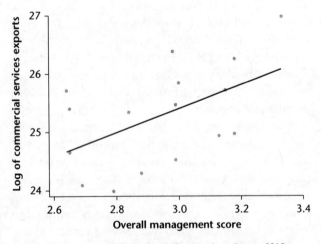

Sources: Trade in Services Database and Bloom and van Reenen 2010.
Note: The overall management score is based on the responses to 18 questions on management practice.

to the adoption and diffusion of ICT. As for policy, the literature suggests that one-size-fits-all management practices are not the solution. For each services sector, policy makers need to carefully assess which management or entrepreneurial skills are necessary to increase output and productivity.

Trade-Related Infrastructure

Trade-related infrastructure encompasses facilities that enable exporting firms to reduce costs related to the delivery of goods and services. This infrastructure includes systems that reduce transportation, transaction, and search costs for firms and consumers. Modernizing customs, for example, makes it easier to trade goods. Documentation procedures, trade facilitation initiatives, and public infrastructure also facilitate trade. Many of these factors help deliver goods efficiently.

Cross-country evidence indicates that economies with large shares of services in value added tend to have better trade-related infrastructure than countries with smaller shares (figure 4.13). Wide variations exist, however, including among countries in the same income group.

Figure 4.13. Value Added of Services as Percent of GDP versus Logistics Performance Index in Selected Countries, 2010

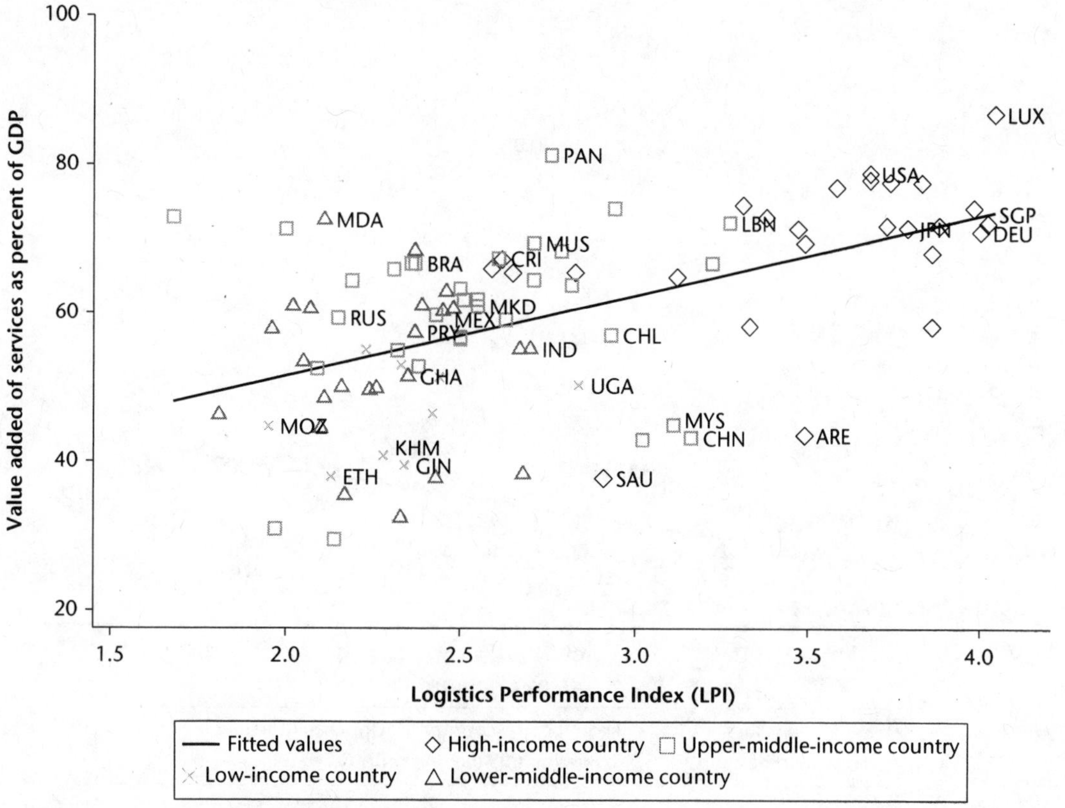

Sources: World Bank Logistics Performance Index and World Development Indicators.
Note: The LPI is a quantitative and qualitative measure assessing the logistics friendliness and the logistics supply chain. For the International Organization for Standardization (ISO) abbreviations, see appendix B.

The increased use of telecommunications has vastly increased the scope of services trade. It is the most powerful symbol of vitality in the services sector. It is also an important source for development of other services. ICT has reduced the costs of delivering many cross-border services to virtually zero.

Empirical research finds that electronic infrastructure has a positive effect on services exports (Freund and Weinhold 2000). Figure 4.14 illustrates the cross-country correlation between Internet penetration and trade in services. It shows that countries with higher densities of Internet connections have higher levels of services trade through Modes 1 and 2. It also shows that developed countries have the highest penetration of Internet users and levels of trade, whereas low-income countries are at the bottom line for both indicators (an exception is India).

Freund and Weinhold (2000) find that a 10 percent increase in Internet penetration in the partner country is associated with a 1.2 percent increase in its imports of business and professional services. Using different measures of telecom infrastructure (such as the number of fixed and mobile phone subscribers per 1,000 people), Shingal (2010) concludes that the quality of infrastructure in the importing country is more important than the quality of infrastructure in the exporting country. Using the OECD's telecommunication index, Lennon, Mirza, and Nicoletti (2009) conclude that telecom infrastructure in both the exporting and importing countries are important. These authors show that telecom and ICT are particularly important for commercial services. One lesson that can be drawn from these studies is that policy makers should target export destinations that are well equipped with ICT and have a high density of telecom or Internet connections.

MODULE 4

Figure 4.14. Internet Penetration versus Trade in Services in Selected Countries, 2010

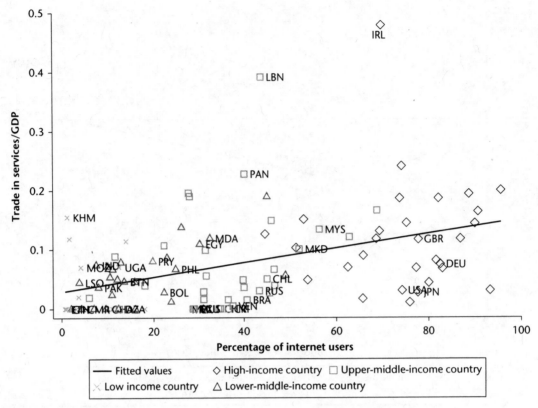

Sources: World Development Indicators and Trade in Services Database.
Note: For the International Organization for Standardization (ISO) abbreviations, see appendix B.

Notes

1. For more on this issue, see Copeland and Mattoo (2008), Deardoff and Stern (2008), and Hoekman and Kostecki (2009).

2. For a discussion of and policy framework on regulations and services trade, see Molinuevo and Sáez (2014).

3. The criteria have not been tested under the WTO dispute settlement system. Although there is an ongoing work program to further develop these criteria, progress has been elusive.

4. Park (2002) assumes an elasticity of substitution of 5.6 for all services sectors; Fontagné, Guillin, and Mitaritonna (2011) use the same value. Walsh (2006) uses a trade-weighted elasticity of substitution for the services sector as a whole of 1.95, calculated from the Global Trade Analysis Project. Francois (2001) uses an elasticity of 4 for overall services trade. Francois, van Meijl, and van Tongeren (2003) use elasticities of 1.26–1.68 for different services sectors.

References

Acemoglu, Daron, and Simon Johnson. 2005. "Unbundling Institutions." *Journal of Political Economy* 113 (5): 949–95.

Amin, Mohammad, and Aaditya Mattoo. 2006. "Do Institutions Matter More for Services?" Policy Research Working Paper Series 4032, World Bank, Washington, DC.

Arnold, Jens M., Beata Javorcik, Molly Lipscomb, and Aaditya Mattoo. 2010. "Services Reform and Manufacturing Performance: Evidence from India." CEPR Discussion Paper 8011, Centre for Economic Policy Research, London.

Arnold, Jens M., Beata S. Javorcik, and Aaditya Mattoo. 2011. "Does Services Liberalization Benefit Manufacturing Firms? Evidence from the Czech Republic." *Journal of International Economics* 85 (1): 136–46.

Arnold, Jens M., Aaditya Mattoo, and Gaia Narciso. 2008. "Services Inputs and Firm Productivity in Sub-Saharan Africa: Evidence from Firm-Level Data." *Journal of African Economies* 17 (4): 578–99.

Australian Productivity Commission. 2011. "Planning and Zoning Regulations." In *Economic Structure and Performance of the Australian Retail Industry*, chapter 8. Melbourne.

Baldwin, R. 2011. "Trade and Industrialisation after Globalisation's 2nd Unbundling: How Building and Joining a Supply Chain Are Different and Why It Matters." NBER Working Paper 17716, National Bureau of Economic Research, Cambridge, MA. http://www.nber.org/papers/w17716.

Balistreri, Edward J., Thomas F. Rutherford, and David G. Tarr. 2009. "Modeling Services Liberalization: The Case of Kenya." *Economic Modelling* 26 (3): 668–79.

Bennet, D. 2002. "Innovative Technology Transfer Framework Linked to Trade for UNIDO Action." World Summit on Sustainable Development, United Nations Industrial Development Organization, Johannesburg, August 26–September 4.

Blomström, Magnus, and Ari Kokko. 1998. "Multinational Corporations and Spillovers." *Journal of Economic Surveys* 12 (3): 247–77.

Bloom, Nicholas, and John Van Reenen. 2010. "Why Do Management Practices Differ across Firms and Countries?" *Journal of Economic Perspectives* 24 (1): 203–24.

Borchert, Ingo, Batshur Gootiiz, and Aaditya Mattoo. 2012a. "Guide to the Services Trade Restrictions Database." World Bank Policy Research Working Paper 6108, Washington, DC.

————. 2012b. "Policy Barriers to International Trade in Services: New Empirical Evidence." World Bank Policy Research Working Paper 6109, Washington, DC.

Borzenstein, Eduardo, José De Gregorio, and Jong-Wha Lee. 1998. "How Does Foreign Direct Investment Affect Economic Growth?" *Journal of International Economics* 45 (1): 115–35.

Cadot, Olivier, Maryla Maliszewska, and Sebastián Sáez. 2011. "Nontariff Measures: Impact, Regulation, and Trade Facilitation." In *Border Management Modernization,* edited by Gerard McLinden, Enrique Fanta, David Widdowson, and Tom Doyle, 215–30. Washington, DC: World Bank.

CEPII (Centre d'Etudes Prospectives et d'Informations Internationales). GeoDist database, Paris. http://www.cepii.fr/anglaisgraph/bdd/distances.htm.

Copeland, Brian, and Aaditya Mattoo. 2008. "The Basic Economics of Services Trade." In *A Handbook of International Trade in Services,* edited by Aaditya Mattoo, Robert M. Stern, and Gianni Zanini, 84–129. Oxford: Oxford University Press.

Costinot, Arnaud. 2009. "On the Origins of Comparative Advantage." *Journal of International Economics* 77 (2): 255–64.

Deardoff, Alan V., and Robert M. Stern. 2008. "Empirical Analysis of Barriers to International Services Transactions and the Consequences of Liberalization." In *A Handbook of International Trade in Services,* edited by Aaditya Mattoo, Robert M. Stern, and Gianni Zanini, 169–220. Oxford: Oxford University Press.

Dihel, Nora, Ana Margarida Fernandes, Richard Gicho, John Kashangaki, and Nicholas Strychcz. 2012. "Becoming a Global Exporter of Business Services? The Case of Kenya." In *Exporting Services: A Developing Country Perspective,* edited by Arti Grover Goswami, Aaditya Mattoo, and Sebastián Sáez, 237–69. Washington, DC: World Bank.

Feenstra, Robert C. 2010. *Offshoring in the Global Economy: Microeconomic Structure and Macroeconomic Implications.* Cambridge, MA: MIT Press.

Findlay, Ronald, and Henryk Kierzkowski. 1983. "Human Capital and International Trade: A Simple General Equilibrium Model." *Journal of Political Economy* 91: 957–78.

Fontagné, L., A. Guillin, and C. Mitaritonna. 2011. "Estimations of Tariff Equivalents for the Services Sectors." Working Paper 2011–24, Centre d'Etudes Prospectives et d'Informations Internationales (CEPII), Paris.

Francois, J. 2001. *The Next WTO Round: North-South Stakes in New Market Access Negotiations.* Adelaide: Centre for International Economic Studies.

Francois, J., H. van Meijl, and F. van Tongeren. 2003. *Economic Benefits of the Doha Round for the Netherlands.* Agricultural Economics Institute, The Hague.

Freund, Caroline, and Diana Weinhold. 2002. "The Internet and International Trade in Services." *American Economic Review* 92 (2): 236–40.

Gibbs, J. Murray. 1986. "Services, Development, and TNCs." *CTC Reporter* 21 (Spring): 51–53.

Gregory, Neil, Stanley Nollen, and Stoyan Tenev. 2009. *New Industries from New Places: The Emergence of the Hardware and Software Industries in China and India.* Redwood City, CA: Stanford University Press and Washington, DC: World Bank.

Grossman, Gene M., and Esteban Rossi-Hansberg, 2008. "Trading Tasks: A Simple Theory of Offshoring." *American Economic Review* 98 (5): 1978–97.

Grünfeld, L., and A. Moxnes. 2003. "The Intangible Globalisation: Explaining Patterns of International Trade in Services." Norwegian Institute of International Affairs Paper 657, Oslo.

Guislain, Pierre, edited by 2004. "The Postal Sector in Developing and Transition Countries: Contributions to a Reform Agenda." World Bank, Global Information and Communication Technologies Department, Policy Division, Washington, DC.

Gwartney, James, Robert Lawson, and Joshua Hall. 2012. *Economic Freedom of the World: Annual Report.* Vancouver: Fraser Institute. http://www.freetheworld.com/2012/EFW2012-complete.pdf.

Hall, Robert E., and Charles I. Jones. 1999. "Why Do Some Countries Produce So Much More Output per Worker Than Others?" *Quarterly Journal of Economics* 114 (1): 83–116.

Helpman, Elhanan. 2011. *Understanding Global Trade.* Cambridge, MA: Harvard University Press.

Hoekman, Bernard, and Michel Kostecki. 2009. *The Political Economy of the World Trading System,* 3rd. edited by Oxford: Oxford University Press.

Inklaar, R., M. P. Timmer, and B. van Ark. 2008. "Market Services Productivity Across Europe and the US." *Economic Policy* 23: 141–94.

Jensen, J. Bradford. 2008. "Trade in High-Tech Services." *Journal of Industry, Competition, and Trade* 8 (3–4): 181–97.

Jensen, Jesper, Thomas F. Rutherford, and David G. Tarr. 2008. "Modeling Services Liberalization: The Case of Tanzania." Policy Research Working Paper Series 4801, Washington, DC.

Jensen, Jesper, and David G. Tarr. 2012. "Deep Trade Policy Options for Armenia: The Importance of Trade Facilitation, Services and Standards Liberalization." *Economics, The Open-Access, Open-Assessment E-Journal* 6 (1): 1–54, Kiel Institute for the World Economy.

Jones, Ronald W. 2000. *Globalization and the Theory of Input Trade.* Cambridge, MA: MIT Press.

Kaufmann, Daniel, Aart Kraay, and Massimo Mastruzzi. 2009. "Governance Matters VIII: Aggregate and Individual Governance Indicators, 1996–2008." World Bank Policy Research Paper 4978, Washington, DC.

Kelle, Markus, J. Kleinert, Horst Raff, and Farid Toubal. 2013. "Cross-Border and Affiliate Sales of Services: Evidence from German Microdata." *World Economy* 36 (11): 1373–92.

Lall, Sanjaya. 1999. "Competing with Labour: Skills and Technology in Developing Countries." Issues in Development Working Paper 31, International Labour Organization, Geneva.

Lejour, Arjan, and Jan-Willem de Paiva Verheijden. 2004. "Services Trade within Canada and the European Union: What Do They Have in Common?" CPB Discussion Paper 42, Netherlands Bureau for Economic Policy Analysis, The Hague.

Lennon, Carolina. 2009. "Trade in Services and Trade in Goods: Differences and Complementarities." WIIW Working Paper 53, Vienna Institute of International Economics Studies (WIIW), Vienna.

Lennon, Carolina, Daniel Mirza, and Giuseppe Nicoletti. 2009. "Complementarity of Inputs in Services Trade." *Annales d'Economie et de Statistiques* 93/94 (April/June): 183–205.

Levchenko, Andrei A. 2007. "Institutional Quality and International Trade." *Review of Economic Studies* 74 (3): 791–19.

Miroudot, Sébastien, Rainer Lanz, and Alexandros Ragoussis. 2009. "Trade in Intermediate Goods and Services." OECD Trade Policy Working Papers 93, Paris. http://dx.doi.org/10.1787/5kmlcxtdlk8r-en.

Miroudot, Sébastien, Jehan Sauvage, and Ben Shepherd. 2010. "Measuring the Cost of International Trade in Services." MPRA Paper 27655, Munich Personal RePEc Archive, University Library of Munich.

Molinuevo, Martin, and Sebastián Sáez. 2014. *Regulatory Assessment Toolkit: A Practical Methodology for Assessing Regulation on Trade and Investment in Services.* Washington, DC: World Bank.

Ng, Francis, and Alexander Yeats. 2000. "Production Sharing in East Asia: Who Does What for Whom, and Why?" World Bank Policy Research Working Paper 2197, Washington, DC.

Nunn, Nathan. 2007. "Relationship-Specificity, Incomplete Contracts, and the Patterns of Trade." *Quarterly Journal of Economics* 122 (2): 569–600.

Nusbaumer, Jacques. 1987. *Services in the Global Market.* Amsterdam: Kluwer.

O'Mahony, Mary, and Bart van Ark. 2005. "Assessing the Productivity of the UK Retail Trade Sector: The Role of ICT." *International Review of Retail, Distribution and Consumer Research* 15 (3): 297–303.

MODULE 4

Park, S.-C. 2002. "Measuring Tariff Equivalents in Cross-Border Trade in Services." Working Paper 02-15, Korea Institute for International Economic Policy, Seoul.

PEZA (Philippine Economic Zone Authority). 2000. "Guidelines on the Registration of Information Technology (IT) Enterprises and the Establishment and Operation of IT Parks/Buildings." Certificate of Board Resolution 00-411, December 29, Pasay City. http://www.peza.gov.ph/issuances/guidelines/Guidelines_IT.pdf.

Reis, José Guilherme, and Thomas Farole. 2012. *Trade Competitiveness Diagnostic Toolkit*. Washington, DC: World Bank.

Rossotto, Carlo Maria, Khalid Sekkat, and Aristomene Varoudakis. 2003. "Opening up Telecommunications to Competition and MENA Integration in the World Economy." Middle East and North Africa Working Paper 33, World Bank, Washington, DC.

Saxenian, Anna Lee. 1999. *Silicon Valley's New Immigrant Entrepreneurs*. San Francisco, CA: Public Policy Institute of California.

———. 2000. "Back to India." *Wall Street Journal: Technology Journal Asia*, January 24.

———. 2004. "The Bangalore Boom: From Brain Drain to Brain Circulation." In *IT Experience in India: Bridging the Digital Divide*, edited by. Kenneth Keniston and Deepak Kumar, 169–81. New Delhi: Sage.

Shepherd, Ben, and Erik van der Marel. 2013. "Services Trade, Regulation and Regional Integration: Evidence from Sectoral Data." *World Economy* 36 (11): 1393–405.

Shingal, Anirudh. 2010. "How Much Do Agreements Matter for Services Trade?" Paper presented at the World Trade Organization Public Forum, Geneva, September 17.

Sudan, Randeep, Seth Ayers, Philippe Dongier, Arturo Muente-Kunigami, and Chirstine Zhen-Wei Qiang. 2010. *The Global Opportunity in IT-Based Services: Assessing and Enhancing Country Competitiveness*. Washington, DC: World Bank.

Teerawattananon, Yot, Viroj Tangcharoensathien, Sripen Tantivess, and Anne Mills. 2003. "Health Sector Regulation in Thailand: Recent Progress and the Future Agenda." *Health Policy* 63 (3): 323–38.

Thomson, R. and J. Nielson. 2001. "Consolidated List of Cross-Sectoral and Sector-Specific Barriers." In *Trade in Services: Negotiating Issues and Approaches*, 11–26, Paris: Organisation for Economic Co-operation and Development (OECD).

Triplett, Jack E., and Barry P. Bosworth. 2004. *Productivity in the US Services Sector: New Sources of Economic Growth*. Washington, DC: Brookings Institution Press.

Trade in Services Database. World Bank, Washington, DC.

UNCTAD (United Nations Conference on Trade and Development). 1999. *World Investment Report 1999: Foreign Direct Investment and the Challenge of Development*. Geneva: UNCTAD.

van der Marel, Erik. 2011. "Determinants of Comparative Advantage in Services." GEM Working Paper, Groupe d'Economie Mondiale, Paris.

———. 2012. Trade in Services and TFP: The Role of Regulation." *World Economy* 35 (11): 1387–429.

Walsh, Keith. 2006. "Trade in Services: Does Gravity Hold? A Gravity Model Approach to Estimating Barriers to Services Trade." IIIS Discussion Paper 183, Institute for International Integration Studies, Trinity College, Dublin.

WEF (World Economic Forum). 2010. *Human Capital Report*. Geneva: World Economic Forum.

Wolf, E. N. 1999. "The Productivity Paradox: Evidence from Indirect Indicators of Services Sector Productivity Growth." *Canadian Journal of Economics* 32 (2): 281–308.

World Bank Governance Indicators. Washington, DC. www.govindicators.org.

World Development Indicators (database). World Bank, Washington, DC. http://data.worldbank.org/data-catalog/world-development-indicators.

WTO (World Trade Organization). 2000. "Korea: Measures Affecting Imports of Fresh, Chilled and Frozen Beef." WT/DS161/AB/R, WT/DS169/AB/R, December 11.

———. 2003. "The Necessity Tests in the WTO." Working Party on Domestic Regulation, S/WPDR/W/27. December 2.

———. 2005. "United States: Measures Affecting the Cross-Border Supply of Gambling and Betting Services." WT/DS285/AB/R, April 7.

———. 2011. "The Necessity Tests in the WTO." Working Party on Domestic Regulation, S/WPDR/W/27/Add.1. January 18.

Yi, Soonhwa. 2012. "Reaching the World through Private Sector Initiative: Service Exports from the Philippines." In *Exporting Services: A Developing-Country Perspective*, edited by Arti Goswami, Additya Mattoo, and Sebastián Sáez, 121–60. Washington, DC: World Bank.

APPENDIX A: EXPORT OF VALUE ADDED DATABASE

Trade data is usually measured at transaction values, which is the price actually paid or payable for goods and services. Transaction values of goods and services are gross values, or value added plus domestic and foreign intermediate inputs. The measure of gross exports may undervalue the real contribution of a sector to trade if value added from this sector is embedded as inputs in other sectors' exports. This is particularly true for services exports. Alternatively, the measure of gross exports may overvalue the real contribution to trade if the sector's exports embed inputs from other sectors. This is particularly true for manufacturing exports. Measuring trade on a value-added basis, as achieved in the Export of Value Added Database, overcomes this shortcoming.

This database follows up on pioneering work of Christen, Francois, and Hoekman (2012) and Francois, Manchin, and Tomberger (2013). It provides information on the domestic value-added content of domestic output and exports across 27 sectors of the economy, including 9 commercial services sectors, 3 primary sectors, and 14 manufacturing sectors.

Thus this alternative measure to trade makes explicit the direct value-added contribution of services sectors to domestic production as well as exports, as well as the linkages that services provide to all other sectors of the economy in terms of value added. In addition to direct potential for export, services have indirect potential as important inputs for other economic activities' exports. The services sector is intrinsically linked with the overall activity of an economy through value chains. By measuring exports on a value-added basis, it is possible to measure these value chain linkages between the services sector and other export sectors of the economy. This includes both **forward linkages**—the contribution of a particular sector as an input to others sectors' exports—and **backward linkages**—the contribution of all other sectors to a particular sector's exports. These value chain linkages not only capture the full (direct and indirect) contribution of the services sector to a country's exports, but also inform a comprehensive strategy to improve export competitiveness of both goods and services.

Why This Database?

The Export of Value Added Database provides a full picture of the economic relationships or value-added structure between sectors that are accounted for in national income, or gross domestic product (GDP). The underlying construction of the database stems from economics and is based on a general equilibrium principle, which means that every income of an economy also has a counterpart in terms of expenditure so that all receipts and outlays correspond with each other. The strength of this database, therefore, is its comprehensive setting out of the interrelationships within an economy of linkages that record intermediate input use and final demand.

This value-added structure can be broken down into direct and indirect value added. Direct value added captures the true sector-specific value added generated within an economy and nets out domestic and foreign inputs. The direct contribution of each services sector to value added, either of the domestic economy as a whole or only of exports, is the value added sold directly to final consumers. For example, in Bangladesh, trade and transport services represent 10.0 percent of the direct value added of the domestic economy and 1.0 percent of the direct value added of exports. However, the contribution of this sector to overall value added and exports of the economy is much higher, since transport services are used as inputs by other sectors but also use inputs from other sectors.

Indirect value added adds to the direct measure the portion of value added of the inputs that are produced domestically, expressed in terms of forward or backward linkages.

Forward linkages represent the contribution of a particular sector as an input to other sectors' value added. More specifically, they are the supply response of a particular sector to all other (downstream) sectors' demand for more inputs. For example, forward linkages will indicate how much other sectors are using financial services as inputs. In Bangladesh, trade and transport services represent 28.9 percent of value added of the domestic economy and 24.2 percent of value added of exports after considering this sector's contribution as inputs in all other sectors' value added.

Analogously, backward linkages represent the contribution of all other sectors to a particular sector's value added. More specifically, they represent how much the demand of a particular sector will pull the supply of all other (upstream) sectors. For example, backward linkages will indicate how much financial services are using other sectors as inputs. In Bangladesh, trade and transport services only demanded 11.5 percent of value added of the domestic economy and 4.9 percent of value added of exports across all sectors.

These linkages represent the interdependence of sectors in the economy. Industries with strong backward and forward linkages play an important role in the development strategy of a country. A sector with strong backward linkages means that an increase in the final demand of these industries' output will have a large impact on industries that supply inputs in the production of these industries' output, while a sector with strong forward linkages means that an increase in the final demand of other industries' output will have a large impact on the industry. Naturally, strong linkages to value added exports suggest an important role in the export strategy of a country.

Manufacturing and services contribute differently to exports due to a different structure of forward and backward linkages. From a policy point of view, when looking at services, the primary interest is forward linkages, as services tend to be used as inputs to other sectors of the economy. On the other hand, backward linkages are dominant for manufacturing sectors because manufacturing tends to use inputs from other sectors of the economy (or imports from other countries).

Data Source

The Export of Value Added Database is constructed using input-output tables. The underlying data come from the Global Trade Analysis Project (GTAP) dataset.[1] This global dataset measures and describes domestic consumption, production, intermediate input use, and trade patterns of goods and services across sectors of an economy. It covers not only key OECD countries but also a wide range of developing countries. Hence, the dataset represents an advanced input-output panel—also known as a social accounting matrix—of incomes and expenditures for the domestic economy and their link to trade over intermittent years between 1992 and 2011.

This database is developed for various years, so one can obtain data for the linkages in recent years and observe how the linkages have changed over time. It should be noted, however, that changes such as a rebasing of the national accounts, for example, may make cross-year comparisons unreliable in some countries. The full set of economies and years in the Export of Value Added Database is listed in table A.2 at the end of this appendix. Table A.3 lists the 27 sectors in the database; table A.4 provides details regarding their classifications.

Methodology to Construct the Export of Value Added Database

The following is a formal representation of how to obtain the direct and indirect (in terms of forward and backward linkages) value-added content of domestic output and exports across sectors of an economy. The variables in the database are explained in box A.1. Equation A.1 provides a simple representation of a domestic economy in terms of gross output and intermediate input requirements:

$$Y = Z - AZ. \qquad (A.1)$$

where Y denotes a vector of final demand of each sector, Z denotes a vector of gross outputs of each sector, and A denotes a matrix of intermediate use coefficients.

First, it is necessary to calculate how much input from each sector is contained by one unit of final output of all other sectors. This is the so-called intermediate multiplier matrix, also commonly known as the Leontief matrix or M-matrix. Equation A.2 is used to construct the M-matrix:

$$Z = (1-A)^{-1}Y = MY. \qquad (A.2)$$

This M-matrix hence holds information on direct and indirect input use in each sector. Each sector uses a different amount of intermediate input from all other sectors, and hence each linkage or intermediate use coefficient between sectors will vary.

Second, it is necessary to have information about the shares of each sector's domestic value added in total

---

Box A.1. Export of Value Added Database Variables

Sector_GMatrix:
This matrix contains the direct and indirect value-added content of domestic output. Depending on whether rows or columns are considered, its sum corresponds to forward (row) or backward (column) linkages. Thus reading a row for a given sector (sector presented on the y-axis) provides information about how much this sector went into each sector (on the x-axis) as inputs. The diagonal corresponds to the direct value added contribution. The matrix represents to the *G*-matrix as described above.

Sector_HMatrix:
This matrix contains the direct and indirect value-added content of exports. Depending on whether rows or columns are considered, its sum corresponds to forward (row) or backward (column) linkages. Thus reading a row for a given sector (sector presented on the y-axis) provides information about how much this sector went into each sector (on the x-axis) as inputs. The diagonal corresponds to the direct value added contribution. The matrix represents to the *H*-matrix as described above.

DomVAshare:
This vector contains the share of each sectors' domestic value added in gross output value. It is the diagonal of the *B*-matrix as described above.

GXshare:
This vector contains the share of each sector's gross exports in total exports based on gross value of exports.

DXshare:
This vector contains the share of each sector's exports of value added in total exports of value added based on direct value added, ignoring linkages.

VXsharefwd:
This vector contains the share of each sector's exports of total value added in total exports of value added based on forward linkages. This vector corresponds to the share of the row-sums in the total sum of the *H*-matrix as described above.

VXsharebwd:
This vector contains the share of each sector's exports of total value added in total exports of value added based on backward linkages. This vector corresponds to the share of the column-sums in the total sum of the *H*-matrix as described above.

---

output, which is then of course consumed domestically or otherwise exported, and is called the *B*-matrix. The output vector (Z) is measured in gross terms whereas the goal of this database is to obtain a cleaner "net" measure of output in value-added terms. As some share of the sector's gross output measure also involves value added created within that sector, the next step is to disentangle the flow of gross activities into the value added activities and intermediate use. The *B*-matrix is a diagonal matrix where the diagonal elements are the value added shares of gross output Z of each sector.

Third, the *M*-matrix (containing the intermediate input use shares) is then multiplied with the *B*-matrix (a diagonal matrix containing the value added shares of gross output) to obtain a *V*-matrix, which identifies the inputs of value added from each sector related to a unit of final demand of all other sectors:

$$V = BM. \tag{A.3}$$

Finally, in order to obtain flows of value added broken down across sectoral activities, the *V*-matrix is then multiplied by a diagonal matrix whose non-zero elements are the vector of final outputs ($\widehat{Y}$) or exports ($\widehat{X}$) of each sector.

This obtains the direct and indirect value-added content of output (*G*-matrix) and exports (*H*-matrix) across sectors of an economy:

$$G = V\widehat{Y} \tag{A.4}$$

$$H = V\widehat{X}. \tag{A.5}$$

Note that each of the matrixes contains each sector's direct value-added contribution on the diagonal and the indirect value-added contribution through forward and backward linkages off the diagonal. Summing across columns within a row provides the forward linkages, while summing across rows within a column provides the backward linkages.

Methodology Example

Table A.1 shows how this methodology is applied for Turkey. It provides some measures based on how value added is measured in the database, both for the domestic economy as well as for exports. Column 1 shows measures

Table A.1. Value Added in Final Output in Turkey, by Sectors, 2007

Sector[a]	Domestic value added share	Gross export share	Direct value added export share	Total value added export share considering forward linkages	Total value added export share considering backward linkages
	(1)	(2)	(3)	(4)	(5)
1 primaryagr	7%	3%	5%	4%	4%
2 otherprim	2%	2%	3%	3%	2%
3 energy	2%	2%	1%	4%	1%
4 procfoods	6%	3%	3%	3%	4%
5 bevtobacco	1%	0%	0%	0%	0%
6 textiles	2%	10%	9%	8%	10%
7 clothing	1%	7%	5%	3%	7%
8 leather	0%	0%	0%	0%	0%
9 lumber	0%	1%	1%	1%	1%
10 paperpub	1%	1%	1%	1%	1%
11 chemicals	2%	6%	4%	4%	5%
12 nonmetmin	2%	3%	3%	2%	3%
13 metals	1%	9%	5%	5%	7%
14 fabmetals	1%	3%	3%	4%	3%
15 transpequip	2%	14%	13%	8%	14%
16 machinery	3%	12%	11%	8%	12%
17 othermanuf	1%	2%	1%	1%	1%
18 water	1%	0%	0%	0%	0%
19 construction	7%	1%	1%	0%	1%
20 distribution	17%	1%	3%	10%	2%
21 transport	11%	15%	19%	16%	16%
22 communication	2%	0%	1%	2%	1%
23 finance	7%	1%	1%	5%	1%
24 insurance	0%	1%	1%	1%	1%
25 obsict	4%	1%	1%	3%	1%
26 oconsumer	1%	1%	2%	1%	1%
27 oservices	18%	1%	3%	2%	2%
Total	100%	100%	100%	100%	100%
Services categories 22–27	**31%**	**5%**	**8%**	**14%**	**6%**

Source: Calculations based on the Export of Value Added Database.
a. See table A.3 for sector descriptions.

of value added for the total economy, i.e. the allocation of value-added across sectors. It shows how much value added (including direct and forward linkages) is produced in each sector whereas column 2 shows the share of exports at gross terms in total gross exports. It shows that services—including communication, finance, insurance, and other business and information and communication technology services—are an important sector because it generates 31 percent of value added in Turkey's economy although it only occupies 5 percent of gross exports. In contrast, in the case of machinery, for instance, these figures are reversed. Column 3 shows the direct contribution of services to total exports, that is, services exported for final consumption. For example, this is the case of software that is ready to be installed in a particular firm information system.

However, as previously explained, with this database, the value-added embodied in exports for Turkey's services sector can be estimated. Because all linkages across sectors are accounted for, it is possible to estimate the total contribution of services to total exports in two ways, namely forward and backward. Analogously to the situation for domestic production, forward linkages tell how much each sector contributes value added, which is exported directly or indirectly in the production of other goods and services. Hence, it represents the contribution of a particular sector as an input to other sectors' value added. Backward linkages represent the contribution of all other sectors to a particular sector's value added. The shares once considering direct plus forward linkages are given in column 4 and backward linkages in column 5. For instance, in Turkey commercial services account for 8 percent of total value

Table A.2. Economies in the Export of Value Added Database

Economy	Income level	Years covered in the database						
Albania	low income	2011	2007	2004	2001	1997		
Argentina	upper middle income	2011	2007	2004	2001	1997	1995	1992
Armenia	lower middle income	2011	2007	2004				
Australia	high income	2011	2007	2004	2001	1997	1995	1992
Austria	high income	2011	2007	2004	2001	1997		
Azerbaijan	upper middle income	2011	2007	2004				
Bahrain	high income	2011	2007	2004				
Bangladesh	low income	2011	2007	2004	2001	1997		
Belarus	upper middle income	2011	2007	2004				
Belgium	high income	2011	2007	2004	2001	1997		
Benin	low income	2011						
Bolivia	lower middle income	2011	2007	2004	2001			
Botswana	upper middle income	2011	2007	2004	2001	1997		
Brazil	upper middle income	2011	2007	2004	2001	1997	1995	1992
Brunei Darassalam	high income	2011						
Bulgaria	upper middle income	2011	2007	2004	2001	1997		
Burkina Faso	low income	2011	2007	2007				
Cambodia	low income	2011	2007	2004				
Cameroon	lower middle income	2011	2007	2004				
Canada	high income	2011	2007	2004	2001	1997	1995	1992
Caribbean Region	–		2007	2004				
Central Africa Region	–	2011	2007	2004				
Chile	upper middle income	2011	2007	2004	2001	1997	1995	1992
China	lower middle income	2011	2007	2004	2001	1997	1995	1992
Colombia	upper middle income	2011	2007	2004	2001	1997	1995	
Costa Rica	upper middle income	2011	2007	2004				
Côte d'Ivoire	low income	2011	2007	2004				
Croatia	upper middle income	2011	2007	2004	2001	1997		
Cyprus	high income	2011	2007	2004	2001	1997		
Czech Republic	high income	2011	2007	2004	2001	1997		
Denmark	high income	2011	2007	2004	2001	1997	1995	
Dominican Republic	upper middle income	2011						
Ecuador	upper middle income	2011	2007	2004	2001			
Egypt, Arab Rep.	lower middle income	2011	2007	2004				
El Salvador	lower middle income	2011	2007	2004				
Estonia	high income	2011	2007	2004	2001	1997		
Ethiopia	low income	2011	2007	2004				
Finland	high income	2011	2007	2004	2001	1997	1995	
France	high income	2011	2007	2004	2001	1997		
Georgia	lower middle income	2011	2007	2004			1995	1992
Germany	high income	2011	2007	2004	2001	1997	1995	
Ghana	low income	2011	2007	2004				
Greece	high income	2011	2007	2004	2001	1997		
Guatemala	lower middle income	2011	2007	2004				
Guinea	low income	2011						
Honduras	lower middle income	2011	2007	2004				
Hong Kong SAR, China	high income	2011	2007	2004	2001	1997	1995	1992
Hungary	high income	2011	2007	2004	2001	1997		
India	lower middle income	2011	2007	2004	2001	1997	1995	1992
Indonesia	lower middle income	2011	2007	2004	2001	1997	1995	1992
Iran, Islamic Rep.	lower middle income	2011	2007	2004	2001			
Ireland	high income	2011	2007	2004	2001	1997		
Israel	high income	2011	2007	2004				
Italy	high income	2011	2007	2004	2001	1997		
Jamaica	upper middle income	2011						
Japan	high income	2011	2007	2004	2001	1997	1995	1992

(continued on next page)

Table A.2. *(continued)*

Economy	Income level	Years covered in the database						
Jordan	upper middle income	2011						
Kazakhstan	upper middle income	2011	2007	2004				
Kenya	low income	2011	2007	2004				
Korea, Rep.	high income	2011	2007	2004	2001	1997	1995	1992
Kuwait	high income	2011	2007	2004				
Kyrgyz Republic	low income	2011	2007	2004				
Lao PDR	lower middle income	2011	2007	2004				
Latvia	upper middle income	2011	2007	2004	2001	1997		
Lithuania	upper middle income	2011	2007	2004	2001	1997		
Luxembourg	high income	2011	2007	2004	2001	1997		
Madagascar	low income	2011	2007	2004	2001			
Malawi	low income	2011	2007	2004	2001	1997		
Malaysia	upper middle income	2011	2007	2004	2001	1997	1995	1992
Malta	high income	2011	2007	2004	2001	1997		
Mauritius	low income	2011	2007	2004	2001			
Mexico	upper middle income	2011	2007	2004	2001	1997	1995	1992
Mongolia	lower middle income	2011	2007	2004				
Morocco	lower middle income	2011	2007	2004	2001	1997	1995	
Mozambique	low income	2011	2007	2004	2001	1997		
Namibia	low income	2011	2007	2004				
Nepal	low income	2011	2007	2004				
Netherlands	high income	2011	2007	2004	2001	1997		
New Zealand	high income	2011	2007	2004	2001	1997	1995	1992
Nicaragua	lower middle income	2011	2007	2004				
Nigeria	low income	2011	2007	2004	2001			
Norway	high income	2011	2007	2004				
Oman	high income	2011	2007	2004				
Pakistan	low income	2011	2007	2004	2001			
Panama	upper middle income	2011	2007	2004				
Paraguay	lower middle income	2011	2007	2004				
Peru	upper middle income	2011	2007	2004	2001	1997		
Philippines	lower middle income	2011	2007	2004	2001	1997	1995	1992
Poland	high income	2011	2007	2004	2001			
Portugal	high income	2011	2007	2004	2001	1997		
Qatar	high income	2011	2007	2004				
Romania	upper middle income	2011	2007	2004	2001	1997		
Russian Federation	upper middle income	2011	2007	2004	2001	1997		
Rwanda	low income	2011						
Saudi Arabia	high income	2011	2007	2004				
Senegal	low income	2011	2007	2004				
Singapore	high income	2011	2007	2004	2001	1997	1995	1992
Slovak Republic	high income	2011	2007	2004	2001	1997		
Slovenia	high income	2011	2007	2004	2001	1997		
South Africa	upper middle income	2011	2007	2004	2001			
Spain	high income	2011	2007	2004	2001	1997		
Sri Lanka	lower middle income	2011	2007	2004	2001	1997	1995	
Sweden	high income	2011	2007	2004	2001	1997	1995	
Switzerland	high income	2011	2007	2004	2001	1997		
Taiwan, China	high income	2011	2007	2004	2001	1997	1995	1992
Tanzania	low income	2011	2007	2004	2001	1997		
Thailand	lower middle income	2011	2007	2004	2001	1997	1995	1992
Togo	low income	2011						
Tunisia	lower middle income	2011	2007	2004	2001			
Turkey	upper middle income	2011	2007	2004	2001	1997	1995	
Uganda	low income	2011	2007	2004	2001	1997		

(continued on next page)

Table A.2. *(continued)*

Economy	Income level	Years covered in the database						
Ukraine	lower middle income	2011	2007	2004				
United Arab Emirates	high income	2011	2007	2004				
United Kingdom	high income	2011	2007	2004	2001	1997	1995	
United States	high income	2011	2007	2004	2001	1997	1995	1992
Uruguay	upper middle income	2011	2007	2004	2001	1997	1995	
Venezuela, RB	upper middle income	2011	2007	2004	2001	1997	1995	
Vietnam	low income	2011	2007	2004	2001	1997	1995	
Zambia	low income	2011	2007	2004	2001	1997		
Zimbabwe	low income	2011	2007	2004	2001	1997		

Table A.3. Sectors in the Export of Value Added Database

Sector name	Sector description
primaryagr	Agriculture, forestry, and fisheries
otherprim	Minerals n.e.c.
energy	Energy extraction
procfoods	Processed foods
bevtobacco	Beverages and tobacco products
textiles	Textiles
clothing	Wearing apparel
leather	Leather products
lumber	Wood products
paperpub	Paper products and publishing
chemicals	Chemicals, rubber, and plastic products
nonmetmin	Mineral products n.e.c.
metals	Ferrous metals and metals n.e.c.
fabmetals	Metal products
transpequip	Transport equipment
machinery	Machinery and equipment n.e.c.
othermanuf	Manufactures n.e.c.
water	Water and utilities
construction	Construction
distribution	Distribution and trade
transport	Transport
communcation	Communications
finance	Finance
insurance	Insurance
obsict	Other business and information and communication technology
oconsumer	Other consumer services
oservices	Other services

Note: n.e.c. = not elsewhere classified.

Table A.4. Service Sectors Mapping to International Standard Industrial Classification (ISIC)

ISIC number	Service sector
Water: water and other utility service	
401	Production, collection, and distribution of electricity
402	Manufacture of gas; distribution of gaseous fuels through mains
403	Steam and hot water supply
41	Collection, purification, and distribution of water
Construction: construction	
45	Construction
Distribution: trade and distribution services	
50	Sales, maintenance, and repair of motor vehicles and motorcycles; retail sale of automotive fuel
51	Wholesale trade and commission trade, except of motor vehicles and motorcycles
521	Nonspecialized retail trade in stores
522	Retail sale of food, beverages, and tobacco in specialized stores
523	Other retail trade of new goods in specialized stores
524	Retail sale of second-hand goods in stores
525	Retail trade not in stores
526	Repair of personal and household goods
55	Hotels and restaurants
Transport: transport services	
60	Land transport; transport via pipelines
61	Water transport
62	Air transport
63	Supporting and auxiliary transport activities; activities of travel agencies
Communication: post and communications services	
64	Post and telecommunications
Finance: financial services	
65	Financial intermediation, except insurance and pension funding
67	Activities auxiliary to financial intermediation
Insurance: insurance services	
66	Insurance and pension funding, except compulsory social security
OBSICT: Other business and ICT services	
70	Real estate activities
711	Renting of transport equipment
712	Renting of other machinery and equipment
713	Renting of personal and household goods n.e.c.
72	Computer and related activities
73	Research and development
74	Other business activities
OConsumer: other consumer services	
92	Recreational, cultural, and sporting activities
93	Other service activities
95	Private households with employed persons
OServices: public services, dwellings	
75	Public administration and defense; compulsory social security
80	Education
85	Health and social work
90	Sewage and refuse disposal, sanitation, and similar activities
91	Activities of membership organizations n.e.c.
99	Extra-territorial organizations and bodies dwellings (no ISIC mapping)

Note: n.e.c. = not elsewhere classified.

added exported directly and 14 percent when including forward linkages; these are the services used as inputs to other sectors' exports. When including backward linkages, on the other hand, commercial services represent only 6 percent of total exports.

Note

1. Available at https://www.gtap.agecon.purdue.edu/. The basic structure of GTAP is explained by McDougall (2001) and McDougall and Hagemeijer (2005). It is produced by a consortium of institutions that include the World Bank, US International Trade Commission, World Trade Organization, OECD, UNCTAD, UNFAO and a number of universities and independent research institutes.

References

Christen, E., J. Francois, and B. Hoekman. 2012. "CGE Modeling of Market Access in Services." In *Handbook of Computable General Equilibrium Modeling*, edited by P.B. Dixon and D.W. Jorgensen. Waltham, MA: Elsevier.

Francois, J., M. Manchin, and P. Tomberger. 2013. "Services Linkages and the Value Added Content of Trade." Policy Research Working Paper 6432, World Bank, Washington, DC.

McDougall, R. 2001. *The GTAP Database, Version 5*. Centre for Global Trade Analysis. West Lafayette, IN: Purdue University.

McDougall, R., and J. Hagemeijer. 2005. "Services Trade Data." In *Global Trade, Assistance and Production: The GTAP 6 Database*, edited by B. V. Dimaranan and R. McDougall. Centre for Global Trade Analysis. West Lafayette, IN: Purdue University.

APPENDIX B:
TRADE IN SERVICES DATABASE

The collection of data on cross-border trade in services is notoriously difficult. This is of course due, in part, to the intangible nature of services. In addition, sometimes national statistical agencies simply do not have the resource capacity to collect services trade data. Quite often this is the case for developing countries. Although some international institutions collect data on services trade, cross-border trade in services is never complete. This database tries to fill that gap by consolidating multiple sources of bilateral trade data in services to provide a broader coverage of developed and developing countries over time. As such, the Trade in Services Database should be seen as the best approximation currently available to capture a comprehensive picture of global trade flows in services.

To combine all these different data sources and to make each bilateral trade relationship between countries consistent, the creators of this database applied a mirror technique and performed many checkups to make data as comprehensive as possible. Mirror technique is a method to retrieve export trade flows of a partner by using information on imports of the reporter country. Yet, although data on many bilateral trade relationships between North-South countries could be recovered, one weakness of this dataset is that a substantial share of South-South trade remains largely unreported. The magnitude of this gap can be verified by comparing trade with the world with all existing bilateral flows in the database.

One should bear in mind that this database measures mainly cross-border trade flows in services together with consumption abroad. As such, other modes of supply within the services framework are left unmeasured. As explained in the introduction of this toolkit, there are four modes of supply. Mode 1 covers cross-border trade, which is mostly services traded over the internet, or more formally, services supplied from the territory of one country into the territory of another. Mode 2 represents consumption abroad. Modes 3 and 4, which are not covered here, are commercial presence of foreign firms that deliver a service and service provided through the presence of natural persons, respectively.

This database has collected data of services trade based on the official information reported on a country's balance of payment (BOP) statistics. Therefore, only Modes 1 and 2 could be included. Although these two categories are also used when constructing (inter)national input/output tables—as used for the **Export of Value Added Database**—one should note that Mode 3 is also a very important channel of foreign services delivery. Mode 3 trade is often proxied by foreign direct investment (FDI) because the official trade statistics for this mode, namely **Foreign Affiliates Trade in Services (FATS)**, are hard to obtain. Unfortunately, currently only a few countries in the world report FATS statistics. Nonetheless, from FDI data it is known that about 60 percent of global FDI stock is undertaken in the services sector, with finance and trade being the most important sectors.

Data Sources

The underlying data sources are taken from Eurostat, International Monetary Fund (IMF), Organisation for Economic Co-operation and Development (OECD), and United Nations (UN). Most of these databases report bilateral trade relationships between individual countries; only the IMF provides solely trade with the world as a partner. All sources also give a breakdown of sectors, which allowed the creators to construct a database by exporter, partner, sector, and year. Services sectors are divided into individual BOP codes at aggregate and disaggregate levels. Table B.2 provides a complete list of the sectors covered, including each BOP code and chapter division and table B.3 lists the economies covered, including each ISO 3-digit country code.

The most comprehensive database of reporting countries for bilateral services trade among the sources used is the UN, which provides data on 190 economies. The other two databases—from Eurostat and OECD—release data for only a limited number of economies. Specifically, the OECD covers 34 country markets, which include its members and various emerging economies. Eurostat covers 28 EU member countries (including Croatia) plus Iceland, Japan, Norway, Switzerland, Turkey, and the United States.

One may wonder why World Trade Organization (WTO) data on services trade has not been included. This information has not been incorporated because the coverage for both sectors and countries is limited and is sufficiently covered by the four other sources used. In fact, WTO data is only provided for three broad sectors and for the world as partner.

Compilation

Not only is the collection of services trade data difficult, the quality of the data is also often poor compared to merchandise trade statistics. One reason is that services cannot easily be taxed when imported due to their intangible nature. To give the best quality possible, the creators of the Trade in Services Database have adjusted the data extensively to assure consistency.

This assurance involved cross-checking across the four data sources to identify inconsistencies where identical bilateral trade relations are reported more than once. For example, sometimes cases were discovered where one data source reported figures with a different order of magnitude compared to the other sources. Through extensive examination of the data these cases have been traced

Table B.1. Variable Descriptions

Variable name	Description
REP	ISO 3-digit code for reporting country (importer)
PAR	ISO 3-digit code for partner country (exporter)
YEAR	Year
BOP	BOP Manual 5 3-digit code for services activity
VALUE	Services imports value (current US$ millions)
DESCRIPTION	Sector description
NAME	Services activity (sector) name

and corrected. In many cases mistakes had already been cleaned up by the UN.

A further verification has been made across sectors. Each individual subsector has been scanned and compared with the reported aggregate flow within that sector. For example, when a higher value of the aggregate figure was found, the authors made adjustments concordantly. Such checks were also performed for trade flows of each reporter-partner with respect to overall trade with the world. If differences were found between the aggregate figure and the sum of its parts—either by sector or partner country—the difference between its initial value and the sum of its components was changed to correct for the aggregate value.

Database Description

Together, the dataset contains bilateral services trade flows for 195 economies as reporters and partners, plus the category "rest of the world."[1] In addition, for each economy, the database reports total trade with the world. Trade flows are reported in US$ millions for 1981–2010, with later years having greater accuracy. Table B.1 describes the variables. The data includes more than 20 economic

Table B.2. Services Sector Components, by Balance of Payments (BOP) Code and Chapter

BOP code			Services sector	BOP chapter
200			Total services	–
205			Transportation services	1
	206		Sea transport	1.1
		207	Passenger	1.1.1
		208	Freight	1.1.2
		209	Other	1.1.3
	210		Air transport	1.2
		211	Passenger	1.2.1
		212	Freight	1.2.2
		213	Other	1.2.3

(continued on next page)

Table B.2. *(continued)*

BOP code			Services sector	BOP chapter
	214		Other transport	1.3
		215	Passenger	1.3.1
		216	Freight	1.3.2
		217	Other	1.3.3
	218		Space transport	1.4
	219		Rail transport	1.5
		220	Passenger	1.5.1
		221	Freight	1.5.2
		222	Other	1.5.3
	223		Road transport	1.6
		224	Passenger	1.6.1
		225	Freight	1.6.2
		226	Other	1.6.3
	227		Inland waterway transport	1.7
		228	Passenger	1.7.1
		229	Freight	1.7.2
		230	Other	1.7.3
	231		Pipeline transport and electricity transmission	1.8
	232		Other supporting and auxiliary transport services	1.9
236			Travel	2
	237		Business travel	2.1
		238	Expenditure by seasonal and border workers	2.1.1
		239	Other	2.1.2
	240		Personal travel	2.2
		241	Health-related expenditures	2.2.1
		242	Educated-related expenditures	2.2.2
		243	Other	2.2.3
245			Communication services	3
	246		Postal and courier services	3.1
		958	Postal services	3.1.1
		959	Courier services	3.1.2
	247		Telecommunications services	3.2
249			Construction services	4
	250		Construction abroad	4.1
	251		Construction in the compiling economy	4.2
253			Insurance services	5
	254		Life insurance services and pension funding	5.1
	255		Freight insurance	5.2
	256		Other direct insurance	5.3
	257		Reinsurance	5.4
	258		Auxiliary services	5.5
260			Financial services	6
262			Computer and information services	7

(continued on next page)

Table B.2. *(continued)*

BOP code			Services sector	BOP chapter
	263		Computer services	7.1
	264		Information services	7.2
		889	New agency services	7.2.1
		890	Other information services	7.2.2
266			Royalties and license fees	8
	891		Franchises and similar rights	8.1
	892		Other royalties and license fees	8.2
268			Other business services	9
	269		Merchanting and other trade-related services	9.1
		270	Merchanting	9.1.1
		271	Other trade-related services	9.1.2
	272		Operational leasing services	9.2
	273		Misc. business, professional, and technical services	9.3
		274	Legal, accounting, management consulting, and public relations	9.3.1
			275 Legal services	9.3.1.1
			276 Accounting, auditing, bookkeeping, and tax consulting services	9.3.1.2
			277 Business and management	9.3.1.3
		278	Advertising and market research	9.3.2
		279	Research and development	9.3.3
		280	Architectural, engineering, and other technical services	9.3.4
		281	Agricultural, mining, and on-site processing services	9.3.5
			282 Waste treatment and depollution	9.3.5.1
			283 Agricultural, mining, and on-site processing services	9.3.5.2
		284	Other business services	9.3.6
		285	Services between related enterprises, n.i.e.	9.3.7
287			Personal, cultural and recreational services	10
	288		Audiovisual and related services	10.1
	289		Other personal, cultural, and recreational services	10.2
		895	Educational services	10.2.1
		896	Health services	10.2.2
		897	Other	10.2.3
291			Government services, n.i.e.	11
	292		Embassies and consulates	11.1
	293		Military units and agencies	11.2
	294		Other government services	11.3
981			Other services, total (category 3–11)	–
982			Commercial services, total (category 3–10)	–
983			Services not allocated	–

Source: IMF, www.imf.org/external/np/sta/bopcode/topical.htm.
Note: n.i.e = not included elsewhere.

Table B.3. Economies Covered in the Trade in Services Database

Economy	ISO3	Economy	ISO3	Economy	ISO3	Economy	ISO3
Afghanistan	AFG	Denmark	DNK	Kuwait	KWT	Qatar	QAT
Albania	ALB	Djibouti	DJI	Kyrgyz Republic	KGZ	Romania	ROU
Algeria	DZA	Dominica	DMA	Lao PDR	LAO	Russian Federation	RUS
Andorra	AND	Dominican Republic	DOM	Latvia	LVA	Rwanda	RWA
Angola	AGO	Ecuador	ECU	Lebanon	LBN	Samoa	WSM
Antigua and Barbuda	ATG	Egypt, Arab Republic of	EGY	Lesotho	LSO	San Marino	SMR
Argentina	ARG	El Salvador	SLV	Liberia	LBR	São Tomé and Príncipe	STP
Armenia	ARM	Equatorial Guinea	GNQ	Libya	LBY	Saudi Arabia	SAU
Aruba	ABW	Eritrea	ERI	Liechtenstein	LIE	Senegal	SEN
Australia	AUS	Estonia	EST	Lithuania	LTU	Serbia	YUG
Austria	AUT	Ethiopia	ETH	Luxembourg	LUX	Seychelles	SYC
Azerbaijan	AZE	Fiji	FJI	Macao SAR, China	MAC	Sierra Leone	SLE
Bahamas, The	BHS	Finland	FIN	Macedonia, FYR	MKD	Singapore	SGP
Bahrain	BHR	France	FRA	Madagascar	MDG	Slovak Republic	SVK
Bangladesh	BGD	French Polynesia	PYF	Malawi	MWI	Slovenia	SVN
Barbados	BRB	Gabon	GAB	Malaysia	MYS	South Africa	ZAF
Belarus	BLR	Gambia, The	GMB	Maldives	MDV	Spain	ESP
Belgium	BEL	Georgia	GEO	Mali	MLI	Sri Lanka	LKA
Belize	BLZ	Germany	DEU	Malta	MLT	Sudan	SDN
Benelux	BLX	Ghana	GHA	Mauritania	MRT	Suriname	SUR
Benin	BEN	Gibraltar	GIB	Mauritius	MUS	Swaziland	SWZ
Bhutan	BTN	Greece	GRC	Mexico	MEX	Sweden	SWE
Bolivia	BOL	Greenland	GRL	Micronesia, Fed. Sts.	FSM	Switzerland	CHE
Bosnia and Herzegovina	BIH	Grenada	GRD	Moldova	MDA	Syrian Arab Republic	SYR
Botswana	BWA	Guam	GUM	Mongolia	MNG	Taiwan, China	TWN
Brazil	BRA	Guatemala	GTM	Montenegro	MNE	Tajikistan	TJK
Brunei Darussalam	BRN	Guinea	GIN	Morocco	MAR	Tanzania	TZA
Bulgaria	BGR	Guinea-Bissau	GNB	Mozambique	MOZ	Thailand	THA
Burkina Faso	BFA	Guyana	GUY	Myanmar	MMR	Timor-Leste	TLS
Burundi	BDI	Haiti	HTI	Namibia	NAM	Togo	TGO
Cabo Verde	CPV	Honduras	HND	Nepal	NPL	Tonga	TON
Cambodia	KHM	Hong Kong SAR, China	HKG	Netherlands	NLD	Trinidad and Tobago	TTO
Cameroon	CMR	Hungary	HUN	New Caledonia	NCL	Tunisia	TUN
Canada	CAN	Iceland	ISL	New Zealand	NZL	Turkey	TUR
Cayman Islands	CYM	India	IND	Nicaragua	NIC	Turkmenistan	TKM
Central African Republic	CAF	Indonesia	IDN	Niger	NER	Uganda	UGA
Chad	TCD	Iran, Islamic Republic of	IRN	Nigeria	NGA	Ukraine	UKR
Chile	CHL	Iraq	IRQ	Norway	NOR	United Arab Emirates	ARE
China	CHN	Ireland	IRL	Oman	OMN	United Kingdom	GBR
Colombia	COL	Isle of Man	IMN	Pakistan	PAK	United States of America	USA
Comoros	COM	Israel	ISR	Palau	PLW	Uruguay	URY
Congo, Dem. Rep.	COD	Italy	ITA	Panama	PAN	Uzbekistan	UZB
Congo, Rep.	COG	Jamaica	JAM	Papua New Guinea	PNG	Vanuatu	VUT
Costa Rica	CRI	Japan	JPN	Paraguay	PRY	Venezuela, RB	VEN
Côte d'Ivoire	CIV	Jordan	JOR	Peru	PER	Vietnam	VNM
Croatia	HRV	Kazakhstan	KAZ	Philippines	PHL	World	WLD
Cuba	CUB	Kenya	KEN	Poland	POL	Yemen, Republic of	YEM
Cyprus	CYP	Kiribati	KIR	Portugal	PRT	Zambia	ZMB
Czech Republic	CZE	Korea, Republic of	KOR	Puerto Rico	PRI	Zimbabwe	ZWE

activities according to BOP classification, as listed in table B.2. Note that not all sectors have the same coverage regarding time and economies. Generally, a more disaggregated level of trade flows will have fewer observations available. Despite all these corrections, some bilateral data on flows remain unallocated. This unmatched information is obtained after carefully mapping all bilateral trade flows against total flows. After comparing total identified bilateral flows with respect to reported total flows, an extra reporter category was created to cover this type of undesignated trade flow: XWD or rest of the world. With the addition of XWD, bilateral and aggregate trade flows are internally consistent. Note that where the bilateral sums exceeded reported totals, no XWD residual was added. This is usually the case if no reported totals were available, but only bilateral flows (including the ones obtained through mirror techniques). XWD is created on both the importer as well on the exporter sides.

Note

1. This database contains 7 variables and a total of 7,117,775 observations. Missing values mean that no source for an observation was available. Zero value means that at least one primary source (such as Eurostat, OECD, or UN) reported zero flows rather than missing. Some bilateral combinations are unreported, which means that they do not appear in the dataset; these observations can be safely assumed to be missing and a reported source of these flows could not be found in any of the underlying databases.